The Spanish Civil War in 100 Objects

The Spanish Civil War in 100 Objects

A Material History of the Conflict and its Legacy

Edited by
Antonio Cazorla-Sánchez and
Adrian Shubert

Translated by
Esther Shubert-Palacios

BLOOMSBURY ACADEMIC
LONDON · NEW YORK · OXFORD · NEW DELHI · SYDNEY

BLOOMSBURY ACADEMIC
Bloomsbury Publishing Plc
50 Bedford Square, London, WC1B 3DP, UK
1385 Broadway, New York, NY 10018, USA
29 Earlsfort Terrace, Dublin 2, Ireland

BLOOMSBURY, BLOOMSBURY ACADEMIC and the Diana logo are
trademarks of Bloomsbury Publishing Plc

First published in 2022 in Spain as *La guerra civil Española en cien
objetos, imágenes y lugares* by Galaxia Gutenberg
First published in Great Britain 2025

ISBN: HB: 978-1-3503-5143-1
       PB: 978-1-3503-5144-8
       ePDF: 978-1-3503-5145-5
       eBook: 978-1-3503-5146-2

Typeset by Integra Software Services Pvt. Ltd.
Printed and bound in Great Britain

To find out more about our authors and books visit www.bloomsbury.com
and sign up for our newsletters.

CONTENTS

The Francoist Dictatorship

CONTRIBUTORS

Vicente J. Benet is Professor of Audiovisual Communication and Director of the Institute for Social Development and Peace at the Jaume I University in Castellón. His research has focused on the cultural history of Spanish cinema and media representations of military conflicts.

Antonio Cazorla-Sánchez is Professor of History at Trent University in Canada. He is the author of numerous books that have been published in Spanish and English. He is a specialist on the history of Francoism and public history of social and political violence. He is co-director of Virtual Museum of the Spanish Civil War and a Fellow of the Royal Society of Canada.

Jesús Espinosa Romero is Associate Director of the General Archive of the State Administration and former Director of the Archive of the Civil War in Salamanca. As a historian and archivist he has specialized in the Civil War and the Francoist dictatorship, especially their cultural and social history.

Plàcid García-Planas is editor of the international section of *La Vanguardia* newspaper. He has covered the disintegration of Yugoslavia and wars in the Middle East, North Africa, and Afghanistan. He is the author of several books as well as co-creator of the exhibition, documentary and book *The Red Box*, about the discovery of Antoni Campañà's photography of the Spanish Civil War.

Arnau González i Vilata is Professor of Modern and Contemporary History at the Autonomous University of Barcelona. He is the author of twenty books about the Second Republic and the diplomatic aspects of the Civil War, including *Cataluña en la crisis europea (1931–1939)*. *¿Irlanda española, peón francés o URSS mediterránea?* (Catalonia in the European Crisis [1931–1939]. Spanish Ireland, French peon, or Mediterranean Soviet Union?).

Alfredo González Ruibal is a specialist in contemporary conflict archaeology and has excavated some of the best-known sites of the Civil War and Francoism. His books include *An Archaeology of the Contemporary Era* (2018) and *The Archaeology of the Spanish Civil War* (2020).

Emilio Grandío Seoane is Professor of Contemporary History at the University of Santiago de Compostela and Director of the HISPONA research group. He has written a number of books and articles about the Francoist period and has been principal researcher on several projects about processes of repression during the Civil War and the dictatorship.

Miren Llona is Professor of Contemporary History at the University of the Basque Country, a member of the Modern Experience research group, and Director of the Oral History Archive. Her research focuses on three areas: the construction of contemporary identities, oral history, and gender history. She is currently the president of the Spanish Association for Women's History Research (AEIHM).

Sofía Rodríguez López is a Professor at the Complutense University of Madrid. She is the author of five books and almost fifty articles and book chapters dealing with the Civil War and Francoism. In 2020 she won the Society for the History of Children and Youth prize for the best article published in Spanish.

Adrian Shubert is University Professor of History Emeritus at York University (Canada). He is the author of a number of books about the modern history of Spain, most recently *The Sword of Luchana: Baldomero Espartero and the Making of Modern Spain (1793–1879)*. He is co-Director of the Virtual Museum of the Spanish Civil War and a Fellow of the Royal Society of Canada.

Verónica Sierra Blas is a Professor at the University of Alcalá de Henares. A specialist on contemporary written culture, especially during the Civil War and the early years of the Francoist regime, she is the author of dozens of books and articles. She is also co-editor of the journal *Cultura Escrita & Sociedad* (Written Culture and Society).

INTRODUCTION

Antonio Cazorla-Sánchez and Adrian Shubert

The hundred brief essays in this book are letters from their authors. They describe and analyze some of the events that happened during the Spanish Civil War and the Francoist dictatorship to which it gave rise, and the way these have been remembered into our own times. The eleven authors come from different professional backgrounds: most are historians, but they include an archaeologist, an archivist, and a journalist. Each has their own voice and their own way of understanding the past about which they write and the places in which they lay their priorities. While we do not always agree when it comes to analyzing historical figures or events, we all share fundamental values that underpin a humanistic and democratic understanding of history. We all recognize that the pain of the victims of the Civil War was the same for every person affected and their families, but we do not consider causes for which they fought to be morally equivalent. This book tries to reflect the suffering that Spaniards, with the assistance of foreign collaborators, inflicted on each other, regardless of the side on which they fought. At the same time, the essays make it perfectly clear that many on the Republican side fought to defend democracy while many others, on both sides, including all on the Francoist side, did not.

The Spanish Civil War is one of the most intensively studied events in Europe's twentieth-century history. Tens of thousands of books have been written about it, and, more than eighty years after it ended, they continue to pour off the presses as scholars refine their interpretations and expand our knowledge. The sad truth, however, is that even after more than forty years of democracy, a glaring deficit in the practice of public history has meant that these developments have not always reached the general public in Spain. How do we understand public history and what do we mean when we say there is a deficit?

There is no single, universally shared definition of public history, even in the United States where it emerged as a discipline in the 1970s and where the term is most widely used.[1] The National Council on Public History in that country currently defines it as "the many and diverse ways in which history is put to work in the world" and describes practitioners expansively as people who "share an interest and commitment to making history relevant and useful in the public sphere."[2] It is a much newer development in the United Kingdom, where it is sometimes conflated with the benign term "heritage."[3] According to the Historical Association:

> Public history is all around us, it brings together heritage, archives, museums, local history societies, history professionals, and active amateurs. Public history is the engagement with history for different groups and professionals but with a level of expertise outside of the fixed university environment (even though some universities have public history departments). It is all of the staff at the Historical Association and many of its members. It is about acknowledging historical knowledge, employment, need and expertise beyond the lecture theatre and into the every day.[4]

The concept of public history is much less well known in Spain and continues to have little impact, even among professional historians today.

We understand public history as a practice whose goal is to inform the general public and to do so by incorporating the most recent developments in scholarship. It takes various forms, most significantly memorials, exhibitions, and especially museums. Spain does not even have a museum devoted to the Civil War although a project for one in Teruel was announced early in 2022.[5] In addition, there are many important symbolic spaces, for example the Valley of the Fallen which is one of the most visited monuments in the country, that do not perform the educational function they should, even to the level of not offering the visitor a decent guidebook, although that began to change following the passage of the Law of Democratic Memory

---

[1]Robert Weible, "Defining Public History: Is it possible? Is it necessary?," *AHA Perspectives on History*, March 1, 2008, https://www.historians.org/publications-and-directories/perspectives-on-history/march-2008/defining-public-history-is-it-possible-is-it-necessary (accessed May 11, 2024).

[2]https://ncph.org/what-is-public-history/about-the-field (accessed May 11, 2024).

[3]The University of York describes its MA in Public History to potential students this way: "You'll study the variety of perspectives on the relationship between the past and the public and evaluate their impact on the modern day heritage sector. You'll analyse how public engagement with the past has evolved with new types of media. Finally, you'll explore the role of museums and other heritage institutions in our society and their impact on our identity throughout history."

[4]https://www.history.org.uk/historian/categories/public-history (accessed May 11, 2024).

[5]An online museum in which we were involved: www.vscw.ca (accessed May 11, 2024), was launched in September 2022.

in October 2022.[6] To coin a phrase, Spain has many places without memory and many memories without places.

This volume was conceived in this context and intended as a modest contribution to addressing this deficit. We believe that using material objects as our starting point is a way of bringing the most recent research to the general public in an accessible and attractive way while not simplifying complex and often contradictory realities.

Some readers may ask why yet another book about the Spanish Civil War? Others may say that it would be better to let that difficult part of the past rest in peace. These are legitimate opinions, but not ones the authors share. For us, the past is not past; it remains very much alive and subject to rethinking on an almost daily basis. This is true for all wars but especially for civil wars, the greatest collective trauma that can befall a society.

Civil wars continue long after the battles end. Because they bring into question fundamental aspects of the way a nation understands itself, civil wars remain alive as long as the nation exists. The United States is the most telling example: almost 160 years after the end of its Civil War (1861–65), the conflict over its meaning and memory continue—and not just verbally. Nobel Prize-winning author William Faulkner, himself a southerner, knew of what he spoke when he wrote "The past is never dead. It's not even past." It should come as no surprise that while the United States has many impressive national museums, there is not one devoted to the Civil War (albeit there are many dedicated to individual battles).[7] And the United States is not alone: very few countries that suffered civil wars have created museums to explain them. Other countries have similar problems dealing with different difficult aspects of their past such as empire and the slave trade. This has begun to change, although slowly and, arguably, nowhere more slowly than in the United Kingdom.

Similarly, the Spanish Civil War continues to inform many people's political identities and its legacies continue to divide Spaniards. It has caused wounds that remain unhealed, especially those caused by the mass graves that hold the remains of tens of thousands of unidentified victims. This does not mean, however, that Spain is a country traumatized by its past. It is sufficiently mature and distanced from the Civil War and its aftermath to be able to look on them critically and with a genuine desire to learn. Spaniards are not prisoners of their history, although to some extent they may be prisoners of their lack of knowledge. The fundamental goal of this book is to help provide people outside academia with some of that knowledge.

---

[6]https://elpais.com/espana/2022-10-21/no-a-la-calle-division-azul-y-si-a-nuevos-lugares-de-memoria-liberales-entra-en-vigor-la-ley-de-memoria-democratica.html?rel=buscador_noticias (accessed October 24, 2022).
[7]For example, the Gettysburg National Military Park: https://www.nps.gov/gett/index.htm (accessed October 24, 2022).

The volume is divided into three chronological periods: the Civil War itself, the Francoist dictatorship that was constructed during the war and survived until shortly after the dictator's death in November 1975, and the democracy that has been in place since then. This appears straightforward, but when it came to placing an object in one of the sections, the editors often found ourselves with a difficult decision. These objects have had long lives and their importance often transcends the period in which they were created or used. Likewise, their meanings, the ways in which a society knows, remembers, or forgets, have evolved over time and continue to do so as that society evolves and its questions and priorities change. Something that was considered important a few decades ago may be insignificant today—and vice versa. How do we decide what is most significant about a monument: when it was erected? When was it forgotten? Or when its name was changed? Or where do we put something that happened in 1936, such as a massacre and the dumping of the victims' bodies into an unmarked mass grave that was not discovered until 2010? Finally, and perhaps most important, which should be given priority: what people experienced and felt during the Spanish Civil War or what we experience and feel today?

By approaching the Spanish Civil War through material objects, this volume offers an innovative approach to that conflict but we did not invent the genre. There have been a number of predecessors, but we were inspired by two written by Neil MacGregor, former director of the British Museum and currently the director of Berlin's Humboldt Forum: *A History of the World in 100 Objects* and *Germany: Memories of a Nation*.[8] These volumes form part of a much broader field of material culture studies that has spread from archaeology to a number of other disciplines, including history, although it is a field without any universally agreed methodology, "nor any single way to go about learning how to read objects."[9]

---

[8]Neil MacGregor, *A History of the World in 100 Objects* (London: Allen Lane 2001) and *Germany: Memories of a Nation* (London: Allen Lane 2014). Other examples include Harold Holzer, *The Civil War in 50 Objects* (New York: Viking, 2013); Roger Moorehouse, *The Third Reich in 100 Objects: A Material History of Nazi Germany* (Barnsley: Pen & Sword, 2018); and Melissa Harper and Richard White, eds., *Symbols of Australia: Imagining a Nation* (Sydney: NewSouth Publishing, 2021).

[9]Dan Hicks and Mary C. Beaudry, eds., *The Oxford Handbook of Material Culture Studies* (Oxford: Oxford University Press, 2010); Jessica Lamb and Clare Smith, "Modern Material Culture Studies," *Encyclopedia of Global Archaeology* (New York: Springer, 2014), doi: 10.1007/978-1-4419-0465-2; Victor Buchli, *The Material Culture Reader* (New York: Routledge, 2021). On history and material culture, see Serena Dyer, "State of the Field: Material Culture," *History*, 106 (370) 2021: 282–92, https://onlinelibrary.wiley.com/doi/full/10.1111/1468-229X.13104 (accessed May 11, 2024); Ivan Gaskell and Sarah Anne Carter, "Introduction: Why History and Material Culture?," in Gaskell and Carter, eds., *The Oxford Handbook of History and Material Culture* (Oxford: Oxford University Press, 2021); and Sarah Jones Weicksel, "Historians and Material Culture," *AHA Perspectives*, January 26, 2015, https://www.historians.org/publications-and-directories/perspectives-on-history/january-2015/historians-and-material-culture (accessed May 11, 2024).

As traces of the past, material objects can bolster historians' understanding of their topic of study and help us communicate more effectively. As French historian Arlette Farge wrote in her reflections on working in the archives, even in those palaces of paper where historians spend so much of our time, a material object like the fragment of a shirt a prisoner tried to smuggle out of the Bastille "can communicate the feeling of reality better than anything else can."[10] And as Serena Dyer commented in her recent survey of the field, "[o]bjects are omnipresent, and act as a uniquely sympathetic point of connection between humans, past and present."[11]

In this volume we use a wide variety of objects to convey "the feeling of reality" of the Spanish Civil War and to provide people today with a "sympathetic point of connection" to that traumatic past. They can be also seen as what have been called "witnessing objects": things that "were present at a pivotal moment in the past and serve as tangible links to that history" including, and perhaps especially, to the experiences of people who are invisible in the written record.[12]

Objects are "mute to those who listen only for pronouncements from the past,"[13] and in this they are identical to written documents. Their stories must be teased out of them by the scholar who beings their knowledge of a range of other sources as well as of the relevant literatures. For any individual object, there are many possible stories: asking the right questions is crucial. The contributors to this volume know how to ask those questions and how to listen for the answers.

The hundred objects in this book do not provide a comprehensive history of the Spanish Civil War, although we have endeavored to include all parts of Spain. They have been selected because the authors believe they can tell stories about important aspects of that conflict and the way it has been remembered. Some are well known, most are not, but they are all pieces of a giant puzzle. Some connect; others have spaces between them. Another great advantage of using material culture as a way of telling stories about the past is that these objects are not all sequestered in museums and archives, accessible only to professional scholars and the most motivated of others. They exist in people's homes and in their surroundings, and we hope that this book will encourage people to think of the stories those objects tell, to discuss them with their families and friends, and even to write to us. Let us share our knowledge and our curiosity and think together.

---

[10]Arlette Farge, *The Allure of the Archives* (New Haven, CT: Yale University Press, 2013), 9–11.
[11]Dyer, "State of the Field: Material Culture."
[12]"Material Culture," *The Inclusive Historian's Handbook*, https://inclusivehistorian.com/material-culture (accessed May 11, 2024).
[13]Stephen D. Lubar and W. David Kingery, *History from Things: Essays on Material Culture* (Washington: Smithsonian Books, 1995), viii.

The War

1. DRAGON RAPIDE AIRPLANE, JULY 1936, MADRID

Antonio Cazorla-Sánchez

In hangar number five of the Cuatro Vientos Air Museum outside Madrid are two De Havilland D.H. 89 airplanes, better known as the Dragon Rapide. One of them is the plane that took Franco from the Canary Islands to Tetuán at the beginning of the Civil War. It is exhibited with its 1936 registration, colors, and the name of its owner: Olley Air Service Ltd.

Beneath the nose of the plane is a plaque that reads: "In this airplane, the Head of the Spanish State and General of the armies His Excellency Francisco Franco Bahamonde traveled from Las Palmas to Tetuán to take charge of the National Uprising. Its owner Mr. Griffith donated it to Spain in memory of this historical event." As tends to occur with historical texts written under dictatorships, this one tells a partial truth in order to construct a great lie.

The true part is that Franco traveled from Las Palmas to Tetuán on that plane; the great lie is that he did so in order to take charge of the National Uprising. This lie forms part of the myth, created during the first months of the war, that Franco had organized the July 18 rebellion and was its natural leader, so designated by God and the people. The truth is less clean, more complex and, of course, less glorious than what the propaganda claimed.

The Dragon Rapide was chartered with money belonging to the financier Juan March, who assured Franco that if things went badly, he would have enough economic support to live comfortably for the rest of his life. Juan Ignacio Luca de Tena, owner of the daily newspaper *ABC*, organized the charter with the help of Luis Bolín, the newspaper's London correspondent. The plane arrived in Las Palmas on July 14 carrying an English man, his daughter and a friend. Until that moment, Franco, who lived in Santa Cruz de Tenerife, was perhaps still unsure whether he was going to join the rebellion organized by General Emilio Mola, which was going to be led by the *caudillo* [chief] of the Spanish right, General José Sanjurjo, then in exile in Portugal. Mola and the other conspirators were furious with the evasive Franco, who had been stalling and flip-flopping for months, and they decided that Sanjurjo would have to take charge of the rebellion in Morocco. It was only the assassination of José Calvo Sotelo, it seems, that led Franco to commit to the revolt. The problem now was that the plane and the general were on different islands, and the Dragon Rapide could not land on Tenerife.

The solution to this problem came in a suspiciously opportune manner. On July 16, the military commander of Las Palmas, General Amado Balmes, died of a supposedly self-inflicted gunshot wound to the abdomen that happened while he was trying to unblock his pistol. With the excuse of attending his funeral, Franco and his family arrived in Las Palmas on the 17th, mere hours before the Army of Africa was to rebel. At midday on the 18th, with Morocco already in the hands of the rebels, Franco took the plane en route to Tetuán. The Dragon Rapide made stops in Agadir and Casablanca, from where Franco called to make sure that the uprising was going well. The mythology around Franco would later invent the tall tale that there were gunmen waiting to kill him in Morocco. That is yet another lie. In reality, Franco was disguised as an Arab, had shaved his mustache and was carrying a borrowed diplomatic passport. This is not exactly the image of a hero convinced of his destiny. Moreover, according to the pilot, Franco threw a suitcase full of documents into the sea. Could it have contained a letter offering to negotiate with the government? There are at least two precedents for this idea: the very ambiguous missive sent to the president of the government, Santiago Casares Quiroga, in June, and the fact that Franco had just proclaimed that he was rebelling to defend the Republican Constitution. In any case, before landing in Tetuán on the morning of the 19th, the mistrustful rebel made sure that the soldiers who were waiting for him at the airport were friendly. Only then did he give the pilot the order to land. The next day, Sanjurjo died in Portugal when his plane crashed during takeoff.

The collections of the Air Museum also include the blueprints for the first jet engine designed in Spain, by Captain Virgilio Leret in 1935. At the time, only the United Kingdom and Germany had plans to build anything similar. Leret was executed by the rebels in Melilla on July 18. His body has never been found. Until May 2018, the plaque in the museum said simply that he had died, with no further details. It now says that he was executed for defending the legal government of the country.

2. QUEIPO DE LLANO'S MICROPHONE, JULY 1936, TOLEDO

Adrian Shubert

Just before 9:00 p.m. on July 18, 1936, General Gonzalo Queipo de Llano, who had just become Nationalist military commander in southern Spain, sat down behind this microphone belonging to Unión Radio Sevilla to deliver the first of what would be a series of bloodcurdling fifteen to twenty minute radio addresses. Intended both to encourage his supporters of the barbarity of the Republicans and to terrify the enemy, these would be broadcast every night at 10:30 until February 1, 1938.

British writer Gerald Brenan heard the harangues in Málaga, where he was living, and described them as "replete with vile anecdotes, jokes absurdities, all extraordinarily colorful but hair-raising when we learned about the executions." On July 23, in one of the most outrageous and controversial of these diatribes, he threatened Republican women with mass rape: "Our valiant Legionnaires and Regulares have shown the Red cowards what true men are. And their women as well. This is totally justified because these Communists and anarchists advocate free love. At least now they will know what real men are, not militia gays. They will not escape, however much they kick and scream."

Queipo de Llano's nightmarish broadcasts were the verbal reflection of the very flesh-and-blood repression that had been taking place, with his authorization, in western Andalucía since the beginning of the uprising. On July 18, he gave his troops and their civilian sympathizers carte blanche to execute anyone who resisted. The conquest of the city of Seville involved using women and children as human shields for the soldiers fighting their way into working-class areas and aerial bombing of La Macarena district. This was followed by his prohibition of any public sign of mourning for those killed. The death toll in Seville was at least 3,000. As such, this elegant object, 58 centimeters tall and made of chrome and Bakelite, can stand as a symbol of the murderous New Spain that was in the process of emerging from a sea of death.

The microphone also represents the importance of this most modern means of mass communication in conducting the war. The first conflict in which radio was the key medium for communicating information and propaganda, the Spanish Civil War has been called "the first radio war." The government of the Republic recognized the power of radio: one of its first responses to the military uprising was to suspend amateur radio, close down local stations, and establish the Madrid and Barcelona stations of the Unión Radio network as the sole outlet for news. It did not take long, however, for regional governments like the Generalitat and political parties and trade unions to set up their own stations.

The rebels also knew the power of radio. Where their coup was successful, they used the facilities at hand, such as Radio Navarra and Radio Asturias, but these transmitters reached just kilometers. Sevilla's Unión Radio, which could be heard in much of the country, was the only powerful station they controlled.

Radio was also part of the internationalization of the war. Radio Moscow presented pro-Republican programming in a number of languages—multi-lingual broadcasting was pioneered by the Soviet Union—while the Nationalists were supported by the shortwave services of Portugal, Germany, Italy, and the Vatican. (Until the fall of Catalonia in January 1939 and despite Franco's protests, Italy's Radio Verdad, which reached Spain's east coast, broadcast in Catalan.) Germany also gave the Nationalists a mobile transmitter that was twice as powerful as any the Republic had. This made possible "ghost radio": Nationalist programs that appeared to be Republican, the forerunner of what during the Second World War would be known as "black broadcasting." As the war continued, the Nationalists would weave their radio facilities into the National Radio network.

Queipo de Llano and his microphone had been the subject of controversy over historical memory. The exhibition of the microphone and Queipo's desk at the Museo del Ejército in Sevilla in 2013 led to protests by civil society associations that the museum was violating the 2007 Law of Historical Memory by glorifying the military uprising. The ongoing controversy over his burial in a prominent place in the church of the Macarena was resolved when his remains, along with those of his wife and his right-hand man, general Francisco Bohórquez Vecina, were discreetly exhumed on November 3, 2022 as a result of the passage of the Law for Democratic Memory, which had come into force only two weeks earlier.

3. MASONIC PIN, JULY 1936, CÁDIZ

Jesús Espinosa Romero

In the New Spain, Masons, Crypto-Jews (although who these might be was unclear), and "reds" were all groups targeted for elimination. There were, however, fewer than 5,000 Masons in Spain in 1936. Contrary to the myths, during the dictatorship of Primo de Rivera, Masonic lodges had been converted into genuine civic schools, social centers, and refuges where liberals and progressives could debate questions of liberty, equality, and fraternity. They had a limited presence, even in places like Andalucía, where they were relatively strong. Studies of that region show that the lodges had only 393 members, although they did produce some Republican and leftist activists. For this reason the Masons, just as much as these other groups, were targets of assassination and persecution by the rebels, who were eager to inflict indiscriminate terror. Such was the case of Miguel Romero Castellano, who was executed in August 1936 in an unknown location somewhere between Cádiz and Puerto de Santa Maria. His body has never been found. Apart from a few photographs and his memory, his family has preserved this small lapel pin of the Gran Oriente Español.

Miguel was 43 years old, had four children, and was a native of Maracena, a small village on the plains of Granada. In the 1920s he moved with his family to Cádiz, where they ran a hostel. On the night of July 20, 1936, his home in the Pópulo neighborhood was searched by the Civil Guard, who found a rifle and a Star pistol, along with their licenses. He was detained and placed in the custody of the Cádiz military authorities.

According to his dossier, generated by the Special Section of the Delegation for the Recovery of Documents, located in Salamanca, Miguel joined the Hermano Vigor no. 23 Lodge in October 1928 and later moved to the Fermín Salvoechea lodge in Cádiz. After ascending through the organization, in the summer of 1934 he became a candidate for National Grand Master. As a result, Miguel Romero was well known within the secretive Masonic circles, whose meetings, called *tenidas,* were known within the city. In addition, his candidacy as a member of the Popular Front in the February 1936 elections meant that his elimination, be it judicial or extrajudicial, was all but guaranteed.

The military proceedings against him began on July 26. After spending several days in the provincial prison, he was transferred to the ship *Miraflores.* The formal accusation against him was of not having surrendered the two weapons the police had seized. On July 30 the decision came down that he had violated the official war mandate and the matter was elevated to the judicial authority of the Second Organic Division, under General Queipo de Llano in Seville, for a summary trial. In the end, this never took place. The official version of events is that Miguel Romero died in October 1936, after the group of Civil Guards that was moving him and other prisoners to Puerto de Santa Maria were attacked. Later documents indicate that his fate was actually decided far more expeditiously.

Following his death, his widow and four children had to deal with the initial confiscation of their property. After the war, Miguel's family, along with many others, were subjected to repressive measures as continued punishment against the deceased and their relatives. First, in February 1942, the Regional Tribunal of Political Responsibilities of Seville convicted him for his political and social activities and imposed a fine. This was suspended because his widow could not pay it with the modest pension she received. Second, the Special Tribunal for the Repression of Masonry and Communism opened another case against him in 1947. This time the case was provisionally dismissed until a death certificate confirming his death could be presented. As such, the case remained open until 1963, when the Tribunal was closed by the dictatorship for having completed its mission.

Miguel Romero's youngest daughter, Chary, who still recalls how she enjoyed her first swims at La Caleta beach with her father, has only a few photographs of him. The majority were burned by her mother, Adoración

Rojas, to avoid further trouble. However, they never disposed of this small pin from the Gran Oriente Español, which his widow could more easily hide and whose significance not everyone understood. Only at the end of the twentieth century did Chary learn that her father was a Mason and a socialist, and that his was the true reason for his death.

4. BOOKLET, "THE SEA. VISIONS OF CHILDREN WHO HAVE NEVER SEEN IT," JULY 1936, BAÑUELOS DE BUREBA, BURGOS

Adrian Shubert

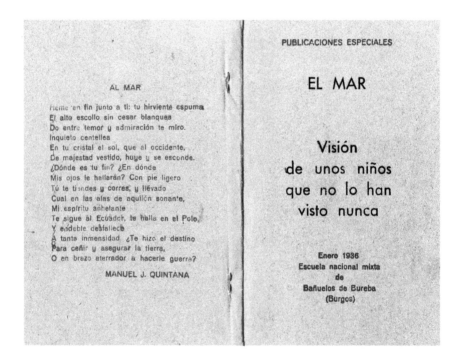

This page from the booklet "The Sea. Visions of children who have never seen it" was created in 1936 by the students of the school in the village of Bañuelos de Bureba (Burgos) under the direction of their teacher Antonio Benaiges. A native of Mont-roig del Camp in Tarragona, the 31-year-old Benaiges had arrived in the village of 198 people in 1934. He was a practitioner of the innovative Freinet method, a pedagogy of work in which students, working in groups, created useful products based on their own interests and experiences. Publishing booklets such as this one using a basic printing press was a key practice. For this project, Benaiges asked his students to imagine "what is the sea like?" and he promised that in the summer he would take them to Catalonia to see it.

He was never able to keep his promise. The day after the military uprising, Benaiges, whose novel teaching methods, which included having students dance to music played on a gramophone he had purchased, had generated suspicion and resentment, was arrested in Briviesca. The day after that, a group of Falangistas went to Bañuelos where they ransacked the school and burned everything they found, including the booklets the students had created. Benaiges was tortured and publicly humiliated before being killed on July 25. Along with as many as 400 others, his body was put in a mass grave in La Pedraja, along the national highway about 25 kilometers from Burgos.

The booklet illustrates three things: the importance of secular, public education to the Republican project; the nature of Francoist repression; and the intersection between them.

Article 48 of the Constitution of 1931 proclaimed that "primary education will be free and obligatory" and that the government would provide "economically disadvantaged" students with the means to access any level of schooling to which their "vocation and abilities" took them. Public-school teachers would be civil servants who enjoyed academic freedom. Education would be secular, "have labour at the heart of its methodology, and be inspired by ideals of human solidarity." The church could run its own schools and teach religion "subject to State inspection." The first governments of the Republic acted energetically to realize these goals, creating new schools, hiring new teachers and raising their salaries, creating a new curriculum for teacher training, bringing in co-education, and creating Pedagogical Missions to reach into villages across the country. There was no single official Republican pedagogy, but approaches such as the Freinet technique was an ideal fit with the goals of the new regime and Antonio Benaiges was a model of the new Republican teacher.

Education also mattered to the rebels. Teachers were a target of the violence of the first months of the war. Even in Burgos, where Francoist repression was relatively mild, forty teachers were killed or reported as "disappeared." After the initial killings, the profession as a whole was subjected to a bureaucratized purge. Decreto 66, published in the Boletín Oficial del Estado (BOE) on November 11, 1936, ordered a sweeping purification of a body that "with only the rarest exceptions" had been "almost monopolized by destructive ideologies and institutions that openly opposed the national spirit and tradition." This was to be followed by a sweeping reorganization of the school system, "tearing out by the roots the false doctrines and their apostles that have been the main cause of the tragedy that has befallen our Fatherland." Teachers were subject to punishments that ranged from temporary suspension and loss of pay to forced transfer to a remote area, permanent dismissal or, in the most serious cases, execution. About one-quarter of all teachers were punished in some way; 10 percent were permanently barred from teaching. They were replaced by clergy, Nationalist veterans and new teachers trained in the beliefs of the new regime. When the school in Bañuelos reopened, it had a crucifix and bicolor flag in the classroom.

The purge even reached into the grave. In December 1939, as a posthumous humiliation, the National Commission for Purging Primary School Teachers punished Benaiges, who had been dead for more than three years, with a "permanent dismissal" from his teaching position.

In 2010, the Association of Relatives of People Murdered in the Montes de La Pedraja began to excavate the pit at La Pedraja and found the remains of 104 people killed between July and October 1936. A second mass grave was found nearby. The exhumation triggered a process that led to the recovery of the memory of Antonio Benaiges and his work. The degraded state of the remains, however, means that Benaiges' body cannot be identified.

5. PILATE'S BALCONY, JULY 1936, NAVARRA

Miren Llona

It is not clear how the Ubaba Overlook in the Urbasa Mountains in Navarra came to be known as Pilate's Balcony. It is a stunningly beautiful place—a 350-meter-tall precipice home to the headwaters of the Urederra River, which flows south toward La Rioja. Beginning on July 18, 1936, this cliff, along with some of the mountain's many caves and chasms became the scenes of horrendous crimes perpetrated by the rebels against the supporters of the Second Republic. The density of the forest and darkness of the chasms made this the perfect place to hide any evidence of the murders, making them effectively disappear.

Some of the most relentless cleansing of Republican sympathizers during the Civil War took place in the province of Navarra, despite the fact that the coup provoked very little resistance there. Once war was declared in Pamplona, General Mola gathered all the mayors of the province and told them: "We have to sow terror … without any scruples or hesitation, among all those who do not think like us." His words reveal one of the fundamental objectives of the rebellion which, in the words of Paul Preston, was to "tear out progressive Republican culture by the roots." This is how this primarily Catholic and conservative province well behind the lines came to lose 2,822 men and thirty-five women, a rate of 8.3 murders per 1,000 residents. This figure was surpassed in La Rioja, another rearguard region, where 2,000 people, including forty women, were executed—a rate of 9.8 per thousand residents. The places most deeply affected in both territories were the villages of the Ribera region, where the Popular Front had won the elections and where labor unions were strongest. With an assassination rate of 67.6 per 1,000 residents, the town of Sartaguda tragically become known as the Village of the Widows.

These figures demonstrate, first, that victims had been targeted for the "crimes" of having voted for the Popular Front or showing themselves to be Republicans, or for having been unacceptably insubordinate as women and workers. Further, the magnitude of these figures shows that the repression was carried out methodically and precisely, and that the civilian population was decisively involved, both in accusing the victims as well as in their execution. This was not solely the work of the Civil Guard, the Requeté or the Falange. Fear, a basic driver of violence and collaboration, and the safety offered by shared values, were two factors that help explain how great number of ordinary people turned into informants against and murderers of their own neighbors.

Pilar, from the village of Larraga, describes the assassination of her father, Vicente Lamberto, a 52-year-old farmer and member of the General Workers' Union (UGT), and her 14-year-old sister Maravillas, on August 15, 1936, this way:

> Around two in the morning two people from the village along with a pair of Civil Guards came to my house to take my father away. My sister told them, "I want to know what you're going to do to my father." She got out of bed, got dressed, and went with them. My father was thrown in the jail in the basement of the town hall. My sister was taken upstairs where she was raped ... They themselves said so and everybody knew it.

They were killed deep in the oak forest around the 12-kilometer mark of the highway connecting Puerto de Lizarraga to the Urbasa-Andia mountains. Vicente's body was found by residents of the Iruñuela village. Maravillas' naked corpse was discovered only later.

The military commanders may have directed the political cleansing, but in practice it was carried out by the Requeté and Falangist militias. The Central Carlist War Council of Navarra (JCCGN) converted the school run by the Piarist order into its main headquarters, the Requeté jail, and the Tercio Movil. The Falange's Eagle Squadron from Pamplona used the Salesian order's school as its central jail. These two organizations also took over the San Cristóbal Fort and the provincial prison. In other words, between them, the Carlists and Falangists were in control of all of the repressive institutions, those responsible for processing accusations, prisoner "releases," and execution orders. An infamous example is the "release" of prisoners from Tafalla on October 21, 1936, in which sixty-four persons were shot to death in Monreal. The murder of fifty-two others in Valcaldera, on August 23, is another.

The magnitude of these numbers contrasts with the startling lack of documentation regarding the activities carried out by these entities; the absence of any records of detentions, release orders, or wanted-persons lists. Just as astonishing is the absence of any trace of who was responsible for this decision-making and for organizing and operating all of this repressive machinery. Expunging the incriminating information regarding all of this criminal activity was also done systematically and with great care. They washed their hands of it, just like Pontius Pilate.

6. EXECUTED TILES, SUMMER 1936, MALANYANES, BARCELONA

Plàcid García-Planas

God has been shot many times. By definition, however, he never dies. His most legendary execution came one morning in 1918, when a group of soldiers fired several rounds from their machine guns up into the Moscow sky. The judicial proceedings of the Soviet State against God, represented by a Bible sitting on the bench, had taken place the day before. After five hours of testimony, appeals, and protests, the court declared Him guilty of the crime of genocide.

Though the early Soviets carried out several trials against God, there is no documented record of his "execution" in Moscow. But for the execution of Saint Ines in the small town of Malanyanes, near Barcelona, there is. Somebody collected and kept all of her pieces; when the fragments ended up in my hands several years ago, I closed my eyes and imagined the group of

Iberian Anarchist Federation (FAI) soldiers standing before the tiles, loading their riles and firing at the patron saint of adolescents.

As in so many places in Spain, anticlerical fervor had taken aim at these eighteenth-century painted tiles adorning the exterior wall of the rector's house—iconoclasm against a thousand years of devotion to this Roman martyr in the village of Santa Agnes of Malanyanes, located within the greenery of the coastal mountains of Barcelona. She was shot, just as the Christ of the Sacred Heart of the Hill of the Angels, near Madrid, was shot, by Republican militias in that summer of 1936.

As the National Confederation of Labour editorialized in its journal *Worker Solidarity* on January 22, 1937: "We have turned the torch of purifying fire on all those monuments that have for centuries cast their shadow over all corners of Spain—the churches—, and we have traversed the countryside, purifying it of this religious plague."

The manner and severity of Spanish iconoclasm, unprecedented in Europe in its intensity, varied across time and place. In the village of Ayna, in the diocese of Toledo, militiamen took images from the church to a bullfight, where the animals charged at them for people's amusement. There were all manner of victims: in Castellar del Vallès, in the province of Barcelona, the head of the socialist trade union, the UGT, was murdered for trying to help the parish priest, who was himself killed.

Indeed, getting rid of local churches and bell towers was one of the libertarian communists' main goals in their quest for a better world. Two decades after the Spanish Civil War, a French urban-planning movement, known as the Situationists, presented an idea for a project to improve the Parisian urban landscape that involved demolishing all of the city's religious buildings. According to its authors, this project was inspired by what took place in Barcelona in 1936.

For Spain's believers the unimaginable happened and the church, taken before the firing squad, fell into the catacombs. Telephone conversations no longer discussed consecrated objects or hosts, but rather "granulates" or "tonics." It is estimated that on Holy Thursday, 1938, some 70,000 people took communion in secret. In June of that year during the Festival of the Book, the House of the Book took out an ad in the newspapers that read: "The first book of your future library. The Bible. A book for your entire being, mind, heart and spirit. A nexus with all of Humanity in its most noble cause." On August 12 of that year, in the middle of the Battle of the Ebro, *La Vanguardia* newspaper printed pictures of the first death notice in Cataluña since the churches had been burned and believers massacred. Josep Maria Sans i Cacho "died a Christian death"; a Christian death, perhaps, while he fought the fascists along the Ebro. He was 20 years old.

My mother was 10 years old when, that same year, her father found a beautiful old wooden Christ tossed onto the road in Balaguer, near Lérida. She is 92 years old now, and still dives from the rocks into the sea. But she is beginning to lose her memory and worries that when it is gone for good, no one will remember why that Christ figure was broken.

The most divine contradiction that remains from all of this history is the Patum festival in the city of Berga, in the foothills of Pyrenees in Cataluña. With its popular ritual of fire, angels, and dragons, this festival has for centuries been held to celebrate the Corpus Christi holiday. UNESCO has declared it part of humanity's "intangible cultural heritage." However, this demon-filled ritual was strictly prohibited in 1936, and the Antifascist Committee even suggested burning all of the medieval bestiary in the town square.

A century later, Catalan leftists and antifascists have repurposed the festival as a symbol of their own identity, eradicating any trace of religion from it. They have adopted the bestiary that they once wanted committed to the flames. We cannot kill God, but we can confiscate his angels and dragons.

7. PLOW, SUMMER 1936, MADRID

Jesús Espinosa Romero

The Roman plow was fundamental to Spanish agriculture up until the second half of the twentieth century. Two thousand years after the Roman conquest of the Iberian Peninsula it was still used by millions of Spanish farmers. In the 1930s, agricultural rhythms and farming tools such as this marked the lives of the 13.5 million Spaniards—57 percent of the population—who lived in places of fewer than 10,000 residents. This was an eminently rural country.

Nevertheless, in the opinion of the Spanish ambassador in Paris, Salvador de Madariaga, Spain was in 1932 the most advanced nation in Europe, second only to Russia. His belief stemmed from the series of reforms being rolled out by the Republicans and socialists. These included agrarian reform, which was of enormous importance. At that time 47 percent of Spaniards were working 16 million hectares of arable land that produced 45 percent of the nation's wealth. Another important characteristic of the Spanish countryside was the high concentration of property ownership. For example, in Badajoz, the country's largest province, just twenty-five families owned one-third of all cultivated land.

In general the social situation in the Spanish countryside was far from pleasant, as the events in Castilblanco (1931) and Casas Viejas (1933), and the Catalan revolution of 1934 demonstrated. The country's greatest levels of inequality and its worst living conditions could be found on the large estates of Extremadura and Andalucía, home to some half a million laborers. This situation worsened between 1930 and 1936, as the global economic crisis forced more than 2 million people back to the countryside in search of a job or a parcel of land with which to feed themselves.

As in other European countries during the interwar period, agrarian reform was on the political agenda in Spain, including for right-wing parties such as the Falange. This involved changing the structure of property rights, and with them, the social relations of production. However, neither the initiatives of moderate Republican Manuel Azaña in 1932 nor conservative Republican Alejandro Lerroux in 1935 could solve the problem.

With the victory of the Popular Front in February 1936, the failed enlightened reforms issued from above transformed into one implemented from below. For many rural people, the hope produced by this new political situation was synonymous with the distribution of land. Between February and June, 1936, 92,000 *yunteros* (tenant farmers), most of them in Badajoz, occupied some 232,000 hectares of land. This action was based on their understanding of the Decree of March 20, 1936, that permitted such occupation for the purpose of social utility in exchange for a fixed rent based on the land's assessed value. Not only did 85 percent of the *yunteros* occupy the land within just a few weeks; more importantly, they ruptured existing agrarian class structures. The land now belonged to those who worked it.

In places where the coup against the state failed, poor country people passed the hot summer of 1936 in waves of angry revolts. In contrast, where the rebels managed take territory from the Republic, the social order and old system of property rights was restored. Agrarian revolution from below was stamped out forever by the "White Terror," and the assassination of nearly 9,000 people in Badajoz.

During the war years, the Republic deepened this reform from below. Its leader was Vicente Uribe, the first communist to serve as a minister in a Western European government. Appointed to Largo Caballero's Victory Government in September 1936, Uribe oversaw the agrarian reforms until the end of war. Far from imposing the Soviet model of forced collectivization, the Republican government defended the property rights of small farmers. Moreover, the Civil Responsibilities Tribunal was preparing to redistribute the lands confiscated from those hostile to the Republic. It is estimated that the Agrarian Reform Institute distributed or recognized the possession of a total of 7 million hectares of land—the greatest transfer of land during the twentieth century, excluding those in Russia and China. This, not the more famous collectives, was Spain's true rural revolution.

With the rebels' victory, property was returned to its original owners and their heirs. This was not a peaceful process. It was accompanied by the death, incarceration, and pillaging of those who had dared to cultivate land which, according to the laws of the New State, had not belonged to them. The old social order had been reinstated.

8. MATEO SANTOS' FILM COVERAGE OF THE REVOLUTIONARY MOVEMENT IN BARCELONA, SUMMER 1936

Vicente J. Benet

No images are more frequently used in audiovisual representations of the Civil War than those from this intense film by Mateos Santos. Before the war broke out, Santos had built a notable reputation for himself as a film critic for different magazines, especially for *Popular Film*, which he founded and directed in Barcelona between 1927 and 1937. After the coup failed in the Catalan capital, the anarchists were initially able to take control of the film industry. Santos, who was a member of the National Confederation of Labor (CNT), was one of the first filmmakers tasked with covering the events taking place in the city in the middle of July.

The film provides valuable documentation of the two days following the clash in which the military rebels were defeated. It shows the scars of the fighting in such emblematic places as the military headquarters and the armory, and the barricades placed in the main streets and in front of buildings, many of which had been seized by the unions and other pro-labor groups. Along with all of this, the video also shows the regular goings-on in the city, which had not lost its usual dynamism. At the same time, however, it reveals glimpses of a revolution that, as the anarchists were claiming, sought to vanquish not only the military but also the existing bourgeois society dominated by capitalists and the church. One of the clearest signs of this was the looting of religious buildings, the most notable example being the monastery of Salesas. Its religious tombs were desecrated, and the skeletons displayed in front of the building's doors in front of a fired-up crowd. Finally, the film shows the militants departing toward the Aragón Front in their improvised vehicles while a joyful crowd sees them off.

These images pulsate with feeling, presence, immediacy, excitement, and a revolution in motion. Yet the editing reveals little trace of manipulation, which turned out to be counterproductive from the propagandistic point of view. They consist above all of descriptive panoramas and static shots organized thematically. Together, they form a documentary report of the events that were taking place, rather than telling a story.

The immediacy of the images, their straightforward revelation of events and the lack of excessive manipulation calls into question how effective they were for their intended purpose. The anarchists' intention was very different from that of the master Soviet filmmakers, for example, who learned early on that for propaganda to have its greatest effect, it must not reflect events but construct them. The primary way of achieving this was through the technique of montage: selecting images and combining them to establish the meaning of events. The anarchists, in contrast, decided to be remain descriptive in their representation of events and praise of the revolution. But this approach created an immediate problem: as soon as the images fell into enemy hands they became an excellent piece of incriminating counter-propaganda, and were systematically used to denounce the brutalities committed in the Republican zone. Thus the images from the Salesas convent ended up in a multitude of films supporting the Francoist cause.

The filmmakers themselves seemed to have realized this situation. Thus, the lack of manipulation of the images themselves was countered by the aggressive tones of the soundtrack, which emphatically established their meaning. They also did not hesitate in using narration to contradict what was right before the viewers' eyes. For example, as the grim images of skeletons are shown, the narrator bluntly affirms that they are "mummies of nuns and friars martyrized by other monks and nuns." And right after this: "The sight of these twisted mummies, distorted by torture, was met with cries of popular indignation. In this and other acts, the Catholic Church, has bared its rotten soul." In short, just eliminating the soundtrack or replacing it with one with a different message made these images very useful to the enemy.

Another important sequence in the film that is often used given its undeniable documentary value is of the militants leaving for the Aragón Front. Even today, the energy conveyed by the images of these determined young fighters leaving for the front successfully conveys the excitement and enthusiasm of those first days of the war.

9. PROTECTIVE ARMBAND FOR AMERICANS, AUGUST 1936, MADRID

Arnau González i Vilata

Sometimes a piece of cloth can render us untouchable; other times it can be a symbol of collective stigmatization. During the first half of the twentieth century in Europe this type of textile was prolific, and it carried dramatic consequences. As is well known, others judged us by our appearance.

The situation was very simple, yet at the same time, complex. When war broke out, some people could be found wearing armbands with different countries' flags. If you were lucky enough to wear one with stars—in this instance round and missing their points—and stripes, you were transformed into someone special, even sacred. This is what happened to Leonides de Diego in Madrid in August 1936, when the four columns of the rebel military as well as the supposed fifth column invented by General Mola, tried to take the Republican capital. Her armband was number 387.

Many citizens of France, Italy, and Peru experienced the same thing. An armband with their country's flag, a lapel pin with their national emblem, or a piece of paper on their front door saying that they were under the protection of the Swedish consulate could make all the difference. Although these pieces of cloth and paper did not have supernatural powers, they did contain something magical and protective. While they could not deflect shells or bombs falling from the sky, they could save their wearers from arbitrary detention or allow them access to foods sent by foreign governments to their citizens in Spain.

Leonides de Diego had black hair, brown eyes and was "5 feet, 3.5 inches" (171cm) tall. But none of this would make her recognizable in the Certificate of Identity and Registration that would be issued to her by the Consul Robert F. Fernando many years later. Looking at her photo one sees in her overly stylized eyebrows, which look almost painted on, the appearance of a young woman yet to venture out into the world. But the most important thing one sees is that combination of red, white, and blue shining from her arm—representing the country that was not yet the world's foremost superpower but that was already determining the course of the European economy following the First World War, and that had already begun to overcome the crisis of 1929 and the Great Depression with President Franklin D. Roosevelt's New Deal.

To have experienced besieged Madrid as an adolescent must have been dramatic. Leonides had been born in Bridgeport, Connecticut, on August 24, only fifteen years before. Six days after her birthday in 1936, the United States embassy sent her, and every other person in Spain with a US passport, a document ordering them to leave, by taking US Navy ships that were making stops in Valencia and Alicante. The same message was sent out by all other diplomatic and consular offices in Bilbao, Barcelona, and Valencia.

There was no time to lose. If she wanted to leave, she would need to meet Mr. Johnson at the embassy, located at number 22, Calle del Cisne, on Monday, August 31. Nobody knew how the war would play out, and the embassies were short on senior-ranking officials to make decisions. Following the tradition of the Spanish nobility, they had all been spending the summer in San Sebastián, and the war had left them trapped on the Basque coast.

What was that fifteen-year-old girl, apparently alone, doing in Madrid? According to a piece of identification that was valid until February 23, 1941, Leonides was a student and lived very close to the Retiro Park, at 27 Calle Lope de Rueda. On November 25, 1936, while still in Madrid, she received a letter signed by Consul John D. Johnson, saying: "Your application to be registered as a US citizen, submitted to this office on August 21, 1936, was approved by the Department of State on November 17, 1936 and is valid until August 20, 1938." In such difficult times this must have happened by a bureaucratic hair's breadth.

Like many other foreigners living in Spain, Leonides did not want to leave Spain, or could not do so. Neither did thousands of French and Swiss citizens in Barcelona, to the desperation of Consul Trémoulet and his Swiss colleague, Gonzenbach, and to the astonishment of the admirals of the French Navy who insisted to the diplomats that they could not wait in the Spanish ports forever.

We don't know if this piece of cloth saved Leonides from any hardships, but it did allow her, it seems, to carry on with her life and remain in Madrid.

10. PIANO STOOL, AUGUST 1936, BARBASTRO, HUESCA

Verónica Sierra Blas

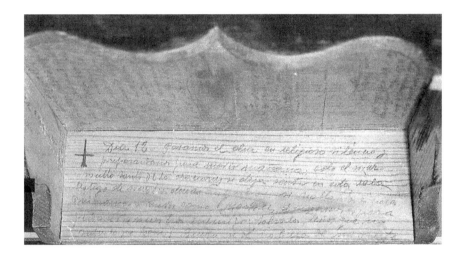

Between August 12 and 15, 1936, fifty-one members of the Claretian Congregation, thirty-nine of whom were students between 21 and 25 years old, were murdered in Barbastro.

In the days leading up to their execution they wrote numerous letters and messages for their congregation and their families in which they say their goodbyes, submit themselves to God's will, and beg His forgiveness for their executioners, thus leaving behind a record of the terrible moments that they lived together. Using worn down pencils that they had been able to hide under their robes, they made use of whatever they had on hand or that they could find to write on: pages from the breviaries and prayer books, instruction cards, prayer cards, pages of sheet music, chocolate bar wrappers, handkerchiefs, walls, floors, stairs, benches, and music stands. They even used a stool at the pedals of a piano that had once filled the hall of the Escolapios seminary, now their prison, with music.

To this day, these messages in Latin, Castilian, and Catalan signed by seven of the seminarians can still be read inside this small, 32-centimeter-long wooden frame. Preceding these messages, written along the edge of one of its sides, is the phrase *Christe, morituri te salutant*. The message from Rufino Pérez, the only one that describes the final moments of their long and cruel agony, stands out:

Day 12. We spent the day in religious silence preparing ourselves to die tomorrow; only the holy whisper of prayer, witness to our harsh anguish, can be heard. If we speak it is to encourage ourselves to die as martyrs. If we pray it is to forgive our enemies. Save us, Lord, they know not what they do!

The majority of the final testimonies from the Claretians of Barbastro were lost. Those written on the walls, the stairs, and the floor were erased when the hall was converted, first into a cafeteria, then a school. Many others were discovered and seized by the militia men who guarded the seminarians before and after their execution, while others were destroyed by the authors themselves so as to not cause trouble for their loved ones. But a select few were saved thanks to the help of third parties and were able to survive hidden away in different places, both within and outside of the village. Pope John Paul II considered them irrefutable proof of the martyrdom of their authors, whom he beatified on October 25, 1992. Together with the seminarians' remains and their personal religious objects, these texts can now be found in the Claretian Martyrs Museum in Barbastro.

Although it differed across time and place, such anticlerical and iconoclastic violence was carried out by systematically by unaffiliated groups and by the more radical elements of the new revolutionary powers that arose in Republican territory in July 1936. Despite much attention and academic debate, there is still no consensus over the extent to which art, books, documents, and other cultural heritage items were destroyed, nor over the number of victims. Yet it is unanimously believed that the Civil War produced the greatest massacre ever suffered by the Spanish clergy. According to Antonio Montero Moreno's research from the 1970s, some 6,832 clergy, including nearly 300 nuns, were murdered during the conflict. This differs from José Luis Ledesma's more recent calculation of 6,770 victims. Both authors agree, however, that the majority of these crimes were committed during the first three months of the war.

Despite the Francoist regime's insistence and its close relationship with the Catholic Church, the first beatification of martyrs from the Civil War did not take place until March 29, 1987, long after Spain had become a democracy. The first were three Discalced Carmelites nuns from Convent of San José de Guadalajara who had been executed on July 24, 1936. From then until July 2019, there were 1,915 more beatifications as well as eleven canonizations in thirty-two ceremonies, the most numerous of which took place on October 28, 2007 and October 13, 2013 (498 and 522, respectively).

This process continues. According to the Dicastery for the Causes of the Saints, the office of the Vatican that oversees the process of canonization, another fifty had been approved through September 2020. In Córdoba in October 2021, 127, including thirty-nine lay people, were beatified, and twenty-seven Dominicans from Seville were beatified in June 2022.

11. SAN SIMÓN ISLAND, SUMMER 1936, REDONDELA, PONTEVEDRA

Emilio Grandío Seoane

The beautiful scenery of the Vigo estuary has been the site of things as diverse as the Battle of Rande in the War of the Spanish Succession, a refuge for novelists like Jules Verne, and a safe haven for submarines bearing the Nazi swastika during the Second World War. At the far edge of this landscape is San Simón island. The island has been the subject of poetry and writing since at least the thirteenth century, including the work *Ondas do Mar de Vigo* by the Galician troubadour Martín Codax. San Simón is made up of two islets which, given their privileged location, have had a complex history: they housed a leper colony in the middle of the eighteenth century, the summer residence of Franco's personal guards until the end of the 1940s, and an orphanage for the children of sailors until the 1960s. But most importantly, and the reason for which they have earned a place in history, they were used as a concentration camp for prisoners from the very beginning of the Civil War. In order for the rebels to hold and classify the residents of territories they dominated, they had to find large spaces that would be easy to control. San Simón was, in this respect, an ideal place.

At first sight, the clash between the beauty of the landscape and the drama of the repressive measures that took place there is shocking. But the architects of the camps at San Simón also sought to make them physically disappear. These camps, whose existence was seemingly known to everyone, were not a source of pride. Bad hygiene and personal dramas were common currency. The prisoners lived with the despair of knowing that they were completely helpless, and that geography made escape impossible. On top of this, the prison's directors had total impunity, as the sea separated them from possible inspections.

Taking into account both islets, San Simón is barely 250 meters long by 80 meters wide. Yet it came to house thousands of people. Its first prisoners came from the provinces of Pontevedra and Ourense, but later, with the fall of the North in 1937, it was increasing filled with inmates from the Basque Country, Asturias, and León. These prisoners would arrive in San Simón after being held in provisional prisons, such as on boats tied up in port. A unique case was the arrival of the "elderly"—hundreds of people of advanced age from centers in Asturias. The humidity and climate in the middle of the sea worsened their infirmities to the point that many died.

There are interesting photographs of these inmates, who formed small groups around prominent or recognized leaders of the area, such as the Poza de Pontevedra. From the images they do not look like they are imprisoned, but rather in a place of leisure. Seen from the outside, San Simón looks idyllic, but on the inside, as days turned into months and then years, it became claustrophobic.

As if comprising different neighborhoods, the tiny space making up the islands was divided according to its use or function, each with its own name. One of the primary sources of the memory of the camp is a documentary called *Aillados* made in the 1980s—when many of the people who passed through these prison camps were still alive and lucid. Their testimonies reveal an attitude quite different from what we would have today. They are the memories of people who, for the simple act of having lived and suffered through them, normalize situations that are today completely outside our comprehension.

Today, San Simón is enormously and dramatically symbolic. Previous governments of the Xunta de Galicia wanted to convert it into a point of reference for remembering the repression in Galicia. It was designated a Place of Cultural Interest in 1999, and a symbol of repression during the Xunta's "Year of Memory" in 2006. Since then, with the help of historical memory organizations, there has been an annual ceremony to remember the Galicians who experienced this repression, thus reaffirming year after year the island's significant symbolic value.

12. *MUJERES* WEEKLY, 1936, MADRID

Miren Llona

The illustrated weekly *Mujeres* (Women) was launched in February 1936 as the official publication of the Antifascist Women's Association (AMA). This organization was created in 1933 in Madrid, and the following year it participated in the International Congress of Women Against War and Fascism, held in Paris. With the outbreak of the Civil War, the group spread throughout Republican Spain and reached 50,000 members in over 255 groups. In January 1937 the National Committee of the AMA in the Northern Front was created and from then on *Mujeres* was also published in Bilbao. Over the course of four months, this ten-page weekly published nineteen issues with a run of 10,000 copies each. It became a fixture in the Home of the Modern Woman.

In Bilbao, the AMA constituted a united front of women belonging to different political parties within the Popular Front, with the exception of Basque Nationalist women's associations such as Emakume Abertzale Batza

(EAB), which was tied to the Basque Nationalist Party (PNV). In the magazine's subscription newsletter, the antifascist women described themselves as "a group of women who love liberty … are the enemies of fascism … and who wish to cooperate in the common project of freeing the people."

The mobilization of antifascist women was as much a part of the strategy of international communism to overcome fascism during the interwar period as it was an initiative of the Communist Party of Spain (PCE) to defeat Franco during the Civil War. We can thus see how the political diversity the local AMA committees diminished at the higher levels of the organization, with PCE leaders having a greater presence in the provincial and national committees culminating with Dolores Ibárruri becoming president of the National Committee at the First Congress of Women Against War and Fascism, held in Madrid in 1934. This guaranteed that throughout the war the communists controlled the organization—which openly rejected revolutionary change and defended the goals of antifascism and the defense of the Republic.

Reading the in-depth articles in *Mujeres*, we can see that the call for women's mobilization broke with their traditional segregation within the public sphere. It defends the emancipation of women from a feminist perspective, demanding their rights to education, culture, work, and equal pay. At the same time, however, it also contains traces of the reactive attitudes towards gender roles that forced women from the front lines to strengthen the home front. In March 1937, the Committee of Women Against War and Fascism claimed in *Mujeres* that "the best way for the antifascist woman in Euskadi to fight against the war today is by getting involved in the tasks on the home front … Basque women's hands are at the disposal of national production." Thus, thousands of antifascist women organized workshops to make clothes for the militants, and groups known as "wardrobes" (*roperos*) to find shoes, mattresses, and children's clothes. They also worked as cooks and nurses and, when the rebel troops were near, the magazine called on them to dig trenches and prepare sandbags for the fortification and defense of the city.

The figure of the "combat mother" was the authentic heroine of the home front. The Republic appealed to the sacrifice, the pain, and the courage of mothers, both to motivate women to join the antifascist fight, as well as to urge their sons to join the militias and contribute to the defense of democracy. The exaltation of traditional female and motherly virtues became common currency in antifascist rhetoric. But not all women identified with this. For a large group of young women, the difficulties they had overcome and the responsibilities they had taken on increased their consciousness of women's worth. Writing in *Mujeres*, Astrea Barrios put it like this: "Lack of preparation is no excuse for keeping women out of certain activities. Just like antifascist men, antifascist women cannot accept professional obstacles if these benefit our common enemy: fascism. Did our male comrades know how to fire a gun on July 19?"

13. LORCA'S LOST TOMB (AND THOSE OF MANY OTHERS), AUGUST 1936, VÍZNAR, GRANADA

Miren Llona

In the early morning of August 18, 1936, Federico García Lorca and Juana Capdevielle were assassinated by two Francoist firing squads. These crimes took place more than 900 kilometers apart. García Lorca was killed at the Víznar ravine in Granada; Capdevielle on the road heading to Rábade in Lugo. The two were friends. During the spring of 1936 Capdevielle, a librarian at the Athenaeum in Madrid, had suggested to Lorca, director of the Barraca theater company, that he stage Lope de Vega's play *The Gentleman from Olmedo*. At the time, Lorca was the most internationally renowned and successful poet and playwright of the Spanish literary scene. For her part, Capdevielle was the first woman director of a university library, at the Department of Philosophy and Letters at the Central University of Madrid. She was a modern and liberated woman, one of those to whom the Second Republic had given wings; he was secular and free-thinking, inheritor of the spirit of the Residencia de Estudiantes, which had been established in 1910 as an Oxford-style college and became one of Madrid's leading cultural institutions. They were both killed for being "reds," and further, she for being a "whore," he for being a "faggot."

They both had plans for the future. In 1935, Capdevielle had married Francisco Pérez Carballo and, when he was named civil governor of A Coruña, they had gone to live in Galicia. Her husband was killed on July 24, after leading the resistance to the coup. Capdevielle was pregnant when, weeks later, they took her "for a walk." Lorca was planning to visit Mexico with his young boyfriend, Juan Ramírez de Lucas, who had worked in the Anfistora theater club run by Pura Ucelay and by Lorca himself. On July 13, with a ticket to New York in his pocket, Lorca traveled to Granada to say goodbye to his family and to spend the July 18 holiday celebrating San Federico with them. He was arrested on August 16. According to Ramón Ruiz Alonso, a prominent member of the Spanish Confederation of Autonomous Right (CEDA) who denounced him, "he has done more harm with his pen than others have done with their guns." For this same reason the Francoists held public book burnings both during and after the Civil War—something which we have come to know only recently as this Nazi-like behavior had been carefully covered up.

Capdevielle and Lorca's executions are among more than 130,000 that can be attributed to the Francoist repression during the Civil War and the dictatorship. Franco's regime did not acknowledge its participation in Lorca's assassination but, given the international response to the news of his disappearance, Ramón Serrano Suñer himself had to publicly deny the participation of Franco's government, declaring in 1948 that it had all been the work of some uncontrollables. Nevertheless, in both his capture and execution, there is evidence of the involvement of the Commander José Valdés Guzmán, civil governor of Granada, and of the Lieutenant Colonel of the Civil Guard, Nicolás Velasco Simarro. They organized his arrest in the plain light of day as a massive operation involving numerous armed guards in the streets and on the roofs who cordoned off the home of the Rosales family in which Lorca had been hiding. Once he was a prisoner in the Civil Government building—which Valdés and Velasco had turned into a place for detention and torture—Lorca faced the same fate as the rest of the condemned who ended up there: to be driven to execution sites without any kind of judicial proceeding. One of the preferred locations for such executions in Granada was the ravine at Víznar.

Although he was dead and his body had not been found, in 1940 the Francoist authorities opened a case against Lorca in order to punish him for his political activities. The charges against him included being a Mason, a "supporter of the Popular Front" and "director of the ideologically communist *La Barranca* newspaper"; denying the existence of God; and maintaining a friendship with Fernando de los Ríos and "other leftist politicians." His public life was "suspicious ..."; "his friendships were very free," and he was a "queer."

In a 1931 interview with *The Literary Gazette*, Lorca had defined himself as a person from Granada (*granadino*) inclined toward "a sympathetic understanding of the persecuted … Blacks, Gypsies, Jews, the Moors, that we all carry inside of us." What is certain is that this way of thinking was subversive and intolerable after the Francoist coup. In fact, as Lorca's cousin Carmen García González has recalled, "amongst the rebels it was considered a source of pride to be the one who had killed Federico García Lorca." To this day they have kept the secret of Lorca's tomb, located somewhere along the path from disgrace to reparation.

14. DRAWING OF BETTY BOOP, AUGUST 1936, LUGO

Sofía Rodríguez López

Women at the Service of Spain (MSE) was an association created in Lugo a few weeks after the beginning of the Civil War. It was founded by Emilia de Tudela Bonell, a former member of Valencia's Regional Right party (DRV) who compiled her activities into a book dedicated to her friend Victoria Fernández Manzano, believing that its contents would serve to convince many women "that they should work for the homeland." The deaths of family members, the persecution of religion and the economic crisis led the thousands of members of this Galician organization to consider themselves the victims of the "political conflict" unleashed during the Second Republic.

Getting involved in the organization was how they took part in the fight against the Popular Front. Their efforts included taking charge of different hospitals and infirmaries, like the Minor Seminary in Lugo, in Monforte, Mondoñedo, and Sarria, as well as collecting donations on the "Day without Dessert" created by the Francoists as a fundraising measure. But their principal contribution was in the sewing workshops that extended to dozens of villages and towns throughout the province. With the feminization of these workshops, now consisting mainly of young, single women fulfilling their Social Service obligation, they came to be represented by sexual icons of the moment, such as Betty Boop. This cartoon, launched by Paramount in 1930, symbolizes the liberal style of the North American flapper or pin-up girl, or the French *garconne*. As this was in diametrical opposition to the gender ideology of the rebels, however, she was drawn to look more demure, while standing in front of her Singer sewing machine and wearing the Nationalist uniform.

In December of 1936, the *Voice of Truth* and the *Progress in Lugo* described daily life in the MSE workshop, where a young woman's voice could be heard praying three Ave Marias—one for the good of the church, one for the Pontiff, and one for Spain—to earn an indulgence from the priest. Hanging on the wall was a Sacred Heart, as well as a portrait of the Generalísimo presiding over the place, next to a wall clock, political posters and a Philips radio for listening to the news, courtesy of the companies sympathetic to the coup. The sounds of prayer blended with hymns from Catholic Youth Action, Popular Action, the Spanish Falange, Carlist Requetés, the Infantry Academy, and of MSE itself, as well as with music of the Spanish Legion.

The Spanish woman
If she has any decorum and shame
Should not for one moment leave the workshop
In order to go for a walk.
Spanish women
Lend themselves to the fight
With textiles and scissors
To make your capes for you.

Making clothes for the Francoist soldiers was a job shared by other, more traditional women's groups, such as the monarchists of the Spanish Renewal and the Women's Section of the Falange. However, the introduction of the Carlist Margaritas, so important elsewhere in Spain at the beginning of 1936, did not take root in Galicia. Their presence was so scarce that they did not reach even fifty members per province. They had no office in Pontevedra, and only in Lugo were there several stable groups. There was a small group in Orense made up of Carlist families. The Women's Section in Orense also remained within narrow family circles, as at least three out of every four members before February 1936 were either the daughters, sisters or girlfriends of militants of the fascist party Falange Española de las Juntas de Ofensiva Nacional Sindicalista (FE-JONS).

In contrast, by 1939 the MSE organization had extended to 125 villages and counted some 5,000 members in Lugo, and 24,640 in all of Galicia. Even Pilar Franco de Jaraiz, Franco's niece, founded an MSE group in Puentedeume and served as its honorary president. The organization's four provincial directors requested a collective medal for their members from the *caudillo* for having made 7,024,841 articles of clothing free of charge, thereby saving the state 1,910,935.80 pesetas in wages, based on what the Administration paid per item. The free use of the physical space, as well as electricity, water, furniture, and the sewing machines, also contributed to the workshops' high productivity and low expenses.

The recognition sought by these women could thus be justified mathematically by the economic benefits they provided to the rebel military. Although there were many groups and organizations dedicated to sewing for the Nationalists, "some called Workshops of the Administration, as in Seville, San Sebastián and Bilbao; Our Lady of Pilar in Zaragoza, Our Lady of Saint Teresa in A Coruña and Santiago, and several others such as ours, the MSE ... only in our workshop has everything has been made for free by the members, who did not receive a single daily wage."

No one should deny these women their due regarding their collective effort toward the Francoist victory. As the dedication in Emilia de Tudela's book says: "When, with the passage of time, everyone will have forgotten the work you and I did for our Spain, this book will take on a great value."

15. ROSARY, SUMMER/AUTUMN 1936, CAMUÑAS, TOLEDO

Alfredo González Ruibal

This metal rosary was found inside a mine shaft along with the remains of a murdered victim. In the summer and autumn of 1936, the abandoned Las Cabezuelas mine in Camuñas, in the province of Toledo, witnessed some unusual activity: the arrival of vehicles full of people, the sounds of banging, shouts, and shots. Afterwards, silence. Between August and November of 1936, an indeterminate number of victims of the revolutionaries' repression met their end at the bottom of the mine. The semi-occult nature of these crimes led to all sorts of speculation, as tends to occur in such instances of indiscriminate violence. Before the bodies in the mine were exhumed, rumor had it that it contained thousands of victims. During the interrogations for the Causa General, the Francoist regime's postwar investigation into what it called the "red domination" of Spain, in 1943, the mayor of the town placed the figure at 600 dead and acknowledged the impossibility of recovering the bodies due to the depth of the shaft.

Between 2008 and 2010, at the request of the Archbishop of Toledo, a team from the Aranzadi Society directed by Francisco Etxeberria descended nearly 30 meters and documented the massacre. The experts calculated that there were around fifty individuals, of whom they were able to separate forty-one. The bodies were in a very degraded state and had traces of carbonization; it is known that cadavers were sometimes sprayed with gasoline and set on fire. Further, the remains were covered over with several tons of dirt. All of this is evidence of the desire to cover up the crime, a fact also implicit in the selection of the mine as the place where the bodies were discarded. The retrieval of cadavers from mine shafts is extremely complicated, and during the Civil War both sides frequently used chasms and mines in order to make the recovery of remains more difficult. The perpetrators were thus conscious of the criminal nature of their acts: the shafts allowed them to "disappear" not only their rivals but also the evidence of their own crimes. The exhumation in Camuñas revealed two levels of human remains separated by a significant layer of lime, evidence of at least two distinct episodes of murders. The lime, which was used to dissolve the cadavers, helped to conserve the bones.

With the exception of one woman, all of the ossified remains identified belonged to male individuals, ranging in age from the very young to elderly people with evidence of arthritis. Archival documentation archives identify sixty-three people from the surrounding villages as having been assassinated between August 3 and September 28, 1936. Other victims ended up in the mine later on, such as Carlos Álvarez Rodríguez, coadjutor in Herencia, whose death is recorded as November 11. Victims for whom there exists a documented record of their death include two women and seven priests. Some of the victims were affiliated with right-wing parties, such as the Falange and Renovación Española [Spanish Renewal]. They also include two mayors and several town councilors. The strategy of eliminating political rivals was adopted both in the rebel zone as well as where revolutionary groups were active.

The plans on both sides of the ideological spectrum to exterminate their rivals were intended to eliminate not only people but also political and religious beliefs. The buried objects testify to this. In addition to the rosary, investigators in Camuñas found the remains of a cassock, a medallion of the Madre del Amor Hermoso (Mother of Beautiful Love), and a crucifix. The last was located near the mouth of the mine shaft, accompanied by various objects associated with the murders: bullets from rifles and pistols and a Mauser cartridge. Other objects were discovered among the remains of the victims: two fountain pens, a carpenter's pencil, hair pins, bits of clothing, shoes, and a small purse with some coins that was found next to the remains of the only woman that it was possible to identify. Several of the victims also had gold dental fillings. These objects tell us not only about the victims' beliefs but also about their professional lives—the carpenter's pencil, the cassock—and their social class—the fountain pens, the gold fillings. These are indications of people with high social status, although many of those murdered by the militiamen belonged to the working class.

The religious elements surrounding several of the victims in Camuñas are eloquent testimony to the savage anticlericalism that characterized the revolutionary violence that cut short the lives of 6,832 priests, friars, monks, and nuns. But the murder of Catholics was not limited to the Republican zone: crucifixes and medallions are among the most numerous types of personal objects found in the mass graves in the rebel zone. Despite increasing secularization, the Christian faith remained widespread in 1930s Spain. During the Civil War, it often united the victims on both sides. The rosary in Camuñas allows us to imagine the final moments of its owner's life: anguished, terrified, saying a prayer and possibly offering words of forgiveness to their executioners, before being gunned down.

16. BULLET STOPPER, AUTUMN 1936, TERQUE, ALMERÍA

Sofía Rodríguez López

According to the Dictionary of the Royal Spanish Academy of Language, a "fetiche" ("fetish") is an idol or religious object to which supernatural powers are attributed. The "bullet stopper" ("detente bala"), used by many soldiers of the Francoist Army—though not exclusively by them—during the Spanish Civil War, is a type of fetish.

Also known as a scapular, it is a textile badge embroidered with the words, "Stop, bullet. The Sacred Heart of Jesus is with me." Originally associated with the Carlist soldiers who fought during the civil wars of the nineteenth century, this tradition actually began in 1686 when the Burgundian saint Margarita María Alacoque had four visions of Christ asking for the creation within the Catholic Church of a prayer or liturgy to the Sacred Heart of Jesus. It would take until the Holy Year of 1900, however, for Pope Leo XIII to institute this ecclesiastical devotion. King Alfonso XIII publicly consecrated the entire country to it in 1919. These were the high points of social Catholicism and mobilization among Catholic lay women. Throughout the entire country there was a proliferation of publications, such as the magazine *The Messenger of the Sacred Heart of Jesus* (1916–41), and associations, like the Sacred Heart Women's Union, whose political mobilization took off in response to the secularizing projects of the Second Republic.

Following the military uprising of July 18, Cardinal Isidro Gomá, the Primate of Spain, informed Cardinal Eugenio Pacelli, secretary to Pope Pius XI, that among the rebels were Republicans who were people "of order" as well as those who fought "with the image of the Sacred Heart of Jesus on their chest and who desire a monarchy united with the Catholic Church." The same thing happened on the Republican side, bad as this may have seemed to many antifascists. This meant that women on both sides embroidered "bullet stoppers" in order to protect their husbands, sons, and boyfriends, as they had previously done when they had left for colonial wars, including the Heart of Jesus alongside images of the Virgin. As described by Luis Ortega Sánchez, a soldier mobilized with the Garibaldi International Brigade: "The Virgin has saved me many times. My mother hung her on me when I left for the war and I've worn her always, the scapular of the Virgin of Carmen. Although I've gone through many difficult things, I have narrowly escaped death many times."

In the moments of greatest anticlerical persecution during the Civil War, this devotion to the Sacred Heart, as well as that to Christ the King, was the perfect target for many Republicans to discharge their anger. In the capital, as well as in places such as Aranjuez, Bilbao, and Almería, militia groups formed firing squads to attack religious images and take town statues, as occurred in the Cerro de los Ángeles in Madrid. After the Francoists conquered the Cerro, on November 9, 1936, they held a church service there in which they asked forgiveness, using one of the blocks that had fallen in August (the monument had been dynamited in July) as the high altar. According to José María Pemán, following the revolutionary fury it was now time to recover one of the symbolic roots of the country. However, Falangists and traditionalists disagreed as to what site should be used as a place of remembrance, to such an extent that, in 1938, the National Delegation of Press and Propaganda of the official party (FET y de las JONS) censored several issues of the *Sacred Heart of Jesus Almanac* for its insistence on uniting those monuments with ones dedicated to the fallen. They were seeking to avoid the secularizing trend inherent in the monuments to the Unknown Soldier that had spread across Europe after the First World War.

The use of the "bullet stopper" continues today. After more than 300 years of tradition, the "fetishes" of the Carlist Requeté were reborn in the hands of the Discalced Carmelites of Toledo who, in 2017, made 600 of them for the Spanish soldiers deployed as "blue helmets" with the United Nations Interim Force in Lebanon (UNIFIL).

17. INTERNATIONAL BRIGADE ID, SEPTEMBER 1936, SANTA FE DE MONDÚJAR, ALMERÍA

Sofía Rodríguez López

Luis Ortega's story is that of an ordinary Spaniard recruited into the Popular Army in September 1936. Or at least this is how he presents it in the memoirs he wrote by hand for his grandchildren, some fifty years later. His diary and documentation are beautiful objects through which to learn about quotidian aspects of the war, including how the troops were fed.

Luis, and another 300 youths from Almería who accompanied him, were stationed in Lérida. He was part of the First Company of the Rakosi Battalion in the XIII International Brigade, which was made up of an unknown number of Hungarian and Czech volunteers. When they went to the front at Jaca, snow prevented the mules with the rearguard's cooking pots from climbing into the mountains. The soldiers could barely feed themselves and were forced to eat the buds of the almond trees that were beginning to bloom. When they were withdrawn to Torralba de Aragón, an evacuated village, they were prevented from using the houses and had to stand guard next to a fire in order to avoid freezing. The toasted garbanzo beans that they were served gave them serious indigestion.

Later, when they were at the Extremadura Front, Luis recalled how they had to subsist on bread crusts, tins of sardines, and sacks of biscuits that were air dropped down to them. When night fell and they prepared for battle, the officers passed around cognac and the nervous soldiers urinated on themselves. The commanders of his battalion, as well as a good number of foot soldiers, were killed between the trenches and the barbed wire. The aid stations were insufficient to stop the bleeding: "I feel as if I am living that moment of my life again, and I cannot help my eyes from filling with tears," he wrote. Although reinforcements arrived from La Peraleda, the advancing tanks and Moroccan cavalry forced the Rakosi to withdraw, suffering casualties of 60 percent. Meanwhile, the sky turned red and a voice on a loudspeaker reached the trenches: "Reds, don't be scared, we are celebrating the capture of Teruel."

In August 1937, on the way to Belchite, a worn-out man entrusted them with a four-year-old girl to return her to her parents at a country house. The bombs would not stop exploding and people were abandoning their belongings along the road. Luis himself would leave behind the corduroy jacket that his mother sent to him at the front along with some chorizos. For this reason, he advised his grandchildren: "If you ever have to go to war, never save anything for tomorrow—God willing you never have to have that experience."

On the Lérida Front, Luis dislocated a bone and spent five days being treated at the military hospital in Badalona before being sent to another recovery center in Montserrat. As he was missing from his company, the clerk in charge of collecting the soldiers' documentation when they went into combat returned his documentation to his parents, mistakenly thinking that he had been killed. For four of five days he was, if not dead, at least officially missing. And while his parents "lost" a child, he was actually in the hospital meeting with the paymasters of the Republican Army and a group of Catalan artists who treated them to a show, some dancing and champagne.

When he was off duty, Luis would go with his girlfriend, Galga, to see variety shows at the Paralelo. He would always be accompanied by doctors trying, supposedly, to get "their things"—threads and tights for the nurses—since "in Barcelona there was nothing to buy unless it was women, or theater, or movies." Interestingly, while the war, and with it the Republic, was waning, Luis concluded that: "That was headed towards perfection … they were the happiest days of my life."

The withdrawal of the International Brigades ordered by the government woke the Rakosi up from that dream. The Hungarians returned to their country, but not before first providing Luis with papers declaring him "a complete invalid." It took nearly two weeks before he was able to get on a boat that would return him to Almería, during which time he survived on two bottles of condensed milk. In this way he was able to avoid both being conscripted to go to the Ebro Front and police raids. After unloading in Valencia, he took the train home. Along the way, he was able to eat some small buns and drink water that was meant for the train engine. It was the end of February 1939. His family had been waiting from him at the station for more than five nights.

18. T-26 TANK, OCTOBER 1936, MADRID

Antonio Cazorla-Sánchez

Aviation played an important and well-known role in the Spanish Civil War. The role of tanks, and the impact of their use on the future of military tactics and technology, is less well known. Among the tanks that were used in the war, one stands out for its quality and longevity: the Soviet T-26.

The first Soviet tanks, including fifty T-26s, reached Spain on October 12, 1936. They arrived at Cartagena, the most important port for the Republican war effort for the duration of the war. Along with the tanks came the first Soviet instructors. They quickly went to Archena, also in the province of Murcia, which had been chosen as the location for the Republican tank training center a few days earlier. On October 29, they entered combat for the first time, in Seseña, near Madrid, and helped to stop the Francoist advance on the capital. Located in the rearguard, well connected and protected, the base at Archena functioned until the end of the war, and every model of tank that was used in the conflict, including fewer than one hundred antiquated French ones, passed through it. The final mission of tanks from Archena was to help snuff out the rebellion of the fifth column in Cartagena, in March, 1939.

In the 1930s the T-26 was the most produced model of tank (some 12,000 units). It was also the one most used during the Civil War: 281 arrived in Spain compared to 155 of the much lighter and less well-armed Italian L-3-33, and 122 of the German Panzer I. Due to the poor way in which they were used and their frequent mechanical failures, the rebels succeeded in capturing and putting back into service some 150 of them, which then served in the Francoist army until they were replaced by American M47s in 1954. One is shown in the photograph. To avoid being confused with the enemy, it was painted over with the colors of the royal flag. It is now on display at the El Goloso military base near Madrid.

The T-26 was based on the British Vickers tank that the Soviets bought in 1930. They eliminated one of the turrets from the original model and installed a 45mm cannon and a machine gun. In the 1930s, it was unrivaled. It weighed almost ten tons, whereas the Panzer I weighted only six and the Italian models barely three. Further, the models from the Fascist powers were armed only with machine guns. Nazi and Fascist military observers in Spain quickly recognized the technological disparity between their tanks and the Soviet ones, and they paid a 500 pesetas reward for each one captured. As a result of their observations, the Germans decided that their new tanks would be heavier and better protected than the Panzer I. In contrast, the Italians did not innovate and their armored vehicles, clearly already inadequate in Spain, were incapable of playing an effective role in the Second World War.

Despite its advantages, the T-26 also had serious problems. Mechanically it was unreliable, and it did not have a radio, which made making complex maneuvers difficult. Its armor was also inadequate: most of the antitank weapons available at the time could destroy one from a distance of 500 meters. These defects become more evident over time. During the Winter War (from November 1940 to March 1941), the Finns destroyed several thousand Soviet armored vehicles, most of them T-26s, by ambushing them and burning them with gasoline bombs or relatively light antitank weapons. The T-26s fared even worse during the Nazi invasion of the Soviet Union, which began in June 1941, in which they confronted heavier and better-protected German models. Some 10,000 were destroyed in just a few months.

Although the T-26 was deployed in the majority of the great battles of the Spanish Civil War (Guadalajara, Brunete, Belchite, Teruel and the Ebro), it did not play a decisive role. The terrain was not always appropriate for tanks, and the Republicans never amassed sufficient numbers of them on the battlefield to destroy and seriously penetrate enemy lines. (They partially achieved this at Brunete.) The tanks ended up playing a supporting role to the infantry. This was a deeply rooted idea among the most conservative strategists which, as a result of the supposed military lessons offered by the Civil War, ended up being imposed on the French and Soviet militaries, as well. (Stalin's execution of Mijaíl Tujachevski, the father of modern tank warfare, in 1937 also contributed to this tendency.) For their part, the

Germans continued developing the opposite doctrine, in which masses of vehicles advanced independently of and preceding the infantry. The result was the so-called *blitzkrieg*, which was so successful in the first years of the Second World War. The Soviets ended up adjusting their tactics and returned to the use of great fleets of armored vehicles preached by Tujachevski. This is, in part, how they succeeded in defeating the Nazis. Another contributing factor was their use of simpler, more versatile and more powerful tank models, including, above all, the mythical T-34.

19. THE SILK EXCHANGE, NOVEMBER 1936, VALENCIA

Antonio Cazorla-Sánchez

At the beginning of November 1936, Madrid, and perhaps the Republic too, seemed lost. Following the Portuguese border, the columns of the Army of Africa advanced from Andalucía in a great arc that had the Spanish capital as its end point. It was a procession of blood and fire that the poorly armed militants could not match. Would Madrid hold up? It did. Firstly, because fighting in trenches with the streets of the capital just behind them was easier than trying to do so in open country. Secondly, because Franco's detour to liberate the Alcázar of Toledo gave Madrid's defenders a few extra weeks to gather reinforcements, including the arrival of the first units of the International Brigades, and, at almost the same time, new shipments of Soviet arms. For a few months, the contest seemed balanced.

Even so, Largo Caballero's government could not be sure that they would retain the capital, which was almost already surrounded. It therefore took the drastic decision to relocate to Valencia. This move offered some key advantages: Valencia was far from the front, it had a very strong tradition of republicanism and—in contrast to Barcelona, the location favored by the president, Azaña—it was a stronghold of Largo Caballero supporters. But, as in other places within the Republican rearguard, not everything went smoothly. In October, at least 150 people died when anarchist and Communist militiamen fought each other in the streets, in what was just one precursor to the more serious incidents that were to take place in Barcelona the following May. In any case, Valencia became the capital of the Republic on November 7, 1936, and remained the capital until October 31, 1937. Government departments installed themselves in the city's most emblematic buildings. The Presidency was located in the Capitanía General (military headquarters), the government in the Benicarló Palace, and the Cortes (parliament) in the city hall, but after the latter was bombed it ended up in the beautiful Contracts Hall of the Lonja de la Seda (Silk Exchange), whose image is reproduced above. The heart of the Republic lay in Valencia.

Valencia also took in and protected the artistic patrimony evacuated from Madrid, especially works from the Prado Museum, the Liria Palace, which had been severely damaged by Francoist bombing, and the Escorial. Valencia was the first stop on a long journey that took these works of art to Geneva, before they were eventually repatriated to Spain after the end of the war. Also notable was that in July 1937 Valencia hosted the World Congress for the Defense of Culture, in which the cream of the leftist intellectual crop of the era participated.

The city paid a very high price for being the provisional seat of the Republican government. From their bases in Mallorca, Italian airplanes and seaplanes commanded by Ramón Franco, the dictator's brother, bombed the port, the railways, and the city's most emblematic places throughout 1937, leveling entire neighborhoods in the process. That November, when the situation on the Aragón Front had so deteriorated that the partition of Republican territory began to look like a live possibility, the government, now led by Juan Negrín, again moved the capital of the Republic, this time to Barcelona. It remained there until the city fell in January 1939. Two and a half years of war had destroyed democracy. When the Cortes met on Spanish soil for the last time—on February 1, 1939, in the castle of San Fernando in Figueras—only 62 of the 473 deputies elected in February 1936 were present. The rest were dead, imprisoned, exiled, or supporting the rebels. The Republic was dying.

Francoist troops entered Valencia on March 29, 1939. The repression began immediately, and it was brutal. As one researcher described it: "The Modelo prison, with a capacity of 500, held 235 prisoners on March 30. That number reached 15,210 on April 1, and even in 1941 more than 10,000 remained." The victors even took their revenge on the dead. The half-built monument celebrating Valencia's most famous son, the writer Vicente Blasco Ibáñez, was quickly destroyed. (It was rebuilt in 1980 and vandalized within days by the very active local extreme right.) All of this served to erase for decades the history of this city that had so quickly and under such dangerous conditions stepped up to defend freedom.

Now that Spaniards have recovered their freedom, today a curious visitor can follow a tourist route leading to all of the places in Valencia referenced here and commemorating what was for one year the capital of Spain.

20. .303 CALIBER BULLET CLIP, NOVEMBER 1936, MADRID

Alfredo González Ruibal

This bullet clip appeared on top of the parapet of a trench in Madrid's Casa de Campo park, which was the site of an archaeological excavation in 2016. Hundreds of shells and clip guides of the same caliber appeared inside the trench. They are testimony to the fierce defense mounted by the Edgar André battalion from November 8 to 15, 1936 against the rebel troops who were advancing towards Madrid.

The .303 caliber could be used with the British Enfield P14 rifle as well as with the Lewis light machine gun, both of which were used by the Republicans during the Civil War. In the photographs from Casa de Campo taken during the month of November 1936, the majority of the members of the International Brigades can be seen armed with Enfield rifles. The cartridges documented in the trench have markings from Lowell, Massachusetts and are dated 1916. But their history actually begins 200 years earlier.

A textile factory was founded in the town of Lowell in the 1820s. Massachusetts was benefiting greatly from the production of cotton in the southern United States, which was massively dependent on slave labor. By the middle of the nineteenth century, Lowell was the country's principal industrial site. As in other textile towns at the time, the working conditions were horrible. Between 1830 and 1840 a worker (most likely a woman as they were dominant in this industry) would have worked an average of seventy-three hours per week. This inhumane schedule was reduced to "only" fifty-four hours per week in the first decade of the last century.

As the textile industry grew, so did another type of factory. In 1869 a new arms factory opened in Lowell: the United States Cartridge Company founded by the Union General Benjamin Butler. The company reached its apex during the First World War when it produced 75 percent of all of the small caliber ammunition in the United States. The majority went to the British Army, which had sent agents there to acquire arms as early as September 1914. (The United States did not enter the war until 1917.) Some other local industries also pivoted to the war effort; they switched from making rugs to making bullets. In total, these factories produced more than 2 million cartridges destined for places such as the United Kingdom, Russia, Italy, France, and the United States, amongst others. The collapse of demand following the end of the war led the Lowell factory to close in 1926, although it relocated to Connecticut where it continued under the name Winchester.

How did munitions from Massachusetts end up in Madrid? Through many twists and turns. The British Army, the primary recipient of .303 caliber ammunition, apparently did not use all of the cartridges they had imported during the First World War. So when the Russian Civil War (1917–1921) broke out, the UK sent assistance to the counterrevolutionary forces, primarily by supplying them with arms: 200,000 (mostly Enfield) rifles and their respective cartridges. When the Bolsheviks won the war, they found themselves in possession of a great number of weapons and munitions of diverse calibers. The Spanish Civil War was the perfect opportunity to make use of them: the .303 cartridges were the among first Soviet military supplies to arrive in Spain.

We know that a shipment of this weaponry was unloaded in Spain on November 1, 1936. The Enfields were far superior to the Vetterli rifles from 1870 that the Soviets had also sent to Spain prior to the battle for Madrid. The standard weaponry of the Soviet Union also included the 7.62 x 54mm cartridge, however, so in addition to getting rid of all types of antiques, they also sold all the ammunition and rifles that were not compatible with their own guns. This is how the Enfields and their bullets arrived in Madrid, just in time for the defense of the capital, where they contributed decisively to stopping the rebel advance.

21. ENIGMA MACHINE, NOVEMBER 1936, TOLEDO

Sofía Rodríguez López

In the spring of 2012, the Spanish press reported the exchange of two Enigma Model K cipher machines from the Army Museum of Toledo that had been used during the Spanish Civil War, for another two given by the British government's Communication Headquarters (GCHQ) in Cheltenham. One of these was an antique model M-209 that had belonged to the Allied forces during the Second World War; the other had belonged to the German navy and was more secure due to the addition of a plugboard.

Enigma machines were a key invention for the transmission of information, permitting messages to be coded in ever-changing ways. According to Ignacio de Torre, a conservationist at the Toledo Museum, the model used in Spain "had only three rotors and one reflector, which permitted some 45,000 distinct possibilities." In contrast, more advanced models, like the one used by the German *Kriegsmarine*, "had four rotors plus the cabling which permitted, depending on how they were arranged, many more combinations—billions. It was practically unbreakable." The Spanish government possessed twelve German machines that had, until 2008, sat unnoticed in a warehouse at the Army headquarters at the Buenavista Palace in Madrid.

The celebrated Enigma cipher machine was first used in Europe in 1923, when Germany took over its production in order to avoid industrial espionage. The Enigma machine first arrived in the United Kingdom in 1927. Spain got its first machines in 1931 when it placed an order for a number of them through the embassy in Berlin for diplomatic and military use. That shipment would not be delivered until the end of 1936, however, and those machines were destined for the rebel army, in order to establish a more secure connection among the Francoist troops, the Condor Legion, and the Italian Corpo Truppe Volontarie. Franco's headquarters in Salamanca acquired ten commercial machines in November 1936, four Model As and six more advanced Model Ks. With them, in December 1936, the Italians and Germans were able to create a common code for the three navies, given the acronym "DEI" (Deutschland–España–Italia) whose primary base of operations was located in Palma de Mallorca.

With the addition of another ten Model Ks in 1937, the Francoist forces had twenty Enigma machines, which were divided among the High Commands of the major land forces, the land units, the General Secretariat of the head of state, which received two, and another two installed aboard the ship *Canarias* under the command of admiral Francisco Moreno. These machines helped them achieve several milestones including, for example, dismantling a Republican plot in Tangiers to trigger an indigenous revolt in the protectorate of Morocco.

It wasn't until in the 1980s that the secret surrounding the decoding of the German Enigma by the Allies was revealed. The Government Code and Cipher School (GC & CS), a secretive arm of MI6, had charged an expert named Dilly Knox with decrypting codes beginning in the First World War. He practiced writing his own messages, but not did not have the opportunity to intercept real messages until the capture of sufficiently audible German signals produced by the commercial machines sent to Spain in 1936. It took half a year, but in April 1937 the first Enigma machine message was decoded.

Despite the fact that the Germans changed the keys and the order of the rotors daily, the Allies were able to surpass the Nazis during the Second World War thanks to the British decryption team, led by mathematicians including Alan Turing, assisted by the "girls" of Bletchley Park and the Polish scientists who succeeded in capturing the first messages. According to reporting by the BBC in 2012, one of their strategies, unknown until then, was that "the English had been able to steal one of [Franco's] machines from a Spanish embassy and thus could learn how it worked."

Taking advantage of the exchange with the United Kingdom, in 2013, Spain's National Museum of Science and Technology organized a temporary exhibition called "QWERTY, the Evolution of a Type of Technology" featuring a German Enigma machine from 1930 on loan from the National Intelligence Center. The Army Museum also loaned theirs for the exhibition "Alan Turning and the Secret in the Messages" organized by the Telefónica Foundation in Madrid in 2018.

22. CHAMBER POT, NOVEMBER 1936, MADRID

Alfredo González Ruibal

A chamber pot is likely not the first object that one would think of in connection to the Civil War, but the truth is that in certain contexts it was essential. The one in the image above appeared in the bomb shelter inside the Santa Cristina Asylum, next to the Clínico Hospital in Madrid. The rebels took the asylum on November 17, 1936, during the Battle of Madrid, and the hospital shortly thereafter. It was the most advanced position their troops reached in the capital. The Republicans surrounded the hospital on three sides and subjected it to an almost constant assault. Rarely did a month go by without a landmine or mortar explosion, or a surprise attack. Under these conditions, the shelters were necessary for ensuring the survival of the troops.

The entire area became filled with trenches, shelters, and subterranean structures for the protection of the soldiers from the Spanish Legion and the

Regulares (Moroccan troops). Chamber pots were ubiquitous in civilian as well as military shelters. In a recently documented private shelter in the city Alcalá de Henares, the only pieces that were found were two clay vessels: an empty one that would have been used as a chamber pot and one for water. Naturally, it was not advisable to leave a shelter during an attack and, given the stressful nature of the experience, it was not unusual for one to need to alleviate oneself: fear is the best laxative. The chamber pot reminds us of the smells that would have impregnated those spaces below ground. The Costa Rican writer María Pérez-Yglesias recounts a familiar memory in her story "Estela." In her description of a prison she writes, "The unbearable stink reminds me of the smell of fear that my aunt and grandmother spoke of when they recalled the horrors of the Spanish Civil War of '36. That smell of excrement, urine, vomit and sweat of the shelters used for hiding from enemy bombs."

The structure where this particular chamber pot was found was not just any shelter; the excavation revealed that it served other functions besides protecting soldiers from enemy bombs. Inside it was an entrance to a countermining tunnel. Republican mines caused massive damage and hundreds of fatalities at the Clínico Hospital and led to an atmosphere of psychosis: one could die at any moment buried under tons of debris and dirt. The rebels were not able to put together a countermining unit until the end of 1937, which began operations only at the beginning of 1938. The Republicans were always superior in this mode of fighting and the Francoists could only try to mitigate the damage. Mine warfare is perhaps the most horrendous form of combat that was employed during the Civil War. The work involved men spending hours underground, armed not only with spades and shovels but also with bayonets, pistols, and grenades in case of unexpected encounters with enemy miners. The stress was extreme. The chamber pot also makes sense in this context.

It is also possible that the chamber pot had belonged to the asylum itself. It is a civilian object, made of enameled metal with a blue gouache design imitating marble. It often came as a set accompanied by a matching basin. It is quite different from the ordinary white bedpans found in more modest homes and in the barracks. It is also worth noting that when the rebels took the asylum, they found it undisturbed. The building had been evacuated and abandoned only a few days before the fighting began, and it was not too badly affected during the first phases of the war. Later it would be destroyed. The chaplain Juan Urra, who accompanied the members of the Legion, writes in his memoirs: "The Santa Cristina Asylum was a strange case. All of the departments, and even the church, were intact and undamaged: the images were well organized inside sacristy next to the holy garments. The pews were in their place."

The asylum's secular objects were also in good condition. During the excavation we came across a large amount of crockery and glassware from the hospice that the soldiers would have used during the two and a half years of the siege of Madrid. The shelter thus offers us a unique image: soldiers armed to the teeth, mines, grenades, and barbed wire, but also porcelain cups, crystal glasses, and an elegant chamber pot. It was a luxury within the trenches. Modern warfare blurred the lines between the civilian and the military, and even more so a civil war, especially one fought inside a city. On the stable fronts, quotidian objects became incorporated into military life and in turn, the war became, in a certain way, domestic.

23. MARTYRS' CEMETERY, NOVEMBER– DECEMBER 1936, PARACUELLOS DE JARAMA, MADRID

Sofía Rodríguez López

At the foot of the mount San Miguel in Paracuellos de Jarama lies the Martyrs' Cemetery. In recent years the rabbits that run among the crosses located there have unearthed religious objects, like rosaries and medallions, from gravesite area 6. They belonged to the people "taken for a walk" (*"paseados"*) between November and December 1936 who took these objects with them as they were supposedly being transferred from the Ventas, San Antón, and Porlier prisons in Madrid. Rather than their supposed destinations of Alcalá, Chinchilla, and Valencia, they ended up in the San José River.

The executions at Paracuellos, as well as those at Torrejón de Ardoz, must be put into the context of the defense of Madrid in November 1936, which coincided with the relocation of the government to Valencia. We can point to several different motives. First, the belief that the Francoist occupation of the capital was imminent and that the prisoners of war would join them as part of the fifth column. Second, the need to reduce pressure on prisons that were already full of right-wingers. Third, revenge for Francoist bombings and massacres, like the one in Badajoz. And fourth and most important, the desire of several leaders, especially among the communists—and their Soviet advisors—to annihilate the enemy within. In the words of José Luis Ledesma, these supposed "evacuations" were part of a maximalist strategy that became the darkest chapter of Republican repression. According to Javier Rodrigo, what we see here is "the desire to annihilate the political other."

What took place there has been well known ever since, not least because the Francoist side has consistently made use of it as rhetorical return-fire against the policies of political memory. Almost 2,000 people were killed in cold blood between November 7 and 9; several hundred more followed in successive *sacas* (evacuations) until December 3. Most were officials and soldiers, but there were also civilians who held conservative beliefs or had a history of activism. Chance also played a role in the selection of the victims, given that the Investigation Council of the General Directorate of Security (DGS) would consult the prison registers alphabetically. It is said that the victims did not resist (unlike the women in the Conde de Tornero prison) because they believed that they were being safely evacuated.

The mass executions were overseen by the Rearguard Surveillance Militias, who read the names of the chosen prisoners in the galleries of the jails. The victims were then stripped of their identification badges and personal belongings and, tied up in pairs, taken to the double-decker buses that would transport them to the Barajas area to be killed en masse.

Responsibility for these acts is usually attributed to the anarcho-syndicalist CNT, who controlled entry to and exit from the city, the Public Order Council, and advisers from the Comintern and the People's Internal Affairs Commission (NKVD in Russian). However, ultimate responsibility has been found to lie with the leader of the United Socialist Youth (JSU), Santiago Carrillo.

According to Julius Ruiz, important collaborators include Carrillo's predecessors Manuel Muñoz and Ángel Galarza, who had tolerated what was going on. Others include the Junta in Defense of Madrid, led by General Miaja; the militia surveillance units and the police of the DGS, as well as the Provincial Committee of Public Investigation, the head of the jail in San Miguel de Los Reyes in Valencia, who signed the evacuation order like a blank check, and the Minister of Justice, Juan García Oliver, a member of the Iberian Anarchist Federation (FAI). It was García Oliver who fired his colleague Melchor Rodríguez, the Inspector General of Prisons, who, together with the president of the Supreme Court, Mariano Gómez, was the biggest obstacle to the *sacas*.

García Oliver was forced to reinstate "the Red Angel" Rodríguez on December 3 following pressure from foreign diplomats and other ministers like Manuel de Irujo and José Giral, to put an end to the repression. The Socialist Party (PSOE), which had been tangled up in its own internal divisions, did not have an active role in the events—though neither did they do anything to put an end to this open secret. Thus, while the people of Paracuellos were interviewed by foreign journalists, a guard at the Modelo prison was able to send lists of the "sacas" to the British and Chilean embassies, and a delegation of British parliamentarians contacted the prisoners at Ventas on November 27.

Ever since, Paracuellos has been a symbol of the "Red terror" and a place of memory by which to recall the Republic's role in the war. Indeed, the Martyrs' Cemetery has so much symbolic and emotional weight that the victims' families have resisted moving their remains to the Valley of the Fallen.

24. NORMAN BETHUNE'S SHOULDER PATCH, DECEMBER 1936, GRAVENHURST, CANADA

Adrian Shubert

This shoulder patch was part of the uniform of Norman Bethune (1890–1939), the Canadian doctor who created the Hispano Canadiense Blood Transfusion Institute at the end of 1936. A distinguished thoracic surgeon, during the Depression Bethune became an advocate for socialized medicine and in 1935, after visiting the Soviet Union, he joined the Communist Party of Canada (CPC). Coming at a difficult moment in Bethune's personal and professional lives, the Spanish Civil War became what his biographers Roderick and Sharon Stewart call "a cause that provided sense and direction."

Bethune arrived in Madrid in November 1936 as head of the medical mission sent by the Canadian Committee for the Defence of Spanish Democracy, an organization created by a number of left wing groups including the CPC. He first tried to join the medical service of the

International Brigades, but when he was turned down he came up with the idea of creating a service to take refrigerated blood to the front. This was something that had preoccupied Bethune since his experience as a stretcher bearer during the First World War where he saw wounded soldiers die from loss of blood.

Bethune was not alone in coming up with innovations in blood transfusions during the Civil War. Spanish doctors on both sides made crucial contributions, but it was hematologist Frederic Durán i Jordà, director of the Blood Transfusion Service in Barcelona, who was the most influential. In September 1936, he began to send blood to the Aragon Front in refrigerated trucks and trains, the first time this had ever been done. Durán i Jordà's system was much more sophisticated than Bethune's and it won him international recognition. In early 1939 he went into exile in the United Kingdom where he contributed to the creation of the British Blood Transfusion Service. Bethune would copy the use of refrigerated trucks pioneered by Durán i Jordà.

After he convinced them that his project would be completely financed from Canada, officials of International Red Aid gave him an apartment in central Madrid to house his Hispano Canadiense Blood Transfusion Institute. It performed its first transfusion in Fuencarral on January 3, 1937, and soon it was taking blood along almost 1,000 kilometers of frontline. Bethune then proposed that the government of the Republic create a unified blood transfusion service under his leadership. Instead, the government folded Bethune's operation into the new Spanish–Canadian Institute that he would run along with two Spanish doctors. The prickly Bethune kicked up such a fuss that he was quickly sent back to Canada. He had been in Spain barely six months.

Norman Bethune was only one of the many foreign medical professionals, women and men, who offered their services to Spain during the Civil War. The Spanish conflict provided a unique opportunity for women. Most were nurses but there were a few doctors as well. There were also a handful of women who filled the "masculine" role of ambulance driver. Women constituted approximately one-quarter of the 1,600 volunteers in the International Sanitary Service of the International Brigades. They came from Australia, Canada, Czechoslovakia, France, Great Britain, Hungary, Ireland, Lithuania, New Zealand, Norway, Sweden, and the United States, among other countries. There were also some nurses among the few medical professionals who served with the Francoists.

Back in Canada, Bethune went on a speaking tour to raise funds for the Committee for the Defence of Spanish Democracy. He also found a new cause for which to fight: China. In January 1938 he was in Ya'nan performing operations while helping train the doctors and nurses in Mao Zedong's army. He died from septicemia in November 1939 after cutting a finger during an operation. Soon after, Mao published his essay *In Memory of Norman Bethune*, which became required reading in China's primary schools in the 1960s and remains part of textbooks today. In his own country, however, Bethune was almost completely forgotten until the early 1970s. Then, following the establishment of diplomatic relations between Canada and the People's Republic of China in 1970, he was turned into a national hero and the house in Gravenhurst in which he was born was made a national historic site.

25. BOWL OF A KIF PIPE, 1936/1937, MADRID

Alfredo González Ruibal

|___ 1 cm ___|

This clay bowl from a *sebsi*, or kif pipe, appeared in a trench in Madrid's Casa de Campo park. The *sebsi* is made up of a thin wooden tube some 45 centimeters long and a clay bowl called a *skuff*. Kif is made from the resinous trichomes of the cannabis plant and has a higher concentration of psychoactive material than other parts of the plant. It has been consumed in North Africa since medieval times, but during the eighteenth century the Rif Mountains became its primary site of cultivation. And it is from here that a significant portion of the North African troops used by the rebels during the Civil War came. As Muslims, the people of the Rif (*rifeños*) could not consume alcohol; they replaced it with cannabis products. The consumption of spirits or cognac, known as "parapet leapers" (*saltaparapetos*) and of kif or "*grifa*" was considered fundamental for maintaining the morale of troops. In fact, soldiers would receive an extra ration of alcohol before an attack. In *Kabila*, Fernando González Martín's 1980 novel about the Rif

War (1921–1927), one lieutenant affirms: "If this war is won, as we can expect, it will be because of the booze and the joints." An altered state of consciousness was particularly useful in the hand to hand combat for which the Maghreb troops had a terrifying reputation.

Cannabis has certain characteristics that make it appropriate for some modes of combat. One study observed that the *rifeños* had improved night vision thanks to the consumption of kif. The supposed ability of the "Moors" to see well at night was mentioned by some combatants and it is possible that this legend has a kernel of truth to it, although not for the biological reasons that were usually ascribed. For example, José Llordés Badía, a veteran of the Francoist Army, claims in his 1986 memoir *Al Dejar el Fusil* (*On Putting Down the Gun*) that the North Africans had "eyes like cats, which is to say, their visual system opens up and they can see in complete darkness." It is possible that the effectiveness of the Moors' nighttime surprise attacks had something to do with cannabinoids. Perhaps the most famous of these attacks occurred on February 11, 1937, during the Battle of the Jarama, when Moroccan soldiers beheaded the sentinels of the André Marty Battalion.

The Moroccan troops' use of drugs was no secret. In fact, the supply of drugs from North African became organized. The routes by which it arrived on the peninsula could be very strange, for example, through the brothels the Francoists established during the war for the Regulares. These brothels were run by Moroccan women and employed Moroccan prostitutes, and some of the madams asked permission to bring great quantities of kif with them to sell in Spain. That the kif came from Morocco and was consumed primarily by Moroccan soldiers does not mean that the Spanish troops did not try it. Father José Caballero, the Legion chaplain during the December 1936 battles in Madrid, writes: "A seriously ill man, with a strange trembling, almost like giddiness. The doctor thinks that he is crazy. He doesn't even know how old he is. Soon after, another arrived in the same state. What is wrong with them? We can't figure it out. The effects of kif?"

The context in which this pipe appeared is very interesting. It was found the in the most northern part of Casa de Campo, in the last trench defended by the Republicans during the Battle of Madrid. The trench was occupied, beginning on November 9, 1936, by central European members of the International Brigades (IBs). They were under constant attack by the Legion and the Regulares until their orderly withdrawal around November 15. The archaeological excavation there unearthed a great number of remains associated with the intense battles of that November (see Chapter 20). How did the pipe get there? One of the shelters within the trench was reused by the rebels in 1937. It is possible that it belongs to that moment. But it is also possible that the pipe was lost by one of the Regulares who took this area after the withdrawal of the IBs in November 1936. Perhaps this anonymous Moroccan smoked his pipe over the remains of the battle in celebration of the rebel victory.

26. BOOKMOBILE AT THE FRONT, 1937, BARCELONA

Verónica Sierra Blas

"Culture is one more weapon with which to fight fascism." This was the slogan on one of Desiderio Babiano Lozano Olivares' (known as "Babiano") best-known propaganda posters. It depicts two militiamen advancing with a firm and decisive step toward their combat positions: one has a rifle in his hands, the other is carrying a large book. The work was commissioned by the Soldier's Education Commission of the United Socialist Youth (JSU), a group to which the artist belonged, and was printed at the Polygraphic Union of Madrid in 1936. This poster, along with others by Babiano and those by other Republican poster artists, demonstrate how the Popular Army made culture one of the key aspects of its identity. The proof lies in the numerous schools and libraries it created during the conflict, with the aim of making soldiers literate so that they could spend part of their leave or recovery time reading and writing.

The Republic's Public Education Ministry had a Popular Culture Department, and their Library Section was in charge of sending batches of free books to Republican soldiers. By March 1937 they had sent 103 libraries worth of books to field hospitals, and another 789 to barracks in both the rearguard and on the Madrid, Aragón, and Andalucía fronts. These books were donations from publishing houses, newspapers, libraries, and individuals; some were requisitioned from abandoned houses while still others were bought with public subsidies. Together with the books, the Popular Culture Department would also send out a catalogue, an order form and instructions for the person in charge of running the library. The offerings were wide and varied, whether it was a "simple" library or a "circulating" one: books about history, society, and politics, school textbooks (especially reading and writing workbooks), works of classic and modern literature, newspapers and magazines, science education books, propaganda brochures, manuals on military strategy, first aid, hygiene, agriculture, mechanics, electrical engineering, etc. Once they received the books, the "librarian" was supposed to cover them "with strong paper" and write the name of the author and the title of the book on its spine in order to help protect and organize them. The librarian's role also included informing the soldiers of the library's existence by hanging posters in visible and frequented places, as well as making sure that the books formed part of their daily life, for example by including news about the library on the units' bulletin boards or organizing reading clubs.

Central to this dispersal of books in the middle of the conflict was the Libraries on the Front Service (SBF) of the Generalitat of Catalunya's Propaganda Commission and its historic bookmobile. The SBF was run by Conxa Guarro, Justa Balló, Jordi Rubió, Maria Felipa Español, Aurora Díaz-Plaja, Rosa Granés, Maria Ponjoan, and Concepció de Balanzó, among others.

The SBF was inspired by experiences during the First World War, as well as by an initiative undertaken by the Madrid Writers' Group years before to spread culture to all corners of Spain. Using a remodeled truck seized by the Army of the East's Rearguard and Transport Command, they created a bookmobile which began its travels in February 1937. Between May 4 and October 6, 1938, the bookmobile made a total of twenty-nine trips and distributed more than 15,000 books to the fronts in Aragón and Cataluña.

Some of these trips were recorded in the diaries that the librarians kept during those six months. Here is an excerpt from that of Aurora Díaz-Plaja:

August 20–22, 1938. We went to Camp No.1 of Division 26. It is set up in an old convent next to the road. It is a bit elevated and in front of the entrance there is a pretty square. We parked the bus there [...] We opened the shelves wide [...] The soldiers begin lining up in an orderly fashion.

They are all big men. The majority choose quickly, some ask where they can find specific material, nobody asks us to choose a book for them [...] The technical works are the most popular; in first place Geography and History, followed by Math and Grammar.

The bookmobile's final "act of service" was not to take books to Republican soldiers, but to save the lives of a group of Catalan intellectuals and their families who, on January 23, 1939, like so many other Spaniards, began their journey into exile. Within a few days all traces of it were lost forever in Perpignan, on the other side of the French border.

27. READING AND WRITING PRIMERS, 1937, SALAMANCA

Jesús Espinosa Romero

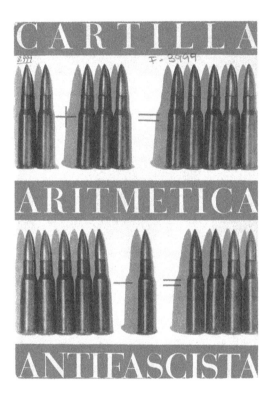

A typical scene in twentieth-century war photography is that of a soldier writing a letter. Mail was the thread that united the front with the rearguard. A soldier could maintain contact with the family and friends that he had left behind, thereby alleviating somewhat the brutality of the campaign. This was also a consolation to those family members, friends, and loved ones who had been left behind—voluntarily at first, then by force as reinforcements were needed. Likewise for the "war godmothers." News helped share the emotions that would overcome the rigor of military censorship, and in this way maintain an emotional connection between combatants and civilians. However, both sides in the conflict confronted the same problem: the illiteracy of their troops. This problem was more accentuated on the Nationalist side given that their primary base of recruitment was rural Spain, whereas the Republicans drew soldiers mostly from urban areas.

Addressing the emotional needs of soldiers was not the most pressing concern among the belligerent's High Commands, however. They had other priorities. In their view, the troops should be educated above all so that they could follow instructions to correctly execute their mission and for their own protection. That is to say, for killing and avoiding being killed. It was thus necessary to educate a great mass of soldiers quickly and efficiently. This was a shared need, but each side found a different solution: Franco's Army found the answer in military chaplains, while the Republican Army found it externally, in the Cultural Militias—an organization of teachers under the Ministry of Public Education led by the communist Jesús Hernández.

The Republic's efforts in this arena greatly surpassed those of the Nationalists, among other reasons because they had a greater conviction in the idea that education was the primary path to human transformation. They believed that ridding a soldier of his ignorance was essential for his personal and social emancipation. It would also improve his capacity in combat because he would understand the reason for the fight. By August 1938 the Cultural Militias had taught more than 362,381 individual classes, and more than 531,000 group ones.

In 1937 the Ministry of Public Education published the *Anti-fascist Student Primer* and the *Anti-fascist Arithmetic Primer*. These basic teaching tools were used by thousands of soldiers in the Popular Army. Their singular quality and importance represent a milestone in the history of education in Spain. Both books were written by Fernando Sáinz Ruiz, a socialist, teacher and school inspector, and by Eusebio Cimorra, a communist and editor of the *Mundo Obrero* [*Worker's World*] newspaper. The illustrations consisted of photographs by José Val de Omar and José Calandín assembled into photomontages by Mauricio Amster, a Polish graphic designer who had been living in Spain since 1930 and who was by that time a Communist militant. These primers employed the most modern techniques for teaching reading and writing: a universal method based on following one's own interests developed by the Belgian educator Ovide Decroly, as well as the use of guide words and Script font. Some 150,000 copies were printed.

The primers came with an introduction and instructions in which one can strongly sense their political bias and communist origins. Even so, their message was ultimately one of class-consciousness that encompassed all forms of antifascism.

Soldiers of the Mixed Brigade were taught to read and write by militiamen belonging to organizations like Culture in the Soldier's Home and Cultural Corners. These groups were linked to military units, and they set up shop right on the front lines. In addition to learning to read and write, soldiers would also go to talks and plays and would collaborate on their units' bulletin boards. Teaching soldiers to read and write became one more form of combat. The number of letters that soldiers wrote to their families became, metaphorically speaking, like the "taking of a hilltop." The ultimate redemption of the illiterate came with their "baptism" in literacy, when they were able to write letters to their family, friends and loved ones, and even to the Ministry of Public Education, to thank it for liberating them from their ignorance.

28. RECORD WITH REPUBLICAN SONGS, 1937, SALAMANCA

Jesús Espinosa Romero

A society's cultural patrimony lies in the products that are preserved and passed down through the generations. A large part of what we identify as cultural patrimony is material, like buildings and works of art; no less important, however, is the part that is intangible and immaterial.

Many of the songs created by Republican combatants form part of the cultural patrimony of Spain, and that of the wider world. The twentieth century saw a profusion of popular songs composed with political messages, and the Spanish conflict was no stranger to this dynamic. Songs became linked to politics due to their malleability, their emotional character, and the efficiency, agility, and brevity with which they could communicate their message. Together with posters and images, such tunes became the primary means by which messages of unity, support, and trust were transmitted among members of the resistance to the fascist enemy, especially during the first months of the siege of Madrid. Composed by Spaniards as well as by members of the International Brigades, this music became a crucible for expressing and reinforcing the troops' group identity over and above their different nationalities. They primarily used musical forms that were popular in Spain, like *coplas* and *romancers,* repurposing and reinterpreting old, local songs. We can see this clearly in the texts, scores, and recordings that have been preserved. A good example is the song "Los Cuatro Generales" ("The Four Generals").

This song is a version of Federico García Lorca's 1931 arrangement of "Los Cuatro Muleros" ("The Four Muleteers") that he recorded with singer and dancer La Argentinita in the legendary album *Canciones Españolas Antiguas (Old Spanish Songs).* The lyrics are a *sextilla* (sextuplet) with an irregular rhyming pattern, and the music has a three-part (ternary) form. It is a festive song; it celebrates the stabilizing of the front at Madrid's University City despite constant bombardment of the capital by rebel aircraft. It begins in heavily accented Spanish, followed by German, and is accompanied solely by classical Spanish guitar.

Although the Republicans had an extensive repertoire of songs, in practice only a small number of songs, including *Los Cuatro Generales,* worked their way into the memory of militiamen and members of the International Brigades. We can attribute this to the songbook complied in 1937 by Ernst Busch at the request of the International Brigades Committee. Busch was a German actor and singer who had worked with Bertolt Brecht before escaping Nazi Germany in 1933 and enrolling in the International Brigades. He would later become famous in the German Democratic Republic. Busch's compilation originally included ninety-eight songs, but in later editions this grew as different versions of the songs were added in Spanish, English, French, and Italian so that they could be sung by the majority of the combatants. In this way, the music generated by the resistance in the trenches became trans-cultural, and its sounds transcended the Spanish war period.

The International Brigade diaspora continued their fight against fascism during the Second World War (as evidenced by the song "Viva la Quince Brigada" ["Long Live the 15th Brigade"]). This allowed the oral traditions that had begun during the antifascist resistance first tried out in Spain to continue. The popularity of Republican songs continued to grow for other reasons as well, including the establishment of veterans associations, and a re-issue of Busch's record in 1940 under the new title *Six Songs for Democracy.*

Following the defeat of fascism in 1945, new resistance contexts gave new life to the Republican songs, some of which took on different melodies. Such was the case with the civil rights movement in the United States, with singers like Paul Robeson, Pete Seeger and Joan Báez, and in Chile at the end of the 1960s and beginning of the 1970s, with Rolando Alarcón and Quilapayún. But these songs remained alive in Spain, too. As the Italian journalists and musicologists Sergio Liberovici and Michele Straniero's 1961 album *Canti della nuova resistenza spagnola (Songs of the New Spanish Resistance)* demonstrates, *Los Cuatro Generales* continued to be sung as a new opposition was forming against the Francoist dictatorship. Indeed, the songs from the Republican trenches that Busch compiled continue to be sung and recorded to this day.

29. LEICA CAMERA, 1937

Adrian Shubert

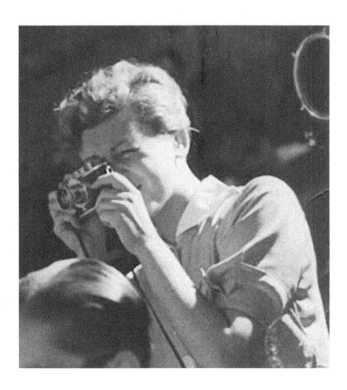

This anonymous photograph taken in early 1937 shows photographer Gerda Taro using the chromed Leica III (Model F) camera that had belonged to her partner Robert Capa. It was largely because of cameras such as this that the Spanish Civil War became, in Susan Sontag's words, the first war ever "witnessed ('covered') in the modern sense." This was the first time that a number of professional photographers were at the front with the technical capability to shoot combat while it was taking place. "Pictures could be taken in the thick of battle ... and civilian victims and exhausted, begrimed soldiers studied up close."

The Leica camera, produced by the German firm Leitz and marketed in 1925, revolutionized photography. The first effective 35mm camera, it was based on the idea of using smaller negatives that could be used to produce larger photographs when developed. Smaller and lighter than earlier cameras, it gave photographers unprecedented freedom of movement. Its faster lens and 36-shot roll of film let them take multiple action shots without reloading. And its viewfinder allowed the photographer to hold the camera to their eye and track moving objects.

The Leica was the perfect tool for photographing a war. Spain was the first major conflict available, and it drew a number of highly talented photographers. The best known are three foreigners: Gerda Taro (1910–37), Robert Capa (1913–54), and David Seymour, known as "Chim" (1911–56). All were Central or East European Jews and all three died while photographing a military conflict. Taro was crushed by a tank during the Republican retreat from Brunete in July 1937. In recent years, the Spanish photographers Agustín Centelles (1909–85) and Antoni Campañà (1906–89) have become much more widely recognized.

The Civil War was also covered by a large number of anonymous photographers working for international news agencies such as Associated Press and World Wide Photos, as well as for Spanish government institutions and organizations. The CNT, for example, had a number of photographers who supplied *Solidadridad Obrera* and its other press outlets with images. In 2019, a cache of more than 500 negatives taken by Kati Horna, a Hungarian Jew who was the official photographer for the CNT's Photo SPA agency, was discovered at the International Institute for Social History in Amsterdam.

The camera, and the men and women who wielded it, were only part of the equation of modern war coverage. The other part was the existence of media outlets that purchased their photographs and made them available to mass publics in Spain and around the world: the photojournalism magazine. Newspapers and magazines had been printing photographs since the 1880s, but the photojournalism magazine deployed photographs in a new way. Rather than simply using an image to illustrate a story, these magazines featured the new genre of the photo essay: an integrated story in which text and image worked together.

The photo essay was a collaboration between photographer and editor, but one in which the latter had the dominant role. The photographer would send contact sheets with all the shots he had taken, but the editor would choose which ones to use, how to crop them, and the sequence in which they would appear in the story, as well as writing the cutlines that connected them.

The pioneer was the *Berliner Illustrirte Zeitung* (*BIZ*) which had put photographs at its heart in the early twentieth century, but the "golden age" of the weekly photojournalism magazine began in the 1930s, with the emergence of *Vu* in France, *Picture Post* in the UK, and *Life* in the United States. *Life*, and *BIZ* on which it was modeled, had circulations in the millions. The Civil War gave them, and many others, the opportunity to bring military conflict into people's homes in an unprecedented way. The cover of the August 26, 1936 issue of the *Berliner Illustrirte Zeitung* featured a photo of the first meeting between Generals Mola and Franco. Robert Capa's *The Fallen Soldier*, the single most famous photograph of the Civil War, and considered one of the most important images of all time, appeared on page 19 of the June 12, 1937 issue of the magazine, above the title "DEATH IN SPAIN: THE CIVIL WAR HAS TAKEN 500,000 LIVES IN ONE YEAR."

New technology like the Leica camera, with talented photographers and new mass media outlets, all combined to make the Spanish Civil War into the first media war, giving it an unprecedented immediacy that undoubtedly contributed to persistence in global memory.

30. *THE LITTLEST ONE OF ALL,* FEBRUARY 1937, SALAMANCA

Jesús Espinosa Romero

Beginning in February 1937, *El més petit de tots* (The Littlest One of All) became the symbol of the new antifascist Cataluña. It is a small figure of young boy wearing a Phrygian cap (a symbol of liberty) and blue work overalls; he marches in a military style with his left fist in the air while sometimes his right hand carries the Catalonian flag. Produced by the Propaganda Commission of the regional government of Catalonia (Generalitat) led by Jaume Miravitlles and created by the sculptor Miquel Paredes, he became "the mascot of the revolution," as the posters that could be bought for 3 pesetas each proclaimed.

El més petit also had his own song, based on the popular traditional melody of "El tres tambors" ("The Three Drums"). The new lyrics, composed by the poet Joan Oliver i Sellarès under the pseudonym Pere Quart, tells of three brothers who show up at the barracks to enlist voluntarily, but the smallest one is turned away because he is too young. He and his mother must instead support the sacrifice made by his brothers and the other men from the rearguard, by holding the flag. The song was recorded and performed by the popular Barcelona tenor Emili Vendrell, accompanied by the Commission's musical group, the Cobla Barcelona.

El més petit was an enormously popular recruitment tool for the Popular Army of Catalonia, which was created in December 1936. In a bold exercise of its sovereign powers, the Generalitat assigned its new force the same status as the Popular Army of the Republic. The new army respected the existing militia columns but recruited young men to fill its new regiments. By the middle of January, the army had almost 50,000 members, 40,000 of whom were the militiamen on the Aragón Front. These men, however, were more loyal to their party or union than to the head of the government of Catalonia. In order to rebalance the composition of the troops and reconstruct the state's—and ultimately the Generalitat's—power, they had to promote enlistment. In addition to *El més petit*, the Generalitat and some Popular Front organizations established pro-Popular Army committees and military instruction camps, like the one located on the confiscated Sant Cugat Golf Club.

However, the military project of the Generalitat was ultimately dealt a decisive blow. The militias, especially those of the CNT, were autonomous, and the communists decided to subordinate theirs to the Popular Army of the Republic. The events of May 1937, when the government's move to take control of the strategically crucial telephone exchange led to street fighting between its forces and CNT and POUM militias, put an end to the Catalonian Army. In June, its militiamen and regiments were reorganized following the structures of the Mixed Brigades and integrated into the Popular Army of the Republic under the leadership of General Pozas, the commander of the newly formed Army of the East.

Despite the dissolution of Catalonia's Popular Army, the war effort and the need for enlistment remained. *El més petit* still had a role to play. Modest reproductions were made. Some stores, like Vilardell located on the Vía Layetana in Barcelona, would gift them with purchases of tights or socks worth more than 25 pesetas. Others were made of more valuable material, like silver, and were reserved for official gifts. For example, General Miaja was offered one during his visit to Barcelona; another was given to the Belgian socialist Émile Vandervelde in Brussels by the children who were accompanying the Cobla Barcelona on tour. It was thought that even President Roosevelt had one of these little symbols of Catalan antifascist resistance.

At the beginning of June 1937, *El més petit* made his debut with children. During the Barcelona Book Fair, the Commission presented the antifascist storybook *El Més Petit*, written and illustrated by Lola Anglada. It became a very popular work in Catalonia's schools, libraries, and homes, due in part to its low price. The story promoted pacifism and a culture of peace and democratic values. This linkage with children led somewhat naturally to the creation of fundraising events focused on getting social assistance to the young orphans produced by the casualties of war. In fact, *el més petit* came to symbolize the children and orphans of the combatants. Additionally, in May 1938, in its first ever issue, which was dedicated to the Catalan front and rearguard, the Barcelona magazine *Mi Revista* (*My Magazine*) announced a new movie, most likely an animated one, based on the character by Paredes. It was never shown, however, and no it appears that no copies remain.

31. TOBACCO, 1937, SALAMANCA

Jesús Espinosa Romero

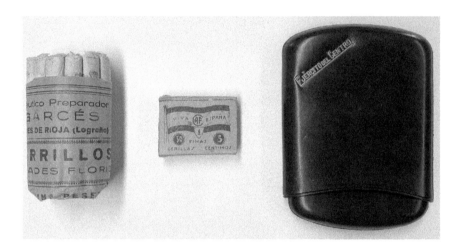

For millions of men during the war, combatants in both armies as well as civilians, tobacco was an indispensable part of daily life. The use of industrially manufactured cigarettes had spread throughout the 1920s and constituted one of the new pillars of working-class masculinity. Although already known to be bad for one's health, smoking represented one of the principal rites of passage from childhood to adulthood. In the military context, moreover, it was a way for the troops to establish internal cohesion as well as hierarchy. Sharing a pack of cigarettes with one's comrades made them the equal beneficiaries of all of the efforts by families and solidarity networks in the rearguard that made such access to tobacco possible.

In January 1937, *Ahora* [*Now*], the United Socialist Youth (JSU)'s Madrid-based daily paper, reported on the failure by the aristocrats of San Sebastián to collect tobacco for the rebel troops, in contrast with the class solidarity shown to the Republican troops via the shipment of cigarettes by the International Red Aid, the International Antifascist Solidarity, and different unions—including that of the female cigarette makers in Valencia who donated 2,500 packs to the wounded soldiers in the hospitals of what was then the capital of the Republic. This type of assistance was also extended in the international sphere; for example, the International Brigades received some 200 kilograms of tobacco from the International Federation of Unions.

On the rebel side, in contrast, soldiers initially received tobacco through individual donations and charity campaigns, something that the

Republic press ridiculed. This was unfounded, however. For example, General Aranda encouraged the Galician organization Women at the Service of Spain to make cigarettes as well as capes and clothing in their workshops as these were a "vehicle of affection and self-denial through which those in the rearguard can support the soldiers, who will be proud to know that there are women looking out for them." Another example was the Center for Feminine Culture in San Sebastián. This organization for women and young ladies was founded in 1932 and described itself as apolitical, its only aim being the cultural education of their members so that they could most efficiently contribute to Catholic social projects. However, after the Carlist Requetés entered the open city of Urumea in the middle of September 1936, the members put themselves at the service of the rebels, channeling their collection campaigns, including of tobacco, to the soldiers.

After the initial shortage of tobacco on the rebel side and the relative abundance on the Republican side, the tables turned in 1937 when a good part of that year's harvest became available to the rebels. Of Spain's five areas of tobacco cultivation—western and eastern Andalucía, Cáceres and the Tajo valley, the Cantabrian coast, and the Mediterranean, including the Ebro valley and Mallorca—the rebels held the first three and gained control of the fourth following their conquest of Vizcaya, Cantabria, and Asturias. The Republic held on to part of the Ebro Valley throughout the war. Despite the rebels' control over these areas, however, tobacco production still did not meet the demand of the internal market. Franco also received donations from the large tobacco companies in Cuba and the Philippines, the latter of which, for example, donated 1 million packs in March 1938.

On the Republican side, the tobacco shortage had become structural by the fall of 1937 (food rationing had already taken effect in March). The civilian market was depleted so a new low quality blend called "war works" was developed in order to make existing supplies and scarce future acquisitions go further. The cigarette shortage led military censors to occasionally take them from the packages sent by Republican "war godmothers." Different blends made up of tea, peanut shells, sawdust, herbs, etc., were being sold in the streets of Madrid, Barcelona, and Valencia.

Smoking remained a vice for soldiers in the New Spain. The National Delegation for Assistance to the Fronts and Hospitals, controlled by the "Margaritas" [women's auxiliary] of the Requeté, was tasked with distributing cigarettes, as a complement to those supplied by the quartermaster. One means for distributing tobacco was through the "war godmothers." The Margaritas would provide them with cigarettes which they would then send to their "god children" in packages using pre-paid postage. While focused on Catholic soldiers, they did not neglect the Muslim "Regulares." For example, the young women of the Requeté's Fronts and Hospitals Delegation gave out sweets and tobacco at a party at the Muslim Hospital in Córdoba in June 1938.

During the final months of the war, the rebels had an overwhelming abundance of tobacco, and they used it as a psychological weapon to undermine the battered resistance of the antifascist soldier. For example, in November 1938, 800 packs of cigarettes were thrown across the government lines using adapted rockets, accompanied by leaflets encouraging them to switch sides because in Franco's Spain one could smoke without limits.

32. 25 CÉNTIMO NOTE FROM GRANOLLERS, 1937, TORONTO

Adrian Shubert

This 25 céntimo note was issued by the municipal government of Granollers (Barcelona) in 1937. On the front, against the silhouette of a factory in the background, a worker and a peasant hold hands behind a horn of plenty and the coat of arms of Cataluña. On the reverse, the word "Emancipation" stands out against a worker and some smoking factory chimneys. This was only one of more than 7,000 different notes issued by some 2,000 local, provincial and regional governments across Republican Spain between the outbreak of the Civil War and the end of 1937. In a mundane yet powerful way it reminded citizens on a daily basis of the fracturing of the Republican state provoked by the military uprising, and the difficulties it faced in restoring even this most basic of government functions.

As the failed military coup turned into a longer conflict, silver and copper coins disappeared across the Republican zone as people hoarded them for the innate value of the metal. In addition, much of the bronze was melted down in foundries and used to make weapons. The government's decision to withdraw all silver coins in order to create a strategic reserve only exacerbated the problem. It issued "silver certificates" to replace the 5 and 10 peseta coins but did nothing to replace smaller denomination 10, 25, and 50 céntimo coins, the small change that was crucial for ordinary people in their daily lives. If someone wanted to purchase a kilo of bread for 70 céntimos or have a coffee in a bar for 20 céntimos, there was no way to get change.

Responses to this situation came from below. First, there was bartering. Then store owners began to issue their own certificates, but these were valid only at a single store and caused protests. The next stage was for all stores in a town or village to issue paper money that could be spent at any of them. The most important response came when municipal and, to a lesser extent, provincial governments began issue notes, usually in denominations of 25 céntimos, 50 céntimos, and 1 peseta, which served as legal tender within the area of their jurisdiction. Some military units, political parties, and unions also issued their own. Most of these local notes were issued during 1937.

This phenomenon was most widespread in Cataluña, which accounted for about half of the notes issued. The Generalitat began the process with a decree on September 21, 1936 establishing its own currency. The government of the Basque Country had already done this on August 1 and the Council of Asturias and León would follow in October, but for the Generalitat this was part of a larger policy of taking over the functions of the central state. The smallest denomination, 2.5 pesetas, was too large to meet the needs of the daily transactions of citizens and in October the Generalitat authorized local governments to issue small denomination notes. Of the regions 1,075 municipalities, 773 did so.

In some cases, the notes embodied more than just practical concerns. There were places that replaced céntimos and pesetas with new units, such as *unidades* and *grados*. And there were places where the town issuing the currency was given a new name, including the more than one hundred municipalities in Cataluña, that removed the word "saint."

The physical objects themselves were tremendously varied. They had different names: *billetes, bonos, certificados, pagarés, valores de cambios*. They came in a wide range of sizes, shapes—including round and rhomboid—and designs. They were made using a number of different materials: paper, leather, cardboard, parchment, and even plastic. Existing items were recycled; in Besora, the parish priest's visiting cards were torn in half and then stamped with the municipal seal.

The Republican government began to reassert its control over the currency in December 1937, when it announced that it would issue 10, 25, and 50 céntimo coins, but only the last was in circulation by early the next year. Only at the start of 1938 did it announce its intention to restore the monopoly over this "irrevocable privilege" it had lost. All notes and coins issued by "individuals, companies or corporate bodies" were to be withdrawn within a month and the people holding them given official ones of an equal value. With the mint unable to produce the necessary coins, the government used postage stamps and other official stamps stuck onto cardboard disks bearing the coat of arms to replace the local notes. Intended as a stopgap, this makeshift system was still in place when the war ended.

33. GAS MASK, 1937, SALAMANCA

Plàcid García-Planas

It has a touch of magical realism to it; or perhaps of the divine. The last specialist to make a plea against the use of chemical weapons, shortly before the outbreak of the Civil War, was a priest, Eduard Vitòria i Miralles, the founder of the very prestigious Sarrià Chemical Institute.

His plea, made in the grand Hall of the Hundred of Barcelona's city council, was delivered as a talk entitled "Dangerous Chemicals," and formed part of a series of lectures called *Protection Against Gaseous Weapons and Industrial Aeroform Toxins*. He delivered it on December 31, 1935—the final day of the final year of peace. In it, he broke down the lethal cloud of elements that could choke one just in trying to pronounce them: chlorine and its derivatives, bromide and benzylbromocyanide, chloropicrin, halogenated ketone, halogenated acetic acids, lewisite (also called "death dew"), and their effects, attempts to create new, "even more toxic," flammable elements, phosphorous, alkali metals, organometallic compounds… and "the uselessness of defensive masks."

Chemical warfare was the most terrifying remnant of the First World War—the world's most recent and most horrific conflagration. In the 1930s, when the coming of the Second World War could already be intuited, European magazines exploited people's fear of a gas-induced apocalypse. This anxiety, deeply felt in Spanish society, was most brilliantly captured by the cover of the French magazine *Vu* in February 1931: a photomontage of *The Marseillaise*—the monumental sculpture by François Rude at the Arc de Triomphe in Paris—in which the angel of war and the revolutionaries' faces are covered with gas masks as a disturbing vapor surrounds them. On the inside pages, the magazine reproduced an image of Murillo's *Nativity* blended with the photograph of a mother and a child both wearing gas masks adjusted to the relative sizes of their heads.

With the threat of "death dew" penetrating mouth, nose, and eyes, the government of the Republic approved the acquisition of 2,000 chemical weapon defensive units as well as 500 gas masks for the army. This was a mere three weeks before the military uprising. But then the war broke out, the country imploded, and chemical attacks between Spaniards ended up being mostly anecdotal. This despite the fact that Spain had been among the first countries to bomb a civilian population with toxic agents—the Rifeños in the 1920s—and despite the fact that Republicans and Francoists both ended up in possession of this type of weapon, to say nothing of the Italian Fascists and German Nazis allied with Franco. It turned out to be more effective— and more terrorizing—to throw massive, indiscriminate conventional bombs at urban centers, large and small. The chemical attacks that had been feared during the 1930s thus did not materialize, neither on the battlefield nor in European cities. Gas was not thrown at the population, rather the population was dragged towards to the gas, in the form of extermination camps. In this Spain also foreshadowed the Second World War.

The gas mask has not persisted as part of the popular imagination of the Spanish Civil War. It persisted, however, in the form of a "non-Christmas" present from the Republicans: on December 25, 1937, the president of Cataluña's regional government, Lluís Companys, received a visit from a group of journalists from Madrid and, as a gift, each was given a gun and a gas mask, all of which, as *La Vanguardia* reported, were made by the Catalan government.

The mask also led to scams. In March 1937, the Board of the Chemical Industries Union of Barcelona denounced the "unscrupulous people who, without any scruples whatsoever" sell gas masks "that do nothing other than cover one's face," and called for severe sanctions against the scammers. The Board warned that masks should be officially approved: "Fifteen days ago, an individual arrived offering a mask that, according to him, worked perfectly. We told him: 'Movement is shown in walking.' So we did the trial and corroborated that less than one minute after he was placed into the gas chamber he came out saying that he could not last any longer."

After the chemist-priest finished reading his asphyxiating list of gases on that final day of 1935, he concluded his presentation by surrendering himself, body and soul, to magical realism. Or more accurately in this case, to the divine. The final point in his talk was called "Universal peace, the aspiration of humankind." According to this Jesuit of universal peace and chemical weapons: "It will not be achieved through these destructive means. The only way is to foment Christian charity between men, as Jesus Christ showed." The Gospel as gas mask.

34. THE CONE OF JINÁMAR, 1937, TELDE, GRAN CANARIA

Antonio Cazorla-Sánchez

There was almost no Civil War on the Canary Islands. The resistance to the coup was very isolated and did not last long. There was no justification, therefore, for the repression that left at least 1,032 people dead and "disappeared," apart from the desire for vengeance and to eliminate the elites and militiamen on the Republican side. And this is exactly what the soldiers, police, the volunteers of Citizen Action, and above all the sadly famous Morning Brigades, set out to do. The latter group was made up of police as well as young men, many of whom had been members of the youth auxiliary of the right-wing Popular Action party and who had recently become Falangists, and/or the children of the wealthiest families on the islands. In contrast to the peninsula, where the worst massacres took place in the deadly summer and fall of 1936, those on the Canary Islands occurred in 1937 at the hands of the Morning Brigades. They went in search of Republicans newly released from the prisons, secret detention centers (*chekas*), prison ships, and concentration camps, like the one at Fyffe's banana warehouses on Tenerife or at Fuencaliente on La Palma. What they did with them was frightening; the Cone of Jinámar is just one example of this horror.

In the Canary Islands it is said that even children were afraid to hear the name "Jinámar." Many stories are told. Some are plausible, like the one about a prisoner who, on being thrown into the chasm, took a Falangist or two down with him. Others are less credible, like the one about an old assassin who had a nervous tick in his cheek because, it is said, a man had spat in his face right before he killed him. Regardless, the Cone of Jinámar does inspire both fear and legends. It is a volcanic chimney some 80 meters deep, located about 20 kilometers from Las Palmas in the municipality of Telde on Gran Canaria. It may hold the remains of as many as 100 people. Many were thrown in while still alive, or half alive, after being tortured at one of the numerous secret detention centers on Gran Canaria and the other islands. According to the people of the island, moaning could be heard emanating from the bowels of the earth. Further, it appears that in 1945, when new times had come and these crimes had to be covered up, explosives were thrown inside to cover up the bottom of the chasm and a group of workers was brought in to throw volcanic earth over top. For years, the Civil Guard kept a subtle watch over this place, but in the 1970s some local speleologists managed to get inside. There, they found complete cadavers, including some that even had bullet holes in their heads.

The "disappearing" of victims and other forms of Francoist repression were a common practice on the islands. On Gran Canaria, some of the dead and dying were thrown into wells: twenty-four bodies were recently recovered from the well at Arucas, and another fifteen have been recovered from the one at Tenoya, despite having been covered with quicklime. Other victims were put into plantains sacks and thrown into the ocean, as occurred at the cliffs of Marfea. (A monument was placed there in 2018.) In the seas around the archipelago, bodies would be seen floating in the water. Some people say that they ended up there via the wells.

The dictatorship, of course, ignored its victims and honored the executioners. Some of the Morning Brigade's worst assassins later became the islands' political and economic elites.

Public spaces filled with homages to the Movement and its leaders. In Tenerife alone, more than eighty public symbols of this type remained in 2018, in violation of the Historical Memory Law passed in 2007. The most famous of these is popularly called the "Monument to Franco." This giant monument was designed by Juan de Ávalos (the sculptor behind the Valley of the Fallen) and was unveiled in 1966. It depicts the flight of the Dragon Rapide, the plane that took Franco from Las Palmas to Morocco in 1936 (see Chapter 1). In 2010, the city hall decided to change its name—apparently without irony—to the Monument to the Fallen Angel. The following year a new administration again changed its name, this time to the Monument to Victory. Of whom, over whom, is unclear. In any case, there it is, in bad shape, yet still on public display.

At the end of 2018, the Canary Islands' Parliament approved a historical memory law. One of its plans includes clearing out the debris that in recent years has been thrown into the Cone of Jinámar, turning it into a garbage dump; the end goal is to recover the bodies. In 2020 a study was done to evaluate the state of the chasm in order to be able to go ahead with the clean-up efforts and the identification of the bodies. In the meantime, whomever wishes to visit this site will have to locate a small, unmarked path that is surrounded by trash. And at the edge of the cone one can read a sign that says: "From the Canary Islands, to the heroes who fell for the cause of the people's liberty." These words, though well-intentioned, do not tell the true story.

35. DRAWING OF A BOMBING BY RAFAEL CERRILLO, 1937, MADRID

Verónica Sierra Blas

One of the Republican government's main objectives following the outbreak of the Civil War was to protect children. Schools in Republican territory that could remain open became their primary refuges, until there was no choice left but to close them. From that point on, any minors who were in danger (injured, sick, the children of soldiers, residents of places close to the front, etc.) were taken in by student colonies (*colonias escolares*). In 1937 alone, Spain had 564 colonies that were taking care of more than 45,000 children. Of these, 158 were boarding schools, where children were cared for by a team of specialists; in the other 406 children were temporarily adopted into families who provided their education, food and lodging, and general care. None of this was totally alien to the rebel side, either, which in addition to reopening schools in the places that they conquered also opened up establishments with similar ends.

Despite the different ideologies and pedagogies that divided the two sides, the war became central to education for both. The conflict transformed schools into the axis of the fight and education became the key element of children's wartime socialization. Children's toys, publications, and organizations also played a crucial role in this project.

Children were generally taught about the war, including the reasons behind it and what was expected of them given the circumstances. But at many education centers, especially in the colonies, those in charge went further and also tried to help children process what they were going through and confront their traumas. One of the most widely used tools for doing so was to get them to draw whatever was tormenting, disturbing, or frightening them. Experiencing a bombing was a frequent subject, as we can see in the above drawing by Rafael Cerrillo. Rafael was thirteen when he drew this picture and attended the Germán de Araujo student colony in Alcañiz, in the province of Teruel. His drawing depicts an aerial attack against his village; it took place on a sunny day that the bombs turned completely black. With other children dressed in shorts and short-sleeved shirts, he was in line at the milk dispensary, taking care of a chore that his mother had asked him to do that morning. The Nationalist bombers released their lethal cargo at least twice. The first bomb split a nearby tree in half and also mutilated a pedestrian whose left arm the children saw fly through the air. Rafael doesn't reveal the consequences of the second bomb, although we can infer that he had time to run far away enough to escape unscathed. Finally, it appears that the enemy airplane was intercepted before it could bomb again, given the presence of the three Republican Tri-motor airplanes that appear in the corner of the page.

In addition to serving as pedagogical and therapeutic tools, the Republican authorities also made effective use of these wartime drawings by Spanish children as propaganda. The drawings were exhibited and put up for sale many times, both inside and outside of Spain. The aim was to raise funds for their cause, to denounce the atrocities committed by the other side, and to gain the support of international public opinion.

Raphael's drawing is a clear example of how these children's drawings served different ends for adults. It formed part of a collection campaign organized by José A. Weissberger at the end of 1937 at the request of the American Friends Service Committee (Quakers) and the Spanish Child Welfare Association of America. The collection of drawings was displayed at the Lord & Taylor department store in New York in 1938, and later toured different cities in the United States. They were also published in the catalogue *They Still Draw Pictures: A Collection of Sixty Drawings Made by Spanish Children during the War* published by Oxford University Press, in 1939, with a prologue written by Aldous Huxley, that was sold around the world. The drawings that were exhibited on Fifth Avenue are currently held in three public institutions: 617 of them at the Mandeville Library at the University of California, San Diego; 153 at the Avery Library at Columbia University in New York City; and 1,172, including Rafael Cerrillo's *Bombing in the Milk Line*, in the National Library in Madrid.

36. SOLDIER'S IDENTIFICATION TAG, 1937, ÁLAVA/VIZCAYA

Alfredo González Ruibal with Josu Santamarina Otaola

This improvised name tag belonged to a Republican militiaman named Manuel Mogrovejo. It appeared during an archaeological excavation in the San Pedro/Askuren hill between the provinces of Álava and Vizcaya. Two Civil War battles were fought there. The first in was December 1936, as part of the battle of Villarreal, which led to the capturing and fortification of San Pedro by the Republicans. The second took place at the end of May 1937 when the Francoists captured it. Since 2016, archaeological excavations there have unearthed the remains of numerous combatants, as well as objects belonging to them. This identification tag, which was found on the layer of earth sealing the ground of a large communications trench, is one example. Such tags tend to be found along with human remains buried precariously in the middle of a battlefield. This one, however, was found without any associated skeletal remains.

Identification tags are relatively common in Republican positions in the Basque Country, compared to their striking absence on other fronts. The first Spanish units to wear a form of personal identification were the troops in Morocco, beginning in 1921. At the start of the Civil War, the members of the Legion wore the 1932 model tags—an aluminum disc that hung from a chain around the neck. The Basque Army created their own type of identification for their combatants, thus making them relatively common in the Northern Front, but many soldiers, particularly the militia battalions, had to make their own. It is possible that they made them in order to imitate the units created by the Basque government. Alternatively, they may have made the tags out of a stronger sense of individual identity and greater political consciousness. Decades after the end of the war, the discovery of these tags is helping to identify soldiers who fell in combat. In the case that concerns us here, it has given rise to an exciting biographic investigation.

Manuel Mogrovejo was born in Amorebieta, in Vizcaya, in 1918. He was one of the first people to enlist in the Communist Leandro Carro battalion, in which his older brother, José Luis Mogrovejo, also fought. The discovery of his identification tag in San Pedro could lead one to think that the young Manuel died in one of the battles that took place there. However, he appears in the battalion's active lists until the summer of 1937, and he continued fighting on the Northern Front until its definitive fall in October of that year. At that point he was able to escape from Asturias, and, after passing through France, rejoined the Republican lines in Cataluña as part of the Anti-Aircraft Special Defenses (DECA). His unit fought in Teruel (December 1937–November 1938) and then in the Battle of the Ebro (July–November 1938) for which his brigade was honored with the Collective Medal of Valor. The Francoist offensive in Cataluña, however, led Mogrovejo to go into exile.

After crossing the border in February 1939, Manuel was interned at the refugee camp in Argelès-sur-Mer, after which he was sent to the camp at Gurs. We know that he was in Bunkhouse 9 of Area B. In September 1939, he volunteered for the French Legion and was sent to the Maginot Line and at the end of May 1940, he entered combat with his regiment against the German Army in the Inor forest, where his unit lost more than 300 men. Mogrovejo was taken prisoner and was sent to different prison camps. Being a Spanish soldier, he was classified as a deportee and interned at the Mauthausen concentration camp. He survived and was liberated by US troops on May 5, 1945. His survival there can be attributed to the fact that he was sent to work in the kitchens of Gusen, where conditions were better. One of the last documented pieces of information about his life can be found in Spain's *Official State Bulletin* from September 15, 1959. He was required to go to court for a crime committed in 1942; he would have been in Mauthausen at the time. Mogrovejo died in Paris in 1993 and his ashes were buried in the Père-Lachaise Cemetery. Two other members of the Legion from Fort de Nogent were present at his burial. The investigation into his story shed light not only on the life of one of the many forgotten Republican soldiers but also put previously unknown family members, both in Spain and abroad, in contact with one another.

37. THE TREE OF GERNIKA, APRIL 1937

Miren Llona

The historic town of Gernika is most strongly associated with its bombing on April 26, 1937, as part of the rebel's full-on offensive to liquidate the Northern Front. It was a market day and many people would have been in town that morning. Over the course of four hours that afternoon, three Savoia SM-79s and ten CR-32s belonging to the Italian Aviation Legion, as well as two Heinkel He-111s and nineteen Junkers Ju-52 of the Condor Legion, attacked the city in several waves. Five Bf-107s and seven He-51s from Germany simultaneously machine-gunned the streets. A relentless combination of explosive and incendiary bombs massacred the civilian population, leaving behind hundreds of victims and completely destroying two-thirds of the city. We can get a sense of the terror it caused from testimony given by one of the last remaining survivors of the bombing. "E." recalls how some militiamen "told us to put a stick in our mouths, so that our ears wouldn't burst. How the bombs rumbled! We were crying, dying of fear."

This attack was a trial run of the total aerial warfare that was later visited upon cities such as Rotterdam, Coventry, and Dresden. In fact, the attack on Gernika was later described by British Prime Minister Anthony Eden as "the first bombing of the Second World War." Although in the days following the massacre Franco denied all responsibility for the attack, placing the blame on withdrawing Republican soldiers, journalists such as George Steer let the world know what had really happened. As soon as April 28, *The Times* of London ran Steer's story: "At two o'clock this morning I witnessed with horror a city engulfed by flames … The buildings kept falling down over the course of the entire night until the streets became filled with mountains of debris, impenetrable and incandescent." Franco's lie was sustained for decades as his regime's official version of events.

Gernika became a symbol of the horrors of war and of fascism thanks to the painting by Pablo Picasso that was commissioned by the government of the Second Republic for the 1937 Paris International Exposition. After the end of the war, *Guernica* was sent to Museum of Modern Art in New York City, but this did not prevent it from touring in more than eleven countries all over the world. The painting became an antifascist symbol and had a significant impact on international public opinion.

From the perspective of the Basque Country, Gernika and the context of the Civil War bring us to the forceful pursuit of the Autonomy Statute and the formation of the first Basque government, and with it the birth of Euskadi as a political entity. The two main architects of the Basque Autonomy Statute were the socialist Indalecio Prieto and the Basque Nationalist José Antonio Aguirre, who co-authored the text in the spring of 1936. Because of the outbreak of the Civil War it was hurried through parliament and approved on October 1. Six days later, Aguirre was elected *lehendakari* (President) and that same day took up his post at the Casa de Juntas (Assembly House) in Gernika, located next to the tree pictured above.

During Franco's dictatorship, reproductions of Picasso's *Guernica* as well as photographs of the tree and the Gernika Assembly House were hung in people's homes as symbols of anti-Francoist resistance and of the hope for freedom. Perhaps for this reason, the tree and the city of Gernika are today universal symbols of peace. On April 18, 1987, on the occasion of the fiftieth anniversary of the bombing, Petra Kelly, member of the German parliament for Alliance90/the Greens, placed a bouquet of flowers under the tree of Gernika in memory of the victims, acknowledging: "I am here today and I am a German and I feel shame for what occurred here in 1937." Kelly also petitioned for the Bundestag to apologize. It took ten years but finally, in 1997, the German ambassador to Spain, Henning Wegener, went to Gernika to read a message from the German president in which he recognized "the fault of the German airplanes" and asked for forgiveness. At the same time, the Gernika Gogoratuz Peace Research Center—another of Petra Kelly's petitions—was created with the aim of organizing an international support network for processes of reconciliation.

38. THE *HAVANA*, MAY 1937, SOUTHAMPTON, UNITED KINGDOM

Miren Llona

On May 21, 1937, a ship named the *Havana* departed Santurtzi, near Bilbao, for England with 3,681 children aboard. In the collective memory of the Basque Country, this evacuation represents the entirety of wartime exile, including the Republican children who were sent abroad as a consequence of the Spanish Civil War. Perhaps the *Havana* is so symbolic because this was the first mass evacuation of children. Prior to this, beginning in January 1937, in view of the danger posed by civilian bombings, some smaller evacuations, from the ports of Ondarroa and Bermeo, had taken place. Or perhaps it is symbolic because this evacuation took place immediately after the bombing of Gernika, whose international repercussions put European nations on alert and helped solidify international solidarity with the Second Republic. Or maybe, because the ship itself had a mythical status. At the time, the *Havana* was Spain's largest transatlantic ship; it had been built in

Sestao's La Naval shipyard and its launch constituted a milestone in local memory.

During the first part of the war, the *Havana*, which could carry 2,000 people, remained in port and was used a hospital ship. However, after the Basque government agreed with the British and French governments to the possibility of organizing a mass evacuation, it ended up making six voyages transporting Basque children abroad. The majority of the children went to France, but some also ended up in Belgium, the Soviet Union, the United Kingdom, Switzerland, Denmark, and Mexico. In April 1938, Basque welfare agencies calculated that around 32,000 children had been evacuated, offering a sense of the scale of the human impact of the evacuations. Of her own departure Helvecia Hidalgo recalls, "I can still hear my mother shouting: 'It will only be three months. It will only be three months.'" But this was not to be the case. After the war, the repatriation process was accelerated, and many children returned to a land that classified them as the sons and daughters of "reds." Many others, however, remained in their adopted homelands, their fates tied to the vicissitudes of the coming Second World War.

For its part, the May 1937 evacuation of those first nearly 4,000 children to Southampton became emblematic of civil society's mobilization to confront the disasters of war. The children sent to England were taken in by the Basque Children's Committee, a movement of British citizens that took action despite the British government's policy of non-intervention. In the end, the British government agreed to take in the evacuated children on the condition that no state resources were used to support them. This prompted the establishment of a large solidarity network throughout the entire United Kingdom: first, to construct a provisional refugee camp in North Stoneham, Eastleigh, with more than 500 tents; then to raise the ten shillings per week that was required to support each child; and finally, to find permanent lodging and foster families for all of the refugees from October 1937 onward. The creation of more than 100 colonies throughout British territory, from London to Wales to Scotland, shows the measure of the British people's enormous generosity and commitment to the Republican cause. It also contributed to the origins of the concept of "humanitarian assistance."

Since its creation in 1986, the Bilbao-based organization Evacuated Children of '37 Association has been an effective instrument for the remembrance of these events and has facilitated the discovery, transmission, and commemoration of those lived experiences through trips, exhibitions, books, and homages. Also in Bilbao, the Mrs. Leah Manning Gardens were created in 2002 in recognition of the Labour Member of Parliament who made the evacuation of the children aboard the *Havana* possible. In 2006, a mosaic by the artist Paco Presa Merodio was made in the port of Santurtzi commemorating the children who departed there for Southampton. In

Great Britain, the Basque Children of '37 Association UK was created in 2002 to teach people there about these events. The Association has tried to tell the stories of these small evacuees and maintain relationships with their families. Their website (http://www.basquechildren.org/association) is a fundamental online repository of articles and information about the events related to the exile of Basque children.

39. DIARY OF A GALICIAN SOLDIER, MAY 1937, FERROL, A CORUÑA

Emilio Grandío Seoane

Faustino, a young man from Monforte de Lemos in Lugo, is conscripted during one of the many military drafts that takes place in A Coruña following the rebels' declaring a state of war in July 1936. Faustino—nicknamed Meana by his friends—loved soccer and had an active social life. But then he, along with many other young men, was submitted to the military jurisdiction of the rebels. Like many of his generation, his political beliefs lay part way between the union-based socialism of which his home city, located at a railroad junction, had a strong tradition,—and headstrong anarchism. Such ideas have no place within the discipline of the barracks.

Meana's world is now very different; it has turned khaki. In A Coruña, his world is transformed into a universe of military exercises and surveillance by the rebels who fear the large numbers of people hidden within the city and in the surrounding hills. They are of course also suspicious of young people with diverse histories and backgrounds within the barracks, who may be tempted to commit daring and courageous acts. Until the complete fall of the Northern Front in late 1937, the military was fearful of a pro-Republican revolt in the city. This fear was not baseless: during that period two insurrectionist plans were discovered within the barracks. This led the rebels to reinforce their security and surveillance teams in the city.

Meana does not have time to see the end of this conflict. At the end of August 1936, the first draftees are sent to Asturias to help the rebel general Aranda relieve the Republican siege of Oviedo. Numerous troops are sent from Lugo; they take the road following the Cantabrian coast and step by step conquer the harsh terrain of the western Asturian mountains. They are accompanied by a large contingent of volunteers, Falangists, paramilitaries, and units of Moroccan Regulares. Together they form the first shock wave against the so-called "red" Asturias of the mining basin, which had revolted in 1934.

Along the way, Meana keeps a diary. His motivation is twofold. First, his love of journalism leads him to write down his observations, recording what was happening with the intention of revising it later on. He observes and describes mass executions, destruction, and misery, the effects of armies in action, the needs of the troops, the first aerial bombings ... But he also notes the contrasts between his personal opinion of what is happening and what they are forced to do, between strict obedience, the cold, the water .... In this way, Meana's writings also serve as a type of "mental hygiene," confiding on the page—where there is no censorship beyond his own imagination—that which he cannot express in daily life.

A few months later, while still on the Asturian front, Meana falls ill and is taken to several different hospitals in the rearguard. He finally lands at the A Coruña General Hospital, one of the area's largest and most important. His diary goes with him. From his hospital bed, he continues writing and revising. One day during his convalescence, a comrade tells the hospital authorities what he has been writing in his diary, which includes negative and sarcastic opinions about a good number of the rebel leaders, including Franco himself. Meana is immediately arrested and sent to a military tribunal where he is sentenced to death. He is executed within a few days, on May 10, 1937. His family is informed about his death by firing squad without any further explanation. I suppose they thought that he could have just as well died in the war from a stray bullet.

One fortunate day many years later, the original diary was found. It had been stored in the Ferrol Military Tribunal Archives, inside the records of his court martial. Faustino Vázquez's diary was published in the summer of 2011, and the recovery of his memory was no doubt transcendent for his family, filling the hole that silence—the tomb stone burying so many people's stories—had covered over.

40. FIFTH REGIMENT GRENADE, JULY 1937, VILLANUEVA DEL PARDILLO, MADRID

Alfredo González Ruibal

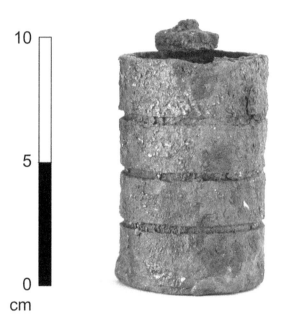

It may look like just an innocent can or metal tube, but the artifact pictured above is an explosive. It is a type of grenade known as the Fifth Regiment, named after the communist unit that created it and put it into circulation. The Fifth Regiment was created out of the Communist Party's Antifascist Workers and Farmworkers Militias (MAOC) immediately after the July 18, 1936 coup; it was dissolved in January 1937 when the militias were folded into the Republican Army, although many of its members remained together in the shock units. With the Republicans facing a scarcity of arms and munitions and with the rebels on their way to Madrid, artifacts like this had to be improvised. Grenades were a key element of urban and trench warfare, and they played a central role in the Civil War, beginning with the battle for the capital.

The Fifth Regiment grenade consisted of a steel tube fitted with horizontal slots to facilitate its breaking apart. It would have been be filled with explosives, paper, and all kinds of shrapnel-like components, such as bolts, bullets, pieces of metal, even rocks. Lacking a ring or other similar mechanism as a detonator, the grenade was activated by a fuse that had to be lit manually with a match or a lighter. It could be dangerous to use even in battles in open country as the shrapnel could injure the person throwing it, but in the kind of house to house and room by room combat that characterized the war in Madrid and surrounding areas during November and December 1936, it was lethal.

Due to the scarcity of supplies at the beginning of the war, the steel tubes were originally taken from the heating systems on trains. Later they would be made from *ad hoc* materials. But despite the crude nature of these grenades, they were likely used throughout the entirety of the war in central Spain. They have been found during archaeological excavations in locations from quite late in the conflict, like Abánades (Guadalajara) and Rivas Vaciamadrid, just outside of Madrid. The grenade pictured above was found in Villanueva del Pardillo, where battles took place between July 1937 (the Battle of Brunete) and January 1939. Further, the weapons inventory lists show that various units of the Army of the Center possessed this type of grenade.

The Fifth Regiment is not the only handmade bomb whose creation was associated with a political group. Another example is the FAI grenade, which was created at the end of the 1920s by Ramón Franco, the future dictator's brother. Franco put it in the hands of the anarchists who began to produce it in 1935. Like the Fifth Regiment, it is heavy and dangerous—and not only for the enemy. It became known as "The Impartial."

Handmade grenades are a characteristically Spanish phenomenon that reveal certain relevant social, cultural, and political aspects of the Civil War. For example, they show how Spain, during the war, was a handyman's workshop as well as the site of experimentation in the latest innovations in arms and tactics. Indeed, the grenades are illustrative of the Spanish revolutionary movement's longstanding tradition of producing its own home made weapons. They also offer testimony to the abilities of the industrial workers of the era who were able to make everything from pistols to tanks, something unthinkable today given modern industry's need for the division of labor and its attendant loss of skills. The homemade grenades are thus in reality the product of a still pre-industrial society made up mostly of workers, artisans, and farmworkers who, during peacetime, would have made most of their own material culture. The grenades are also a reminder of the autonomy enjoyed by the different parties and unions within the Republic, both before and during the war. There is no equivalent of the union grenades in the rebel army. Finally, they remind us of the quotidian nature of the violence that afflicted not only Republican Spain, but all of interwar Europe.

41. CERTIFICATE OF SERVICE IN EOIN O'DUFFY'S IRISH BRIGADE, AFTER JUNE 1937, LIMERICK, IRELAND

Adrian Shubert

This "Certificate of Service" signed by Brigadier General Eion O'Duffy and "Generalíssimo" Francisco Franco testifies that James Roche had fought in the Irish Brigade with "Loyalty, Courage, and Good Conduct" as part of its "Crusade in Spain." Roche was one of approximately 2,000 Irishmen who joined the Irish Brigade. Around 700 actually served in Spain. In comparison, around 200 fought in the Connolly Column of the International Brigades.

Ireland was unique in that many more men there volunteered to fight for Franco than for the Republic, but this reflected the weight of public opinion in this recently independent country where Catholicism and national identity were deeply intertwined.

In Ireland, the Spanish Civil War was interpreted primarily as a religious rather than as a social or political conflict. The church and the Catholic press had been hammering the religious issue since the birth of the Second Republic, and the Irish Church responded quickly to the outbreak of the Civil War, and especially the murder of thousands of clergy in the early weeks of the conflict. In September 1936, Cardinal Joseph McCrory, head of the Irish Church, stated that what was at stake in Spain was extremely simple: "It is a question of whether Spain will remain as she has been so long, a Christian and Catholic land, or a Bolshevist and anti-God one." And it was McCrory who had encouraged O'Duffy to create the brigade in the first place.

Irish society had already started to mobilize in support of the military rebels, most significantly in the form of the Irish Christian Front (ICF) which was created in August 1936. The next month it was able to bring out 40,000 people to a demonstration in Cork. In scenes similar to those in Navarra, when the Brigades left for Spain they were blessed by priests, given religious medallions, and seen off by enthusiastic crowds singing songs like "Faith of our Fathers."

There was also a political element to this mobilization. Some ICF leaders, as well as O'Duffy himself, were fascists and members of the paramilitary Blueshirts. Eamon de Valera's government also came under intense pressure to rescind its recognition of the Spanish Republic and abandon its support for non-intervention.

The experience of the Irish Brigade in Spain was brief and unhappy. It first saw action at the Battle of the Jarama, and soon found itself in a lethal firefight with a Falangista unit. Plagued by drunkenness and indiscipline—on one occasion the officers mutinied when ordered to attack a village—the unit was ordered back to Ireland by Franco in June 1937. It had been in Spain only six months.

The Irish Brigade constituted the bulk of the approximately 3,000 foreign volunteers who fought on the Nationalist side. There were also the 300 members of the Jeanne d'Arc unit of the Spanish Legion, some members of the Romanian Iron Guard, as well as some White Russian veterans of the Russian Civil War and assorted adventurers and right-wingers.

One of the right-wingers was English writer Peter Kemp, who served in the Carlist Requetés and then the Spanish Legion before being seriously wounded and returned to the UK. He claimed that volunteering to fight for the Nationalists was much more difficult than joining the International Brigades. "Had I wished to join the International Brigades there would have been no problem; in every country there were organisations to attract volunteers. But the Nationalists showed no interest in recruiting in Britain."

This lack of interest is unsurprising. The Francoists were receiving massive assistance from Germany and Italy, as well as a lesser but still significant support from Portugal. They had no need to recruit individuals or small numbers of men elsewhere, especially when they were not proper soldiers in real military organizations and, as in the case of the Irish, turned out to be more trouble than they were worth. The Republic's embrace of the International Brigades was a sign of the desperation created by the decision of the democracies to embrace non-intervention that they knew in advance was only a charade.

42. LETTER TO FRANCO, JULY 1937, MADRID

Antonio Cazorla-Sánchez

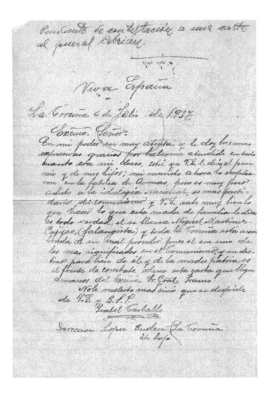

This letter to Franco is preserved in the Royal Palace Archives in Madrid, along with hundreds of thousands of others written by Spaniards, as well as some foreigners, over the course of nearly forty years. Although Franco lived in the El Pardo Palace after the war, his official office was in the Royal Palace. The letter pictured above was written by a woman from A Coruña in July 1937. In it she accuses her husband, with whom she had a terrible and sometimes violent relationship, of being a communist, and asks Franco to send him to the front. In a previous letter, she accuses him of returning from the front, of hitting her, of abandoning their children and going to live with another woman. We know that the authorities investigated the case and forced the husband to provide for the children.

In reality, this letter was an exception to the norm. Franco received many letters from people making accusations against neighbors and, occasionally, against family members. Some were from women asking for justice for feeling betrayed after having been seduced by soldiers. In general, however, the letters sent to the dictator, as well as to his wife and daughter, were petitions for favors and clemency. During the Civil War, many soldiers and their families asked Franco for special permissions, economic assistance, information about "disappeared" people, rewards, etc. Many people, especially women, begged Franco for forgiveness for their husbands, sons, fathers, or brothers condemned to death or sentenced to many years in prison. These supplicants would tell heartbreaking stories to try to soften the Caudillo's heart and get him to see their families' suffering. Franco's wife, Carmen Polo, who held the Office of the First Lady, also received such letters. The women writing to her would try to establish empathy on the basis of their shared gender, to forge a woman-to-woman conversation, and to show that they shared her domestic and Christian values. The same occurred with the children who wrote to Franco's daughter Carmencita, begging her to intercede before her father for the sake of theirs, claiming that they were innocent children who just wanted joy to return to their homes.

The women who wrote to Franco knew that their slim chances of success rested in showing complete submission to the power of the Caudillo and to the values of the New Spain. For this reason, they filled their missives with praise for the dictator and wishes for God to shine light upon his government. They also presented themselves as devout Catholics and selfless mothers who just wanted their men back home to begin new and apolitical lives. Part of their strategy to inspire the dictator's clemency included presenting the condemned men's actions as a momentary error, one for which they had certainly already repented, or due to circumstances beyond their control. In other words, Franco's victim was also the victim of bad luck, or, at worst, of bad influences. In this way, those who meekly put themselves at the mercy of this all-powerful man were also trying to use the regime's official rhetoric, according to which Franco was kind and full of Christian piety, to their own advantage.

It is difficult to know how well these letters worked, particularly those asking for commutations of the death penalty. Some of them would have arrived in the dictator's hands after the condemned man had already been executed. We know that influential people within the new regime had a greater chance of saving their friends and family members than did ordinary people. In any case, the letters would have served for little in 1936, when executions of the enemy were extensive and often immediate. However, they had a greater chance of success as the war went on, and even more so after the end of the conflict, when the Francoist prisons came to house nearly 300,000 prisoners while executions were reduced to 30,000. Beginning in 1942, the prisons began to empty after a series of partial pardons were issued, and at the same time many people condemned to death had their death sentences reduced to long terms in prison. In any case, although the prisoners were set free, their lives were rarely the same as those of other Spaniards. To the authorities they always remained suspect, and they and their families were often socially ostracized and discriminated against, both legally and in practice.

The letters to Franco reveal a cruel and miserable Spain where death and hunger destroyed lives, families, and dreams.

43. *THE SPANISH EARTH* BY JORIS IVENS, JULY 1937

Vicente J. Benet

On July 8, 1937, President Franklin D. Roosevelt, accompanied by his wife Eleonor and others in his inner circle, watched the movie *The Spanish Earth* in the White House. Filmed barely a few months earlier on the battlefields of Spain, the movie had just been completed. A decisive factor in it reaching such a select audience was its endorsement by some of North America's most prestigious writers and intellectuals, like Ernest Hemingway and John Dos Passos, who had been involved in making it. The film was the brainchild of the Dutch director Joris Ivens and editor Helen van Dongen, who had been working in New York for several months. Ivens' usual cinematographer, Johannes Fernhout, known professionally as John Ferno, also joined the project.

The film shows heart-pounding scenes of a war that found great resonance in the United States in the news, the press, and in illustrated magazines. Just four days after the screening at the White House and as the film was beginning a profitable West coast tour, *Life* magazine published a forceful report on Spain prominently featuring Robert Capa's famous photograph of a militiaman being killed on Cerro Muriano. The following week, the film arrived in Los Angeles where it was screened at the Philharmonic Auditorium in front of an audience of 3,500. Other screenings were held at places such as the Ambassador Hotel and the home of actor Fredric March for selected members of the public willing to make generous donations. These donations went toward the purchase of ambulances for Republican combatants.

The film was the rather strange product of a fight that was also occurring within the realm of media and propaganda. *The Spanish Earth* differs from the militant cinema typical of the period by opting for a subtler approach, depicting the political battle more generically and metaphorically. As the title suggests, the earth itself is given a starring role as the primal space in which the battle for survival and justice takes place. Entering into the specifics of the political conflict and employing the usual rhetoric of Communist propaganda from that time—highlighting the fight between the people and fascism—could have been counterproductive for a North American public. For this reason, the film's strategy for achieving their sympathy was to offer a personalized yet transcendent vision, in which the word "fascism" is barely mentioned and the Communist identity of certain protagonists, including José Díaz, Dolores Ibárruri, Enrique Líster, Vittorio Vidali, and "Commander Carlos," is concealed.

Another unique feature of *The Spanish Earth* is the hybrid nature of its composition. Its opening sequences show the splendid sobriety of Castilian countryside, work on the irrigation system, and the archetypal image of the men and women of the village of Fuentidueña. With this, it exhibits traces of the ethnographic cinema that was so popular during the 1930s. However, the almost atemporal nature of these images is broken by images of maps, sometimes animated, that locate this area in the context of the war, and by diverse scenes of the armed conflict shown from different points of view, typical of war reporting.

Later on, the film employs yet other modes of cinematography, such as the testimonial documentary, to show the victims of the bombings and report on the daily life of soldiers, and, in its depiction of a meeting celebrating the creation of the Republican Popular Army, including the Communist leaders mentioned above. Despite its use of eclectic discursive devices, the film is held together and given continuity by three organizing threads. The first is a minor plot featuring a farmer-soldier from Fuentidueña named Julian, who serves as the connection between the eternal, seismic forces of the Spanish earth and the concrete context of the war. The second is Hemingway's text. In accordance with the well-known sobriety of his style, the voice-over adheres for the most part to direct commentary on the images, although there are times when it shifts to a more literary style where it is quite effective in accentuating the social or emotional dimensions intended in the film. Finally, there is the music, which was composed by Virgil Thomson and Marc Blitzstein. Based on traditional Spanish musical themes, mostly from Calatuña, it is somewhat surprising for a local viewer to find them paired with images of the Castilian landscape.

44. *JOINT LETTER OF THE BISHOPS OF SPAIN TO THE BISHOPS OF THE WHOLE WORLD REGARDING THE WAR IN SPAIN, AUGUST 1937, BARCELONA*

Adrian Shubert

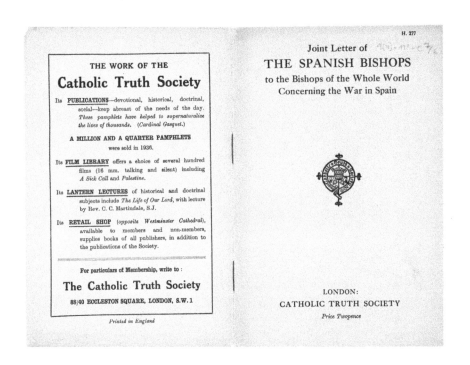

The *Joint Letter of the Bishops of Spain to the Bishops of the Whole World Regarding the War in Spain*, published on August 1, 1937 in English, French, and Italian as well as in Spanish, is the most important statement made by the Catholic Church in Spain during the Civil War.

The document was created at Francisco Franco's express wish. Two weeks after the destruction of Guernica on April 26, 1937, Franco met with the Primate of Spain, Cardenal Isidro Gomá. The bombing had been widely reported in the international press and Franco was desperate to diminish the damage to the reputation of the Nationalists. At that meeting, he asked Gomá to publish a statement supporting his cause. This fifteen-page booklet was the result.

The *Joint Letter* was signed by forty-three bishops and five *vicarios capitulares* [interim administrators], but the names of two very important members of the church hierarchy were missing. One, Cardinal Archbishop Francisco Vidal y Barraquer of Tarragona, refused to sign because he believed that the church should have been working towards reconciliation rather than taking sides. Barraquer had been in Italy since 1936 and the Franco regime never allowed him to return to the country. The second, Mateo Múgica, Bishop of Vitoria, objected to the fact that the *Joint Letter* made no mention of the Basque priests executed by the Francoists after their conquest of the Basque Country. In October 1937, he was expelled from Spain. Although Gomá complained to Franco about those executions in private, he justified them to the Vatican by arguing that the priests had been involved in politics. Not until July 2009 would the church publicly recognize the execution of the Basque priests.

According to the bishops, the conflict in Spain was easy to understand. It was simply a struggle to the death between "two Spains ... the spiritual ... and the materialistic." It was, in the document's most famous words, "an armed plebiscite." (The document did not call it a crusade, as bishop Enrique Pla y Deniel had done in his October 1936 pastoral letter, *The Two Cities*.) The war was also the direct result of a Communist plot hatched and financed by the Comintern immediately after the elections of February 1936 to launch a revolution in Spain. (There was in fact a plot being hatched then, but it was the work of generals opposed to the electoral victory of the Popular Front.) The alleged Communist plot included "the extermination of the Catholic clergy and leading rightists, the sovietization of industry and the implantation of communism."

This revolution "against the divine" was itself the logical conclusion of secularizing measures initiated with the Constitution of 1931. This "inhumane [and] extremely cruel revolution" was also profoundly "anti-Spanish," driven by "hatred for the national spirit." It left the real Spain with a brutally simple choice: either "assume the titanic task of resistance or perish in the assault of destructive Communism." Franco's genuinely "national movement," which started only *after* Republican authorities ignored warnings about the "imminent Marxist revolution," was precisely that resistance. In those parts of Spain where they had triumphed or conquered, the Francoists had restored order and people enjoyed "true authority, which is the cornerstone of justice, peace, and progress ... religious services abound and new manifestations of Christian life are appearing."

This vision of the Civil War was partial, partisan, and distorted. For the terrible violence perpetrated by the Francoists, there was only justification. However, it was precisely these characteristics, as well as the clear black and white story it told, including the alleged holocaust of which the church was a victim, that made it such a powerful piece of propaganda. Even though the Vatican refused to comment on the *Joint Letter* and would not even acknowledge having received it for nine months, hundreds of bishops around the world endorsed it and it was widely publicized in the Catholic press.

Not only did the *Joint Letter* have the effect on global Catholic opinion that Franco desired, it has had an ongoing impact on the way the Civil War is understood.

45. COLOGNE BOTTLE, AUGUST 1937, BELCHITE, ZARAGOZA

Alfredo González Ruibal

The Battle of Belchite (August 24–September 6, 1937) was part of a greater Republican offensive against Zaragoza that ended up failing. The Popular Army made it as far as Mediana de Aragón, just 30 kilometers outside of the city before Francoist reinforcements stopped their advance. Neither were the rebels able to break the Republican lines and help their own units situated in Belchite. The front was thus at a standstill in the Mediana steppe for several months, until Franco's Army renewed their offensive in March 1938.

Trenches many kilometers long belonging to both sides can be found in that area, still conserved today. The soldiers of the 15th International Brigade dug and defended the trenches from September 4 to 7, 1937, although the battle lasted several more days and involved both Spanish and international troops. At some points the lines are nearly a kilometer apart, while at others they almost touch. According to a report from that time: "The distances between the Republican and Fascist positions were small. The English battalion and the Fascists both had forward positions in these hills. In one place there was a small separation of some 40 meters; grenades would frequently be thrown by hand from one group to the other." This description coincides with the zone known as the Parapet of Death, close to the road connecting Belchite with Zaragoza. The trenches here are exactly 40 meters apart at their closest point, separated by a thin slice of land perforated by craters and covered, to this day, with bullets and shells, and thousands of fragments of grenades, artillery and mortar shells (some still undetonated).

During an archaeological excavation of this area, a strange object appeared between the munitions and the shrapnel: a purple-colored bottle. It is different from the other pieces of glass that litter the area. Those come from the bottles of anise and brandy which the soldiers would have used to deal with the brutality of the war and fight their fear. The purple glass belongs, in contrast, to a cologne bottle. It looks completely out of place given the context we find ourselves in, but the truth is that soldiers the in Civil War did not go without their cologne. The American International Brigade member Alvah Bessie thought that this was an absurd obsession, and in describing the extremely young Spanish soldiers sent as reinforcements to Alicante in May 1938, he notes how they brought mirrors, bad-smelling soap, talcum powder and "the inevitable bottles of cologne without which the Spanish soldier seems incapable of confronting the enemy, even in the frontline trenches."

However, the presence of perfume on the front lines is not really so illogical. First, we should recall that soldiers had very few opportunities to wash themselves while they were in combat; the only way to deal with their body odor (as well as parasites) was by applying cologne. Further, smell is the most powerful sense, and the one most strongly associated with memory. In such a hostile and extremely stressful situation, cologne would have provided the soldiers with a mental escape, recalling their homes and ordinary lives far from the trenches. Finally, in the case of the Parapet of Death, we can contemplate yet another reason for the cologne—perhaps the most plausible given the context. The Battle of Belchite was fought during the summer, in a desert area with soaring temperatures and no shade. In the no-man's-land of Mediana, the dead would have been decomposing and rotting under the sun, just a few meters away from the fortifications. The smell would have been unbearable. So unbearable, in fact, that after the fall of Belchite soldiers had to wear gas masks to deal with the stench of the bodies as they were buried or cremated. War does not smell only of gunpowder and explosives; it also smells of cadavers rotting in the sun. And so cologne, like wine and bullets, is a useful thing to have in the trenches.

46. CHILDREN'S GRAVES, AUGUST 1937 AND MARCH 1938, MICHOACÁN, MEXICO

Verónica Sierra Blas

On May 20, 1937, one of the first expeditions organized by the Republican government to evacuate children abroad left for Mexico. Facing the unstoppable advance of the rebel troops and given the high mortality figures recorded during the first months of the conflict, many parents signed up their children for such expeditions, convinced that sending them away from the dangers of the war was the best way to protect them.

Thanks to the Spanish Children's Assistance Committee founded by Mexican President Lázaro Cárdenas in October 1936, 456 children boarded the *Mexique* in Bordeaux. The first group of children had begun their journey in Valencia and were joined by others in Barcelona. The majority were between 3 and 15 years old and came from working-class families in Madrid, Barcelona, Valencia, Sevilla, and Córdoba. They were accompanied by twenty-seven adults, including doctors, nurses, assistants, and teachers.

The journey took fourteen days. When the expedition made a stopover in Havana, they received a visit from the poet Juan Ramón Jiménez, who had been living in exile in Cuba since November 1936. One of the little evacuees, Francisco González Aramburu, as representative for the entire group, presented the writer with an unforgettable and symbolic gift: a new edition of his book *Platero y Yo* (*Platero and Me*) that had been published in Spain by Espasa-Calpe after he had left the country. In an interview given to the newsletter *Ayuda* in July 1937, the poet remembered the moment this way:

> "Sir, will you remember me?" and he give me a little coloured book, an edition of *Platero y Yo* published in Madrid last July that I had not seen finished. On its cover in a steady hand he had written this dedication: "Juan Ramón. In the name of the Spanish children heading to Mexico, we greet you and dedicate this book, which has entertained us and taught us so much."

The *Mexique* docked at the port of Veracruz on July 7, 1937. The children were taken to Mexico City where the older ones were sent to different schools. The remaining 440 went by train to Morelia, in the state of Michoacán and became boarders at the Spain–Mexico Industrial School. Located in two former seminaries expropriated from the clergy, the school had been set up and was run by Mexico's Ministry of Public Education and offered a military-style education. Those running the school faced many difficulties, including insufficient resources, lack of training, and inadequate space. There was also the added complication of trying to work with children who, due to the trauma they brought with them, struggled to adapt.

Occasionally this had irreparable consequences, as in the case Francisco Nevot Satorres' death. According to Emeterio Payá Valera's memoirs, on August 19, 1937, Francisco went to the movies with his sister and two other friends. As they had left school without the principal's permission, however, they returned to find the doors locked. Francisco jumped the wall to open the door for his friends from the inside, but in doing so grabbed an electric cable which killed him instantly. He was the first of the children to die in Morelia. The second was Tárcila García Sorulla, who died on March 1, 1938 of pleurisy. The tombs of both children, located in Morelia's Municipal Civil Pantheon, are easily recognizable as they are crowned by enormous stone fists sculpted by their friends and inscribed with an epitaph that can leave no one unaffected:

> Here lie the remains of ... who died in the city of Morelia on ... a victim of the fascist barbarism that took them from their parents and their homeland, and who lived in Mexico under the custody of the Government of General LÁZARO CÁRDENAS

The Spain–Mexico Industrial School remained open until December 1943. The Assistance for Spanish Republican Children's Fund's

Administration Committee (CAFARE) then took charge of the children, many of them now adolescents. Different boarding homes were set up for them in Mexico City, but in September 1945 they were closed due to lack of funds, leaving the fate of the "children of Morelia" up in the air. Some were able to rejoin their parents in Spain or France; others were able to reunite with them in Mexico; some were adopted illegally or disappeared without a trace; and some, orphaned or unable to locate their parents, were welcomed into the collective of the exiled, remaining in Mexico for the rest of their lives.

47. FILING CABINETS, SUMMER 1937, SALAMANCA

Jesús Espinosa Romero

Among the holdings of the Historical Memory Documentation Center are some 3.5 million files that were created by the State Document Recovery Delegation (DERD) and the Army of Occupation Auditing Unit starting in the summer of 1937. The immense majority of them contain information about people affiliated with organizations loyal to the Republican side.

After the conquest of Republican territory by the rebel army, its occupation and policing units would confiscate information from the archives of local political organizations and unions. Following that, the army intelligence services would arrive. From the end of 1937 onward, these were centralized into the Military Police and Information Services (SIPM) under the command of Colonel José Ungría. The SIPM would separate out the information that was useful for the corresponding High Commands. The rest was sent to the Document Recovery Services, led by the Carlist Marcelino Ulibarri and located in Franco's general quarters which, as of April 1938, was shared with the all-powerful Ramón Serrano Suñer, the dictator's brother-in-law and right-hand man.

After an initial organization of the seized papers in situ, the documents were then sent to Salamanca for analysis. There they were divided among three centers based on the nature of their contents: documents relating to Masonry were sent to the Diocesan Seminary (currently the Pontifical University), while documentation from political organizations and unions went to the San Esteban Dominican convent and the Jesuit novitiate. The different centers were also staffed by distinct personnel. While the Masonic documentation was dealt with by the Civil Guard, political and union papers were processed by Falangists and Requetés—primarily members of the latter who had been relieved from active duty due to injury. Their tasks included reading the seized documents and recording names, as well as the call number for the archive where the reference could be found. Women unaffiliated with the DERD would then help to compile these lists into files. No one escaped: there was even a file on Franco referencing a letter he had written as the head of the Army of Morocco in March 1935 to Alejandro Lerroux's secretary expressing interest in a junior officer.

For its part, the Army of Occupation Auditing Unit, headquartered in Zaragoza, had an office within those of the DERD in Salamanca, as well as its own archive organized by provinces and towns. Every suspect resident in any location would have a file card created on them, and they would be required to appear before the rebels' military court. For the most part, the information gathered in these files came from prisoners of war, escaped soldiers, and right-wing civilian refugees, as well as from the document recovery process. As a result, officials from Franco's Army Audit knew whom to look for before entering any town, no matter how small. In an interview given to the Vice President of the Associated Press, James Miller, in November 1938, Franco was thus able to boast of knowing the names of more than 2 million "criminals." Some of these people would atone for their guilt by facing the death penalty, as nearly 130,000 people were executed during and after the war; another 294,000 civilians would spend time in the regime's horrid prisons. Additionally, 60,000 prisoners of the defeated army would become forced laborers due to their political affiliation. (Denying their military status in this way directly contravened the Geneva Convention that Spain had signed in 1929.) Another nearly 450,000 Spaniards went into exile.

The Salamanca filing cabinet was a key component of the dictatorship's repressive system. Military Courts, the Tribunal for Political Responsibilities and the Tribunal for Masonry and Communism would solicit background information on the indicted. So did the General Directorate of Security for their own investigations when deciding whether to issue someone a National Identification Document. The documentation center was also significant when it came time for the state and the National Movement to select its civil servants, as it could provide a report about the candidates. Further, during its two purification processes in 1941 and 1945, the National Movement made use of these files to collect information about its members and remove those with a suspicious past.

48. PHOTOGRAPHS OF WET-NURSES, AUGUST 1937, SALAMANCA

Sofía Rodríguez López

There is a series of photographs of a shelter in Almería for refugee mothers from Madrid that forms its own niche within the photojournalism of the Civil War. The photographs were taken by Kati Deutsch, the Hungarian anarchist photographer who would end up taking the name of her soon-to-be husband, the painter and sculptor José Horna. She met him after her political loyalties led her to Spain in 1937, just like Gerda Taro and Tina Modotti before her.

Like many other reporters who passed through the Madrid Defense Junta, Horna collaborated with the Republic, capturing images for use by the propaganda services. She also worked in Barcelona for *Tierra y Libertad* (*Land and Liberty*) and the magazine *Mujeres Libres* (*Free Women*). The magazine *Umbral* also featured Horna's work: its twelfth issue, from October 2, 1937, includes a double-page centerfold jointly published with one of its founders, Lucía Sánchez Saornil, called "Maternity under the banner of the Revolution."

Horna's pragmatic interest in studying daily life in the villages of the Republican rearguard took her to many places, such as, Monte Aragón, Banastas, Carrascal, and Vicién, then through the towns of Xàtiva and Silla in Alicante. Finally, in the middle of summer, she arrived in Vélez-Rubio, far from the front lines in the northern part of the province of Almería.

Salvador Martínez Laroca, a doctor at the Hospital for Evacuees in Valencia, had previously been mayor of Vélez-Rubio and director of its Maternity Center, whose mission was to provide refuge, education, and protection to 300 women and their children from Madrid. According to Saornil, the Maternity Center "is located in a former convent, but what love, what tenderness, what exquisite care it has been given in order to erase the austerity of the monastic residents and give it the appearance of a joyful inn, offering glimpses of a family home."

In contrast to the photographs by Horna that ended up being published, the series she took that day begins with an image of a mother breast-feeding her baby. The photograph extracts the woman from her context; although she is shown in the company of other refugees and their babies, Horna does not try to identify any specific people or places, emphasizing only the tenderness and intimacy of breast-feeding. The photograph ran in *Umbral* with the caption, "The instinct of life, stronger than of death and destruction, palpates in this scene."

The war is absent from Horna's images, whose subject is a safe and peaceful place, yet it is implicit in the symbolic absence of any men, with the exception of the doctor. The Vélez-Rubio Maternity Center was an oasis, a citadel of life and hope for pregnant women and families broken by the horror of the war that surrounded them. The white cribs in the garden looked like an offering. In the words of Saornil: "They are watched over by two nurses. Six babies! Six pieces of life that science and love, which burns in the eyes of our companion attend to day after day, warding off death."

The mothers who resided there could bring their children up to age 14, allowing them to continue their education and function as "family units with the independence that the conditions in the building permit." As the doctor expressed:

Look, the residents have been evacuated with all of their children. How could we have thought to leave those children without their mothers? Are we new men or not? Do we not have new ideas about things? By proceeding in this way, we kill two birds with one stone. We reduce the pregnant women's resistance to abandoning their homes, and we get the children out of Madrid, which is also beautiful.

Horna also photographed a mixed-gender classroom with the boys and girls sitting on their benches, as well as other spaces for recreation and communal living. These images are preserved only in the article's photomontage, taken in Vélez-Rubio and Alcázar de Cervantes (whose previous name, Alcázar de San Juan, with its religious connotation, had been changed) in the province of Ciudad Real, in September. Shortly after her marriage, Horna would escape to Paris where she published *Lo que va al cesto* (*What goes into the basket*) (1939) before leaving definitively for Mexico. She took the negatives, which she then left to Spain's Ministry of Culture in 1979. Together with Robert Capa's "Mexican suitcase" and that belonging to Agustí Centelles, they form part of a "postponed" visual history of the Civil War.

49. LETTER FROM A WAR GODMOTHER, OCTOBER 1937, TERQUE, ALMERÍA

Sofía Rodríguez López

During the Spanish Civil War, many young women offered their services as "war godmothers." In this role, women volunteered to maintain an epistolary relationship with soldiers at the front they did not know, thus serving as an emotional link and source of extra-familial support from the rearguard.

Diverse authors agree on the importance of wartime writing for popular memory, bearing in mind that this was the primary means of communication at the time. Men at the front awaited the mail call with a special kind of eagerness, as this was how the combatants would be informed about loved ones far away; conversely, mail sent by the combatants became proof of their continued survival.

The form these letters took depended on the availability of paper at the front. The paper was often cheap and of poor quality, and not always readily available, although sometimes the two armies would provide soldiers with campaign postcards. Given the high levels of illiteracy among the troops, their letters did not abound with literary flourishes, and some soldiers had to delegate this task to others more capable than them. The letters tended to describe daily hardships and traumas more than political ideas or conditions at the front, as this type of information was censored and often targeted by women spies. For their part, the godmothers would send tobacco, ski masks, food, reading material, embroidery, etc., in addition to letters, and in turn received photographs of their "godsons" or handmade gifts. To make it easier for them, postage for their correspondence with the soldiers was free. These writing relationships were organized through newspapers and magazines, like *La Ametralladora* (*The Machine Gun*), which published both requests for and offers from godmothers.

The front page of the September 5, 1936 issue of the illustrated magazine *Estampa* carried the headline, "The first three hundred war godmothers for the militiamen are workers from Madrid." Inside, there was a report featuring interviews with these women while they took turns writing to the brave members of the Mangada Column from inside a warehouse. This reveals the hasty way in which these services were organized, as well as the role that both sides wanted women in the rearguard to fill.

The connection between soldier and godmother was sometimes established via countrymen or acquaintances who informed the soldiers of young women who were available to correspond with them. From that point, a three-stage protocol was followed to establish the relationship: the request and statement of intent by the soldier; the godmother's reply; and then the continuity of the relationship, featuring a greater or lesser degree of intimacy.

The correspondence on the Republican side is usually considered to be more spontaneous than the institutional and patriotic correspondence on the rebel side—although both were motivated by their respective political organizations. Both sides also made use of formulaic greetings to begin their letters, such as "Health and the Republic" for the antifascists, and "¡Arriba España!" (Arise Spain) for the Francoists. In addition to being an unspoken rule at the time, the use of such phrases can also be attributed to the publication of templates for letters requesting a godmother and the appropriate responses that could be purchased for around 30 céntimos. One such example was the *Manual de cartas de amor y de amistad* [*Manual for letters of love and friendship*] published in Santiago de Compostela by Librería Gali in 1937.

Despite the "maternalism" that the relationship between "godmother" and "godson" symbolized, the letters were also meant to encourage romantic aspirations between the two young correspondents. These extremes can be seen in the letter from Antonio Castillo to María Luisa dated October 9,

1937 shown above. The author speaks as much about disinterested curiosity as about sincere love; about the girl's beauty, sympathy, kindness, and intelligence; as well as his need for solace to survive his loneliness and lack of friendships. Another striking feature of the correspondence between the "new youth that is forging itself in Spain today" is the tenor of the writing: frank, without prejudices, and cognizant of the credit that women deserved.

After the end of the Civil War and with the emergence of the Second World War, the Women's Section of FET-JONS was newly charged with establishing these relationships, this time with the volunteers of the Blue Division that fought alongside the Germans in Russia. The harshness of the Eastern Front led them to organize province-wide groups of war godmothers, who were active between August 1942 and March 1944.

50. ITALIAN OATH, NOVEMBER 1937, BARCELONA

Arnau González i Vilata

It may seem like an historical oddity, but for part of the Civil War, for a small handful of Italians, Salamanca became the new Barcelona. Mussolini's allies in Spain, a group of Italian diplomats, spies and journalists, living in Barcelona, were reunited in the Castilian city of Salamanca after being forced to leave. They made themselves a promise—indeed, swore an oath—that in the event of a Francoist victory they would return to Barcelona.

Barcelona was the great European capital in Spain, the center of the labor movement and of the eternal "Catalan problem," and the door to

France with its the border along the Pyrenees. It was a key geopolitical location in which thousands of Italians lived and owned business: clothing stores like Pantaleoni, hotels like the Falcón on the Ramblas, and the Pirelli factories. There was an annual Italian Dance and the Italian colony lived similarly to those in other great cities in Europe and America.

The Italian Consul General Carlo Bossi, the Vice Consul and military espionage service agent Sandro Majeroni, and the *Corriere della Sera* correspondent Alfredo Giorgi escaped aboard the *Mirabello* at 20:55 on November 18, 1936, following "123 days in a trench in Red territory." They had sworn their oath, with an almost religious fervor, a few days before. They renewed it one year later in Salamanca.

For weeks, Bossi and his acolytes had been asking their superiors in Rome not to close the Italian Consulate after granting Franco's government diplomatic recognition. This despite the fact that things had not been easy for Italians in Barcelona after the failure of the coup in Cataluña and the following revolutionary reaction. Some Italians had been murdered for being fascists or simply for being Catholic; thousands were evacuated aboard the *Regia Marina* while others, who had come fleeing Mussolini, had kept a watchful eye on the consulate. The official order from the Ministry of Foreign Affairs was to leave before the danger increased. This is not what Bossi et al. had wanted; they were compelled to leave Barcelona.

On November 4, 1937, Bossi and his group were in Salamanca after a journey that took them through Genoa and Rome. There was no sea on their route to this province on the border with Portugal. Nor was there any great port, with everything that brought in terms of modernity and vice. People didn't speak Catalan, although bishop Enrique Pla y Deniel did come from Barcelona and Catalan could sometimes be heard on the radio. The only water was the Tormes River, or further afield the Cantabrian Sea or Portugal's Atlantic seaboard. Despite all these differences, Salamanca became their "new Barcelona" while they waited to return to the one they had left.

This was the second year of the war and Salamanca already seemed like the center of the Axis. Miguel de Unamuno, the great philosopher and Rector of the University of Salamanca had died following his famous altercation with General Millán Astray. Francisco Franco, head of state and Supreme General (Generalísimo) of the army, had chosen the Episcopal Palace in Salamanca as his headquarters. Nazi ambassador Wilhelm Faupel and the Italian fascist Filippo Anfuso, commanders of the Condor Legion and the Corpo Truppe Volontarie (CTV) respectively, were also there.

During this time, Bossi, with his famous monocle, headed the Consulate General in exile and, along with his followers worked for Italian propaganda office Uffcio Stampa e Propaganda Italospagnolo, where, along with some Catalans, they wrote messages in Catalan and Spanish to be transmitted from Rome over Radio Verdad. They persisted throughout in their desire to fulfill their oath and return to Barcelona.

The finally did so after two more bloody years, during which time they saw Italian war planes brutally bombard their beloved city. This was the city in which they had established so many relationships within conservative Catalan circles. It was the city in which Giorgi had been married and in which he would live until his last breath, in 1991; to which Consul General Bossi would return until being sent to San Francisco, California in 1940; to which Majeroni—who in 1939 married a girl from Salamanca whom he had met in 1937—was able to return before dying in a plane accident.

The Barcelona they had known had been destroyed. It was no longer "red," nor atheist, nor Catalanist. It was perhaps not at all the same place where they could resume "the normal activities of Barcelona."

51. MILITIA WOMEN WEARING JUMPSUITS, NOVEMBER 1937, SALAMANCA

Miren Llona

From May to November 1937, the government of the Second Republic was represented in the Spanish Pavilion of the Paris International Exposition by a woman wearing a jumpsuit. The photomontages displayed inside were the work of Josep Renau, an avant-garde artist from Valencia and General Director of Fine Arts, who believed that art could be an important tool of social change. At the base of the photomontage of the militia woman is the caption: "Freeing herself from the veil of superstition and misery, THE WOMAN, eternal slave, has been reborn, capable of taking an active part in shaping the future." In this way, the Second Republic recognized the woman, dressed in her jumpsuit, as the embodiment of the future.

Although it may seem surprising to us today, during the 1930s, women wearing pants was still a transgression and cause for social alarm. Actresses like Marlene Dietrich and Katharine Hepburn would flauntingly wear pants, challenging gender roles and leaving a disturbing question floating in the air: Who wears the trousers?

By vindicating the militia-woman's jumpsuit at the International Exposition, the Second Republic showed the world just how strong its commitment to the emancipation of women was. Indeed, the new Republican Constitution had proclaimed the equality of the sexes and, thanks to the political battle waged by women like Clara Campoamor, in October 1931, it approved female suffrage, allowing women to vote for the first time in the 1933 elections. Further reforms were also introduced, including the legalization of divorce, maternity insurance, and co-education. During the Civil War, Minister of Health Federica Montseny attempted to legalize abortion, but her initiative ended up falling by the wayside and was only ever applied in Cataluña.

Perhaps for these reasons, from the very beginning of the Francoist rebellion in the summer of 1936 many women threw themselves into the defense of the Republic. This was when the figure of the militia woman took center stage. Dressed in her blue jumpsuit, she became a symbol not only of the revolution but also, especially, of women's liberation. Rosa Vega, a school principal in Madrid, recalls how "we women were no longer objects but rather humans, people with the same status as men," and Rosario Sánchez Mora, known as "la Dinamitera" (the Dynamiter) reflects: "It was such an unexpected thing that women would throw themselves at the front, so unexpected … that it took everyone by surprise. The Republic opened up the way, we pioneers paid a great price."

The mythical character of these women, gun over their shoulder—the embodiment of the modern woman and of the ideal of gender equality—was directly related to their representing the defiance of the gender order. Public anger was unleashed toward them, and not only on the rebel side. By the autumn of 1936, with the creation of the Popular Army and the extension of military discipline to the militias, being a man became a formal prerequisite for recruitment. Women were expelled from the front, and from then on their lives during the war played out in the rearguard, working on helpful yet basic tasks for supporting the front. At the same time, a campaign to discredit the militia women began. They were identified with prostitutes, a classic form of stigmatization against the woman transgressor, which this time helped to counteract the subversion of gender norms that the militia women, in their jumpsuits, had unleashed in the middle of the war.

52. BINDING, DECEMBER 1937, VILLAVERDE DEL DUCADO, GUADALAJARA

Alfredo González Ruibal

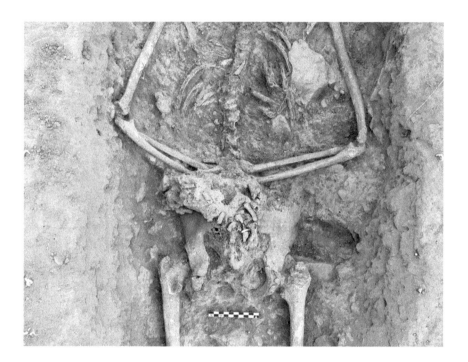

Some objects cannot be seen yet we know that they were there. They leave their mark, like the imprint of a fossil. Such is the case with the binding that was used to tie the hands of a man in Villaverde del Ducado, in the province of Guadalajara, who was executed during the Civil War. We do not know his identity; we only know his initials, A.M., which were inscribed inside of a silver ring still worn on his right ring finger. According to oral testimony, he was Basque, and he was executed after cheering for the Republic during a Christmas Eve midnight mass in front of soldiers from the rebel army. The date of the crime is unclear. From the available information we can infer that he was probably a Basque prisoner captured during the campaign on the Northern Front and sent to Guadalajara with a battalion of soldier-laborers. Military documentation reveals that Francoist Army soldiers, specifically 450 men from the IV Battalion of the America Regiment no. 23, which was part of the Army of the North, were present in Villaverde del Ducado between December 9 and December 25, 1937, which coincides with the date provided.

We don't know if it was really A.M. who cheered for the Republic during that midnight mass or if those in charge chose him for punishment at random in order to set an example. What we do know is that A.M. had his hands tied behind his back with a rope or piece of cloth, was taken in front of the town cemetery, was shot in the head and buried face down in a shallow grave from which his feet and head protruded. He remained there until he was exhumed on July 18, 2019.

When exhuming graves from the Civil War and postwar period, it is very common to find the victims with their hands tied behind their backs. This is usually a sign of extrajudicial killing, although it has also been observed in some cases where execution followed a trial, such as in the cemeteries of Paterna, in Valencia, and San Rafael, in Málaga. The most commonly used materials were wire, cable, rope, or cloth. The latter ones rarely appear in the exhumations because they are biodegradable, but their presence can be inferred when skeletons are found with their wrists together. The bindings provide important information about the context of the crime and its perpetrators. For example, in one of the graves in the cemetery in Castuera, in the province of Badajoz, the victim's hands were tied with wire identical to that found at the nearby concentration camp. Together with other evidence, this confirms that the victims were part of a *saca* ("walk" [see Chapter 23]) from that camp. In Puebla de Alcocer, also in Badajoz, the ways the victims were bound suggests the intervention of different perpetrators. In Villaverde, it demonstrates the improvised nature of the executions: the executioners must have used the first piece of rope or cloth they came across, perhaps a torn up shirt.

Hand-tying was employed not only to prevent victims from escaping; the aim was frequently to inflict additional harm. Tying the prisoners up tightly would lead them to develop injuries around their wrists, which could be especially painful if the journey to their destination was long. Uncertainly and terror were added to this physical torture—a form of psychological punishment. There are also documented cases of blatant cruelty. For example, among the victims of the *saca* from the concentration camp in Castuera were two victims found tied to each other, one person's neck to the other's wrist, before being shot with bullets to the head. In a grave in Aguilar de la Frontera, in Sevilla, one victim had their hands tied to their ankles.

The executed can appear on their own or tied together pairs. In the former case, the victim's hands are usually tied behind their back. In the latter, the wrist or elbow of one prisoner is tied to the elbow or wrist of another. Examples include the above-mentioned grave in Castuera and the trenches in Puebla de Alcocer, which were converted into an improvised burial site where forty-two people who were killed at the end of May 1939 appear tied up two-by-two, with one victim's wrist tied to the elbow of the other. This would have made escape even more difficult. In the mass grave at Costaján, in Burgos, where there are several documented cases of hand-tying, three skeletons were also found with their legs tied together by belts, suggesting a possible escape attempt, or perhaps simply resistance on the part of the victims.

53. SOLDIER'S GIFT BOX, 1937, SALAMANCA

Sofía Rodríguez López

Beginning in the early twentieth century, groups such as the Santa Rita Charity Workshops, the Sagrada Familia sewing workshops (*roperos*) and the Ladies Workers Protective Association used part of their endowments, raised from dues, donations, raffles, and lotteries, to buy Christmas gift boxes. They would also collect gifts for soldiers who had to spend the holidays away from home at the front. The gifts they collected would measure in the tons, and a gift box would usually contain a bottle of liquor, biscuits, preserved meat, cheese, *turrón* (nougat), condensed milk, and rolling paper. This tradition seems to have originated in Spain with the creation of the protectorate of Morocco in 1906 and the establishment of permanent military forces there.

The first gifts to these soldiers were sent by their families, but with the prolongation of the war, this practice was extended and became more or less official.

As early 1911, the city of Ferrol sent hygiene products—which they called the "sailor's bonus"—to local men stationed abroad. In 1921, a group of young women from Malpartida de Cáceres collected funds for the forty-five residents of that town who had been sent to Africa, which the local town hall sent to them in envelopes with 10 pesetas for each. Similarly, Valencia held a bullfight to benefit locals going to Melilla, while the cultural association (*Ateneo*) of Albacete organized a theater and circus event in December 1924 for the same cause. In 1925, under the dictatorship of Primo de Rivera, this work was officially entrusted to the Women of the Red Cross.

During the Civil War, young women on both the antifascist and the fascist side, such as those belonging to the Falangists Winter Auxiliary, organized fundraising events, soccer matches, and variety shows. In the Red Aid workshops and in the *roperos* of the Carlist Margaritas, the women would spend the winter making sweaters, capes, and ski masks, as well as collecting toys for the Twelfth Night (*Reyes*) holiday, which in the Republican rearguard was replaced by the Day of the Child (*Día del Niño*).

The greatest contributors to these causes were the provincial institutions, since they could record their donations as business expenses. However, public sentiment led people from each judicial district to contribute anonymously as well. Mayors would publish proclamations encouraging even children to participate, and in Salamanca, the *El Adelanto* newspaper encouraged them to compete to see who could raise the most money. The province of Salamanca's Civil Government issued a bulletin officially opening up donations on December 11, 1936, although in many towns the mass for collecting gifts coincided with Santa Lucía day, two days later. The aim was to extend the ties between the front and the rearguard, as well as to get people involved in the mission of the war. As such, the cover of the gift boxes on the rebel side usually featured a Spanish flag along with the message: "The rearguard is with you. Hail Franco. Arise Spain! [*¡Arriba España!*]"

In Vizcaya, after the fall of the Iron Belt, the new Francoist authorities encouraged people to fulfill this moral and patriotic duty by contributing to the Christmas campaign of 1937/8. Of particular note was a guitar recital in Bilbao held in the Trueba theater in front of an audience of 900. Similarly, they organized the so-called "single course meal days": once or twice a week restaurants would serve a reduced menu and donate the value of the unprepared meals to the combatants. The Bilbao press once reported on a surprising collection of 962,046.27 pesetas, in which everyone from individuals to companies, businesses, workers, and farmers had collaborated.

In 1938 the *Diario de Cádiz* newspaper reported on its successful collection campaign for gift boxes, claiming that they had collected 800 tons of food from across the entire nation, worth more than 9 million pesetas.

In addition to the gift boxes, collection drives were also organized for the most in-demand products, such as the "Wounded Soldier Tobacco Charity Collection" and the "Soldier's Liquor Day." During the Christmas campaign of 1937, the anise company La Castellana proposed this remedy for fighting off the cold: "Listen now, sirs; there are thousands of soldiers / who by the light of the stars / spend freezing nights / in Somosierra and Madrid. / Send them some bottles!"

On October 25, 1938, the Ministry the Interior, in coordination with National Benefits and Social Works Service and Rosa Urraca Pastor's Fronts and Hospitals Delegation, sent out the final order regarding soldiers' gift boxes. Donations were requested by December 10 of that year in order to provide the necessities for the final winter of the Spanish Civil War.

54. SCHOOL NOTEBOOK (WITH THE MATHEMATICS OF BOMBS), JANUARY 1938, BARCELONA

Plàcid García-Planas

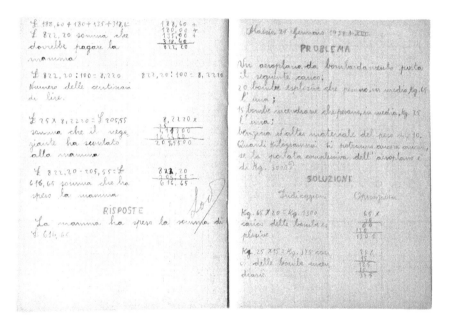

On January 21, 1938, the mathematics teacher at the Morteo Ollandini school in Alassio, in northeastern Italy, posed a problem to his students. It was a terrible calculation; yet he presented it as if it were no big deal, following another problem concerning meters of linen and cotton in a textile business.

The problem went as follows: "A bomber has the following cargo: 20 explosive bombs that weigh an average of 65 kilograms each; 15 incendiary bombs that weigh an average of 25 kilograms each; gasoline and other material that weigh a combined 25 kilograms. If its total capacity is 3,000 kilograms, how much capacity does this airplane still have available?"

There in that classroom, in the sixteenth year of the Fascist era, my father, Josep Maria García-Planas, was meticulously taking notes in his school notebook. After writing down that day's date, he begins his multiplication and addition calculations in order to arrive at the solution to the problem.

My grandparents—Catalans, uncomfortable with both warring sides in Spain—opted to spend the Civil War in Alassio, close to the French border. They did not make this choice for political reasons—they came from a Republican tradition and never raised their arms in a fascist salute—but rather because they had personal contacts in Liguria who helped them survive. It wasn't easy, but they ended up finding a school for their children, albeit one with all of the ideological and imperial baggage of the time and place: after religion, the most important subject matter was military culture (*cultura militare*).

How many more bombs could the airplane take? Was this Italian teacher's question an accident?

In January 1938, the Royal Italian Air Force bombed Barcelona with a violence and intensity previously unknown. In just the first twenty days of that month—my father's teacher posed that math problem on January 21—the number of dead already surpassed that of all the aerial bombings from the previous year.

The first bombing was carried out on New Year's Day by a plane that took off directly from Italy. In response to Italian pilots' uncertainty that their Savoia-Marchetti SM-79s could carry out nighttime attacks, Musolini's own Under-Secretary of Aviation, Giuseppe Valle, took off in a Savoia from Italian territory directly for Barcelona to drop bombs onto its port. Italian planes returned to bomb the city on January 6th, 7th, 8th, 11th, 14th, 15th … Republican airplanes took revenge by bombing Salamanca, Sevilla, and Valladolid, though much less intensely.

On January 19, two days before the math class, Italian airplanes carried out their harshest attack on Barcelona yet, with seventeen Savoia-Marchetti SM-79s machine-gunning the center of the city at noon, killing more than 170 people. The time and location of that bombing made it, according to historians Joan Villarroya i Font and Josep Maria Solé i Sabaté, "without a doubt the first terrorist aerial bombing to take place in Barcelona." A delegation of British Labour Members of Parliament had been in the Catalan capital that day, and the bombing received a lot of attention in the international press. Newspapers like *L'Humanité*, *The Times*, and *The Daily Express* denounced the killings while France tried, without success, to get the Vatican to pressure Franco to put an end to this aerial fury.

What compelled the math teacher, only two days later, to decide on bombs for teaching children how to count?

Since Italian school books were highly critical of the Spanish occupation of Italy that had taken place centuries before, my father's history teacher told him that he could skip that chapter. Thanks to the that teacher's thoughtfulness, the Spanish student was spared having to "learn," amongst other "nice" things, "that the bad Spanish government [in Italy] promoted a life of leisure and frivolity, provoking anarchy" and that "the Spaniards ruined our people morally and intellectually by introducing them to flattery, frivolity and hypocrisy." What did Spanish fascists think when they read such things coming from the movement that had inspired them?

And what about the math teacher? Did he have the aerial attack on Barcelona and other Spanish cities in mind when, in that terrible month of January, he posed that question to his students, among whom was my father, who came from the very place being bombed?

We will never know. The only thing we can know for certain is the solution to the problem: 325 kilograms. This is how much additional capacity the airplane had, sufficient for another explosive bomb weighing 250 kilograms, like the one that, nine days after the math class, was dropped by Italian aircraft onto Barcelona's Sant Felip Neri square, killing forty-two people.

If, of the forty-two people killed by that bomb, twelve were adults, how many children did it kill?

55. WHITE AID CREDENTIALS, APRIL 1938, ALHAMA DE ALMERÍA

Sofía Rodríguez López

The Central Carlist War Junta of Navarra signed its new constitution on August 28, 1936, in Burgos. The normal activities and structures of this ultra-conservative organization were to be suspended in those places where the National Movement had triumphed: some offices and functions, such as the Youth Organization, the Requeté militia and Propaganda, were absorbed into the War Commissions and Juntas, except for "the Margaritas [young women's auxiliary], Press and White Aid" which were fundamental to efforts in the rearguard.

As part of the Carlist party, the White Aid organization existed before the Civil War, although its work in the Republican zone was heightened beginning in 1936. According to the "Glorious Deeds of the Requeté in Madrid," the postwar accounting of its activities, White Aid became a fifth column, coordinated and controlled by clandestine members of the Falange with whom it shared an "absolute understanding" and "mutual identification." However, it never reached the same size as the Falangists' much more famous Six Thousand Women of the María Paz Blue Auxiliary in the capital.

Madrid had four White Aid regiments, which were in turn sub-divided into different companies, sections, and groups. The Special Services Regiment consisted of 200 "Margaritas" who were divided into groups of fifty and performed four main tasks: collecting and distributing money, clothing, and food, as well as making equipment, armbands and chains in their celebrated *roperos* (clothing workshops). White Aid was connected to other auxiliary organizations that helped persecuted people on the right. They had agents infiltrate the food supply organization and the Red Cross and would provide coupons and stamps like the one in the image above. Those who were in need, in hiding, had escaped, were imprisoned, sick or taking refuge in the embassies would be set up with lodging with friendly families and provided with money for their basic needs.

One of the most important networks was created in Madrid by a thirty-year-old teacher named Pascual Cebollada García. According to a Republican court, it functioned "under the mask of a philanthropic and altruistic Society" thus helping people on the right avoid "the worry of having to find a job to sustain themselves." It was discovered in April 1938; among the twenty-three people tried for espionage and high treason, seven were women.

Some female members of White Aid in Madrid could be identified by their rings made out of two silver *reales* coins. By this time, the Republican government had ceased minting the peseta out of precious metals and was making them out of brass. From 1937 on these were known as *rubias* (blondes). However, they stopped wearing the rings after June 1938 when three members of the underground who had been wearing them were tried for disaffection.

Among the female members of the Falangist Blue Auxiliary who received medals in 1940, at least two had previously belonged to White Aid. The group extended across all of Spain. In May 1937 the Madrid daily *ABC* announced the dissolution of a White Aid cell in Santander. In other regions, like Cataluña, the incipient White Aid—protected and legitimized by the Nationalists through domestic masses and collections—tried to avoid association with the more politicized church. In Alicante, before his detention in February 1939 for being a member of the fifth column, lieutenant colonel Luis Romero Sanz organized the militias in Orihuela under the cover of a school for border guards to carry out collections for White Aid. The driving force of the Hataca Network, which connected Cartagena to Lanjarón in Granada, was a woman named Carmen Góngora

López. Before Francoist intelligence took control of her network in 1938, Carmen had knit together a web of collaborators out of people linked to the cathedral and the Catholic Seamstresses Union.

Recognition for the women of White Aid's clandestine efforts came after the war, in publications like Y. *Magazine of the National-Syndicalist Woman*:

> One day it will be known exactly what White Aid did in the rearguard. And how it provided prisoners with food and encouragement. In such a way that, when the troops arrived, they found an extensive and secret Falangist organization, which naturally did not have the form or structure of the official one, but which represented an attempt, a desire, and above all, an unheard-of level of daring.

56. LETTERS FOR THE THIRD CATALUÑA, 1938, BARCELONA

Arnau González i Vilata

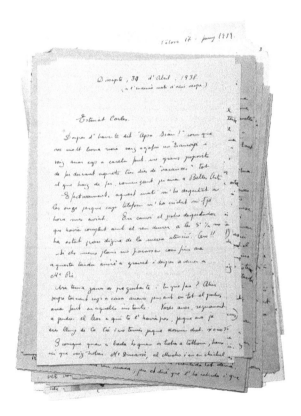

In 1914, after the First World War had broken out, Stefan Zweig reflected on humanity's unsettled sleep: "In today's world there are few who can sleep; the nights are long, but the days are even longer. In all countries, across all of Europe, in every city, in every street, in each house, in each room, the calm breath of sleep becomes shorter and more feverish." Years later, Concepció Ció Rubiés (1919–2020), a daughter of the First World War distressed over the imminent beginnings of another, would have responded: "While you sleep I will come and place my hand on your forehead, and I will say nice things so that your dreams may be simple, clear, firm, sweet, and above all, peaceful."

In interwar Europe, such sound sleep was disturbed by fear, euphoria, and, especially, by complexity. Although this young woman's May 1938 letter to her future husband, Carles Eugeni Mascareñas, promised clarity, real life was a far cry from her wish. The *leitmotif* of that year in Ció's life consisted of confronting adulthood, recognizing her position as a woman in the middle of a disaster and facing a new world that Mascareñas starkly presented to her.

With her precocious intelligence, the eighteen-year-old Ció was able to define in a few words what would come to be known as the "third Spain"— those who were neither with the Republic nor with Franco. Mascareñas was one of these. In a May 1 letter that Ció sent to him—in Catalan, like all of her correspondence—she wrote: "What do all of these important people think about the things going in our house, the third solution to our problems, pardon, to Spain's problems, which cause our own? Can it work?" It was all a learning process—as a woman, as an adult, and as a citizen of a world that could not sleep. A complex and turbulent world in which Mascareñas and others like him—his friend Ramon Sugranyes, the cleric Carles Cardó (both Catholic Catalantists like Mascareñas), the Aragonese jurist Alfredo Mendizába—could not sleep. Likewise, for renowned European Catholics like Luigi Sturzo, the priest who had led Italy's Popular Party after the First World War, and French philosopher Jacques Maritain. Was there an option between Franco and Stalin? Non-Francoist Catholics? What would happen to Cataluña?

Like thousands of others who could not and would not support the revolution, Mascareñas left Cataluña for exile in the summer of 1936. They ran from it; from the violence that, in the face of the Catalan government's weakness, was directed against the church, the bourgeoisie, and the conservatives of Francesc Cambó's Catalan League. Once in France, where he met Ció in January 1938, Mascareñas was plagued by doubt. Siding with the Francoists—Cambó's side—was not an option for a Catalan Nationalist and Christian democrat like himself.

Everything was complicated, a headache, and the future mother of his children rebelled against this. In a letter dated May 25 she wrote: "I hate people with too many problems (because I hate complicated, tortured, and torturing problems). Just like I hate all things that are not simple and clear. I like clear problems," adding, "I think that if I were to marry you and go around the world with you, I would also sink into the unhealthy mud of the too-complex psychological problems of the world and of all the people who enter them." Who could sleep with such a weight on their shoulders?

From August 1936 to 1940, Mascareñas wandered throughout Europe in search of a livelihood. Ció, whose family had sent her to l'École Normale in Toulouse in 1937, would end up suffering the same fate. A good night's sleep continued to elude her.

Ció's personality was forged over those years and is revealed in dozens of letters and in the photo from her wedding to Mascareñas, conducted by the Basque priest Alberto Onaindía, in Paris in 1939. Their relationship was built on the foundation of accepting the great mess that Europe had become. Having accepted this, sleep was everything: "Carles!! Look, I pass my hand through your hair and you sleep. I put it on your forehead, bright red from the intense working of your mind. Each night I imagine that a fairy has granted me its power and I use it to keep watch over your sleep."

But life was meant to be lived, even with all of the risk, and with no guarantee of being able to act with any certainty. Ció put it bluntly: "We live, imagine, love, feel intensely in every moment! How we would have profited from our short life like that ... if I could tell you nothing, I would send you an envelope and inside of it would be my signature. Ció!"

57. *DEFENDERS OF THE FAITH* BY RUSSELL PALMER, 1938

Vicente J. Benet

The movie *Defenders of the Faith* by the American Russell Palmer was rediscovered thanks to its April 2006 broadcast on Televisión Española (Spanish Television). There is still a great deal left to learn about this singular film, which is exceptional in many respects. Not only is it a war documentary filmed in color, for which there seem to be no precedents, but it also involved an unusually high degree of collaboration with Francoist military commanders, who allowed Palmer, amongst other things, to film an aerial attack mission from on board one of the planes. He was also allowed to be present for some aspects of combat, like the taking of a hill, which he filmed during its different phases—the artillery barrage, the infantry advance, recovering the wounded—thereby offering a truthful view of the experience of war. In contrast to most propaganda films of the era, a descriptive focus on the battles was more important than manipulation in the editing process or the artificial construction of events. The use of images apart from those filmed by Palmer's crew itself was practically non-existent.

As such, the film's main objective consists in extolling the Francoist cause through a propagandistic strategy far removed from the dominant forms of the time, in an attempt to create something that would be effective for an American audience.

When the Civil War broke out, numerous members of the Spanish diplomatic corps defected to and collaborated with Franco's side. Some of them organized in New York, working intensively on pro-Franco propaganda. Russell Palmer became an important piece of this process as a collaborator with and figurehead of the Peninsular News Service, a branch of Franco's Press and Propaganda in the United States. Its primary tasks included organizing pro-Francoist activities at Spain House and publishing the magazines *Spain* and *Cara Al Sol* (*Face to the Sun,* named after the Falangist anthem). Palmer tried to counteract the pro-Republic campaigns taking place in North America led by influential intellectuals, writers, and Hollywood stars. In a report preserved at the Ministry of Foreign Affairs archive, Palmer offered insights on how to create effective propaganda for the US public. His suggestion was to elide the complexity of the politics of the conflict and emphasize instead a more sentimental, quotidian, simple, and religious vision of the situation in Spain. We can call this strategy, which attempts to reconstruct a sense of normalcy and divert attention from what was happening on the battlefields, "positive propaganda."

Keeping with this approach, Palmer's documentary begins with images from the rearguard, showing the beaches and streets of San Sebastián in which, the narrator tells us, the people are well-dressed and well-fed, and the war is present only in a number of soldiers walking around. He also shows us images of an orphanage in Málaga, and the social housing set up in Seville under General Queipo de Llano. There are also scenes of a bullfight which serve as a transition to the scenes of combat. Although the film also takes us to the ruins of University City in Madrid and the scars of battle in different places, it frequently returns to depictions of everyday life: the farmers of Aragón working the land, women engaged in their domestic labor, soldiers in moments of rest, the terraces of the cafés in Burgos full of people, dances in the recently captured city of Castellón, and even members of the cavalry bathing on the beach with their horses.

As previously mentioned, the film's images of the war are novel and infrequent. However, it does not fail to also include the inevitable motifs of ruins and cadavers, which it blames on the cruelty of the enemy. The film also emphasizes the importance of new military tactics and the use of armored vehicles. Yet together with all of this are more positive images, like that of a group of women showing up to donate blood, and of wounded Moroccan soldiers being treated in their special hospitals. The film highlights Muslim troops, members of the Legion and the air force, while the intervention by the Germans and Italians is treated in a very cursory way. Of all the valuable documentation the film provides, its tours of the battlefields in Teruel and Belchite, as well as images of the occupation of Castellón de la Plana, are of particular note.

Some of the film's final images, which show American members of the International Brigades who were captured by the Francoists, are especially interesting. The camera pans over their faces, lingering on those with African American or Asian traits. This explicitly racist element gives us a profile of the type of viewer for whom the film was intended.

58. STALE BREAD (AND THE MARKETING OF HUNGER), JULY 1938, BARCELONA

Plàcid García-Planas

"Each contestant may send as many short phrases as they wish. There is no word limit, although brevity is encouraged."

In the spring of 1938, the White Hen (*Gallina Blanca*) company organized the most amazing contest in the recent history of Spain. The contest was open to all. The goal was to come up with brief messages. But expressing what? Pain? Hope? No. The brief phrases they were asking for were to advertise their famous bouillon cubes. "By way of example," the company wrote, "we offer this model phrase: *An old hen makes a good stock, but a WHITE HEN makes an even better one.*"

Who better than the hungry to convince people of how delicious a meal is?

The phrases "should be sent in a sealed envelope, omitting the name of the contestant, addressed to Francisco Figueras Subietas, 259 Aragón Street, mezzanine #1, Notary of the Illustrious College of Cataluña. On the envelope please write: Letter for the WHITE HEN and SOP Contest. The author's name and address should be written on another envelope contained inside the first."

The contest lasted from May 16 to June 16. The phrases could be written in Spanish or Catalan. "It is not necessary to include a ticket from one of our cubes with the letter since this contest is open to the entire public and being a consumer of White Hen and SOP is not required."

The jury consisted of three representatives from the company, the writer Josep Maria Folch i Torres, the tenor Emili Vendrell, the actors Enric Borràs and Pius Daví, and the actor, dramaturgist, and theater impresario Joaquim Montero.

There were thirty-seven prizes: 1,000 pesetas for first place, 500 pesetas for second place, 250 pesetas for third place, 100 pesetas for fourth place, and another thirty-three prizes of 50 pesetas each. According to the entry form: "The company reserves the exclusive publication rights over the winning phrases, without obligation to publish them. The top five winners will be the subject of engravings by our in-house artists, which we also reserve the right to publish as our motto."

When there is a war going on and one is hungry, in such a situation, one might hold onto a piece of bread—not to eat it, but to remember, when it is all over, what it feels like to have an empty stomach. This is what one resident of Gavà, near Barcelona, did. During the 1970s he gave his piece of wartime bread to the writer and politician Josep Soler Vidal. Today it can be found preserved in the government of Cataluña's (*Generalitat*) Democratic Memorial historical memory agency and is pictured in the image above.

Or, encouraged by the White Hen company, one could close one's eyes and come up with a gastronomic slogan, write it down and put it in an envelope in the hopes of winning a cash prize to help fill one's stomach. This is what thousands upon thousands of people choose to do in that springtime of hunger. The contest shattered all predictions and White Hen received 87,475 entries. This bombardment of slogans and "their high degree of ingenuity makes it impossible to choose four for our four top prizes." White Hen ended up giving out more prizes—fifty-four instead of thirty-seven—raising the total cash amount—from 3,500 to 3,775 pesetas—and redistributing the value of the prizes—100 pesetas for the first ten winners, 75 pesetas for the second group of thirty-three, and 50 pesetas for another group of twenty-one. The first person on the list of winners was named Leandre Tarrida who lived at 72 Avenida Mistral, fourth floor #2, in Barcelona.

On July 31, White Hen assured the winners that "Our in-house artists are already drawing and painting the fifty-four posters that will be displayed in a great exhibition whose date will be disclosed more conveniently later on." The Battle of the Ebro was raging.

There never were any posters displaying the winning phrases, nor was there any great exhibition. Six months after the prizes were awarded, the Francoist Army entered Barcelona. Hunger continued. So did the advertisements for White Hen bouillon cubes. Two weeks after the fall of Barcelona, the company wrote the following announcement:

> Hail Franco!!! Arise Spain!! Among the arsenal of foodstuffs that the red Government had stored in different warehouses throughout Barcelona and that have been raided by hungry members of the public were a number of gold-coloured, cylindrical tin cans, 21 centimeters in diameter and 18.5 centimeters tall, weighing approximately 20 kilograms, containing raw material in paste form. These tins were taken by the red "government" from the factory that produces the famous White Hen and SOP bouillon cubes. That raw material is unsafe for domestic consumption and impossible for use by individuals. We beg anyone who has been able to save some of these tins from the shameful neglect that they were subjected to by the looters to please take them to the factory that produces the well-known White Hen and SOP bouillon cubes, where you will be handsomely rewarded.

We don't know if the thousands upon thousands of contest entries still exist. If they do appear one day, those 87,475 food marketing slogans written by hungry citizens will likely be the most spectacular poetic, promotional, sociological, and linguistic monument to hunger in the history of Europe.

59. PHOTOGRAPHS OF THE BEACH, JULY 1938, BARCELONA

Plàcid García-Planas

"Deauville? Palm Beach? Miami? Nothing like that. Simply Barcelona. And here you have what is for some the unexpected physiognomy of the Catalan capital. Of the city that has suffered more than a hundred bombing raids and has seen thousands of its citizens fall victim to the shrapnel." This appeared on the July 28, 1938 front page of *La Vanguardia* newspaper, three days after the beginning of the Battle of the Ebro, the longest and bloodiest battle of the Civil War.

La Vanguardia's front page from that day was—is; bodies pass, the paper remains—pure sensuousness.

Was this front page to some extent propagandizing normality under Juan Negrín's government, which controlled *La Vanguardia* at that time? Without a doubt. Everything had as its purpose raising the morale of citizens, even sunbathing and swimming next to the remains of the l'Escola de Mar, recently destroyed by Italian airplanes. Were these photographs of happy young women in bathing suits taken before the war? Probably. The paper had previously used idyllic images of rural areas taken during peacetime to suggest that there was not too much of a war going on.

Nevertheless, this propaganda tapped into a reality: during the summers of the war, in places along the coast, quite a few people would go to the beach. To swim, to escape, to tan, for everything all at once. In Barcelona there was a bus service between the university square and the beaches at Castelldefels. The municipal government of Badalona had to prohibit bathers from going into the trenches that were dug into the sand. The children's magazine *En Patufet* poked fun at the aerial bombings, and the joke went all the way to the beach: "They say that the sirens could be head today." "From where?" one bather in a vignette asks another. "From these beaches," replied the other. "Oh, from the beaches, that's not surprising. You can hear the Sirens from here, and even Neptune!"

As in all wars, people feared that the bombs would kill them. But the months and years passed and the fear of death persisted even though you were unscathed, a simple imposed agony. What does the fact that the great dance halls and fifty movie theaters were open in Barcelona on March 19, 1938 tell us? That was the day after a brutal three-day bombing campaign by Italian fascists that killed between 880 and 1,300 people in the city. *Java Seas, Satan's Five Warnings, Paradise in the Jungle, Seductive Arms, Montecarlo Nights, The King of Broadway, Dracula's Daughter, Kill Yourself with Music* ... All movies to enjoy before or after a bombing. Or during.

People had to keep living, with the intensity that each was able to muster. Going to the pergolas, losing oneself staring at a fish tank, relaxing in a monumental fountain, watching a puppet theater, drinking champagne, and eating lobster. *La Vanguardia* informs us that none of this was metaphorical.

"Barcelona, brutally bombed. Yesterday morning seven enemy trimotors dropped a great number of explosive and incendiary bombs. The fascist shrapnel produced many victims and caused enormous destruction," the Catalan paper reported on its May 30, 1937 front page. On the back page of the same issue, the department store Jorba del Portal de l'Àngel ran a nicely illustrated advertisement for the champagne and lobster that they served on their fantastic terrace. "The most central and refreshing place in Barcelona, so high up that one can admire the view of the capital's marvelous topography—the same one that the Italian pilots must see when they drop their bombs!—with attractions like pergolas, gardens, a monumental fountain, an aquarium, a panoramic view and a puppet theater."

Pleasure and pain. Those two pages from *La Vanguardia* summarize the history of the world.

"I recall that the summer of the Battle of the Ebro was very hot in Barcelona," an elderly woman sitting next to me on a train told me. "The people said it was because of the heat from the bombs dropped during the battle." Did the people tanning themselves on the beach in Barcelona during those days think of that heat? What were they thinking about?

"Much has been said about the morale in the Republican rearguard" *La Vanguardia* wrote on that front page. "But perhaps nothing really gives voice to it like this smiling picture. In the luminous frame of the beach, the laughter drowns out the echo from the galloping of the four horsemen of the apocalypse. Indifference? No, serenity. Serenity and faith in a triumph and in a peaceful tomorrow."

Six months after this serenity at Camp de la Bota, in the same line of sand, the mass shootings began.

60. SUBMARINE POSTAGE STAMP, AUGUST 1938, BARCELONA

Antonio Cazorla-Sánchez

The tragedy of the first days of the Civil War, when soldiers and police had to hastily take sides in the conflict, was particularly bloody within the Spanish Armada. Its officers were mostly conservative, whereas there was a strong Republican contingent among the sub-officers and sailors. When the former rebelled, the latter responded, first by arresting them, and then, under varying circumstances, executing them. Of the nearly 350 officers executed by the Republicans, almost 300 were killed without a trial. The most extreme cases were those on the prison boats *España* and *Sil*, which had been anchored in Cartagena. After setting sail, 159 people aboard the former and fifty-two people aboard the latter were thrown into the sea, many of them apparently while still alive. For their part, the rebels killed some 170 sailors, mostly from the base in El Ferrol. To these we must also add those executed after the war. In April 1939, some Republicans were thrown into the sea when the boats and crews interned in Bizerta, Tunisia passed by the location of the sunken ship *Baleares* on their return trip to Spain.

As a consequence of detaining and executing their officers, the Republican fleet had a marked operational inferiority compared to the rebels, despite an initial clear numerical superiority. This was as much due to the rebels' aerial hegemony as to the overt help they were receiving from the powerful Italian fleet, in particular its submarines, as well as the generally more subtle assistance they received from the Germans. (I say generally because in May 1937 the Germans openly and illegally bombed the city of Almería.) The lack of capacity on the Republican side significantly affected places like Menorca which, in July 1936, was the only one of the Balearic Islands to remain loyal. The Francoists tried to invade it several times, and it was bombed repeatedly by their fleet and, above all, by rebel and Italian aircraft based in Mallorca. Menorca's isolation was even greater after the fall of Barcelona in January 1939. In February 1939, a pro-Francoist fifth column uprising was organized in Menorca. Things were at a standstill but mediation by the British helped negotiate a surrender, and on February 10, 1939, the island went to the victorious Francoists.

The C-4 submarine is an important symbol of Menorca and of Republican naval history. Received in 1929, it was among the most recent additions to Spain's Navy. In July 1936, its crew detained their officers, who were disembarked in Málaga, where they were later shot. The C-4 played a significant but ultimately ineffective role in the Straights of Gibraltar and the Cantabrian Sea. The Francoists almost captured the submarine in Bordeaux in 1937. It later returned to the Mediterranean, under the command of a Soviet officer, G.I. Kuzmin, who went by the fake Spanish name Víctor Nicolás.

Under Kuzmin's command the C-4 carried out a mission that was to be immortalized on various postage stamps. On August 12, 1938, it left Barcelona for Mahón, with the American journalist Wernell Kerr from the *Saturday Evening Post* aboard. It was also carrying a sack of mail, containing some 1,000 fictional letters and forty real ones, for the demoralized garrison at Mahón. Tomás Orós Gimeno—a postal official, Mason, and UGT militant—was also aboard. The trip was meant to help lift morale, but it also had a second purpose: printing a new series of stamps that, due to their rarity, would be well-sought out by international collectors and bring some much needed foreign currency into the Republican coffers. The operation raised no less than the equivalent of 20 million pesetas in pounds and francs. This was the first mail delivery by submarine in history, although in reality the ship actually sailed on the surface. However, rebel aircraft from the base in Mallorca forced the C-4 to submerge on its return trip. Thanks to reporting by the American correspondent, the trip also helped produce an important round of propaganda that, to some degree, helped compensate for the lack of military success of the Republican submarines.

Many of the protagonists of this story faced a tragic ending. Tomás Orós was exiled from Spain. When he returned in 1941, he was unable to recover his job and was ridiculed by the authorities. Kuzmin died in 1942 when his submarine collided with a German mine in the Black Sea. For its part, the C-4 submarine was returned to duty after being recovered by the Francoists in March 1939. On June 27, 1946, when it was maneuvering near Sóller, in Mallorca, it came to the surface in front of the destroyer *Lepanto*. The collision nearly broke the submarine in half. It sank immediately and all its forty-four crew members perished. During the Second World War, its captain, Francisco Reina Carvajal, had participated in a number of missions around the Baltic as a member of the German navy (*Kriegsmarine*).

In 1988, to commemorate the fiftieth anniversary of the C-4's mail mission, the Navy's S-74 *Tramontana* submarine undertook the same voyage.

61. ITALIAN MODEL M1915/16 HELMET, AUTUMN 1938, ABÁNADES, GUADALAJARA

Alfredo González Ruibal

This helmet appeared during the excavation of a crenellated parapet in Abánades, Guadalajara. The fortification was used by the rebels between the fall of 1938 and the end of the war. There was also a second helmet of the same model, the Italian M1915/16s, which was based on the French Adrián M1915 but is smaller in size. The Adrián was the first modern steel helmet and its later, more solid 1926 version remained in use throughout the Second World War. In contrast, the Italian version was replaced during the 1930s by the M1933. It was three times stronger than the Adrián and the Italian army continued to use it for several decades. The M1915 helmet was the Italian response to the massive and industrialized violence brought about during the First World War.

Soldiers in the trenches were exposed to continuous and unexpected storms of steel, which were the single greatest cause of casualties during the conflict. A significant percentage of these were due to head injuries. When the war began, no nation had helmets that were effective against shrapnel. Most soldiers were outfitted with caps, while the German Pickelhaube, made of hardened leather, offered some limited protection. Over the course of 1915, Germans, Italians, French, and British soldiers were provided steel helmets that were effective against shrapnel, even if they could not stop bullets. For Italians on the Alpine Front, such protection was necessary, not only against fragments from artillery projectiles but also against the shards of rock thrown up by explosions, which killed as many people as did the grenades.

Even though they represented an improvement over the caps that preceded them, the Italian M1915's thin veer, like that of its French counterpart, offered only meager protection. As a result, both were modified or replaced during the conflict. However, the Volunteer Soldiers Corps (CTV) that Mussolini sent to fight in Spain continued to use these helmets in addition to the more modern M1933. We know that the Adrián was worn by many members of the CTV who fought in the Battle of Guadalajara, the failed bid to capture Madrid, in March 1937. Following that battle, the Republicans made off with great deal of Italian equipment, from uniforms to tanks and pieces of artillery. One testimony to the abundant war materiel that remained in the area of La Alcarria, outside of Madrid, is a pigeon house in the town of Ledanca whose owner recycled dozens of helmets as nests for the birds. Moreover, archaeological excavations undertaken in positions held by the rebel army in Guadalajara have revealed different types of Italian-made objects, like flares, driving glasses, and bullets, that came into the hands of Francoist troops either as supplies or from bartering with the Italian combatants.

Spain got up to date in terms of individual protective gear that could better resist shrapnel with the fabrication of the M1926 helmet, made by the weapons company in Trubia, Oviedo. During the first third of the twentieth century, the Spanish army's experience of war was limited primarily to the war in Morocco, an asymmetrical conflict in which the enemy had very limited artillery and no air force. The so-called Trubia helmet was superior to the French and Italian Adriáns because it offered greater protection and was made with a thicker veneer. However, it wasn't until the Republican era that the troops were outfitted with these helmets to any significant degree. When the war broke out, only a small percentage of solders on either side had this or some other form of protective headgear. The factory in Trubia also became isolated on the Northern Front, forcing the Republic to urgently import thousands of French Adriáns and Czech M1930s. Even then it was unable to meet the demand, and soldiers could be observed wearing simple caps or berets late into the war. Further, some rebel units, such as the Regulares, the

Legion and the Carlists, preferred their distinctive traditional headgear, like the fez, the Legion hat, or red beret, over steel helmets; all of them suffered very high numbers of casualties during the war. This was due partly to their role as shock troops and their characteristic fearlessness, but the fact that they lacked steel helmets must have also unnecessarily increased the number of dead and wounded. In this case as in other military contexts, ideology is key when it comes to adapting to or rejecting technological innovations.

62. BREAD BOMBS, OCTOBER 1938, SALAMANCA

Adrian Shubert

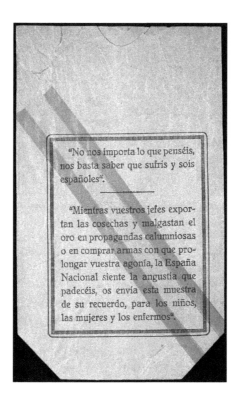

"No nos importa lo que penséis, nos basta saber que sufris y sois españoles".

"Mientras vuestros jefes exportan las cosechas y malgastan el oro en propagandas calumniosas o en comprar armas con que prolongar vuestra agonía, la España Nacional siente la angustia que padecéis, os envía esta muestra de su recuerdo, para los niños, las mujeres y los enfermos".

On October 3, 1938, Francoist planes flew over Madrid yet again. This had been a frequent occurrence ever since the rebels had started to bombard the capital from the air eighteen months before, but this time was different. Instead of explosives, the planes dropped 110 bags full of bread like this one, adorned with the Nationalist colors and a text that read: "We don't care what you think. It's sufficient to know that you are suffering and you are Spaniards ... In the 'One, Great and Free' National Spain there is no home without fuel and no family without bread." There was a second such raid on Madrid two weeks later and then on other Republican cities.

Republican authorities did everything they could to undermine the impact of these unusual attacks. General Miaja warned the people of the capital not to risk tasting "any of the food sent by those traitors since it could well be laced with microbes that cause serious illness and even death." For his part, the civil governor discounted microbes but did claim that the bread contained "a kind of moral poison." The city government claimed that citizens were handing the loaves into municipal offices but other evidence suggests that this bread, "so white that it looked like cotton," ended up elsewhere.

This act of Nationalist propaganda put its finger on one of the major problems facing Republican authorities, and not just in Madrid: the immense difficulties they faced in supplying big cities with food. This was a problem that began with the war itself. The Republic remained in control of Madrid and Barcelona and most of the country's other major cities, but the Nationalists had taken over many of the most important agricultural regions. And the problem only got worse as the conflict dragged on, especially as refugees from areas conquered by the rebels flooded in. For example, Madrid traditionally sourced fruit and rice from Valencia, but the Battle of the Jarama brought this to an end. Nor did it help that many of the agrarian collectives were reluctant to sell their produce at fixed prices in return for paper money they did not trust.

Republican authorities used a variety of methods including posters, pamphlets, and magazines, to persuade people that they could help the war effort by consuming less, changing the way they ate, and even producing their own food. Cookbooks such as *Wartime Menus* (1936) and *Wartime Dishes* (1938) promoted less use of meat and more of low-prestige items like sardines. The authorities also imposed rationing and controlled the times stores could be open. Citizens, almost always women, had to spend more time in lines, which made them more vulnerable to Nationalist air attacks. The National Hygiene Institute reported that between February 1937 and February 1939, the average daily calorie consumption fell from 1,514 calories, less than an adult needed to maintain body weight, to only 852. It is not surprising that there were fewer cats on the streets of the capital.

Changing official responses to these food shortages contributed to undermining faith in Republican authorities and encouraging the flourishing of practices such as hoarding, bartering, and the black market. When people went to villages surrounding the capital to get their own supplies, authorities limited them to just 15 kilos. This only provoked people to find ways to get around the rules. The train to Arganda became known as the "hunger train," and lentils, the most widely available foodstuff, were called the "pills of victory" and, more sarcastically "Doctor Negrín's pills," after the Prime Minister behind the policy of resistance at all costs.

Without a doubt, this inability to properly feed the home front played an important role in undermining morale in the Republican zone and contributed to the final outcome of the war.

63. LAXATIVES, OCTOBER 1938/MARCH 1939, RIVAS VACIAMADRID, MADRID

Alfredo González Ruibal

The archaeological excavations of the Republican positions at El Piul in Rivas Vaciamadrid, which were in use between October 1938 and March 1939, turned up a jar of laxatives. It was produced by the Esteban Bruni laboratory, located at 13 Felicidad Street in Madrid, next to the Almudena Cemetery (then known as the East Cemetery). The jar appeared at the same level as an abandoned refuge for troops, which means it comes from the final days of the war. A bottle of Carabaña mineral water was also found at the same position. With its high concentration of sodium sulfate, it was considered at the time to be an effective purgative. This Madrid spring water was very popular from the 1920s to the 1940s and bottles of it were even exported outside of Spain. In neighboring Vallecas, archaeological excavations of the Republican position at Casas de Murcia revealed a bottle containing castor oil, which also has purgative effects.

There were two omnipresent elements in the Republican trenches during the final months of the Civil War: laxatives and vitamins. Both are related to the same phenomenon: the poor nutrition of the Popular Army's troops. The vitamins were used to complement a diet lacking in vegetables, fruits, and fresh products in general; the laxatives were to counter the constipating effects of this same diet. Advertisements for anti-constipation medicines, nutritional supplements and products for calming the nerves were very common in the Republican press and are eloquent testimony to the difficulties that those on the government side were facing at the end of the conflict. Constipation became part of daily life. The Chilean diplomat Carlos Morla Lynch organized a variety show at the embassy featuring "Fakir Normacol and his helper Agarol," both the names of laxatives.

Poor nutrition was common throughout the Popular Army; the few letters that remain to us mention it repeatedly. A good collection of such letters comes from the Army of Andalucía's censorship services that has been studied by James Matthews. One censored letter reads: "We suffer a great deal of hunger in this village. We cannot resist because half of us are in hospital for lack of food. I'm telling you, they give us no more than four chickpeas and to eat them we have to mash them in a mortar, and that is the only way that we can eat them."

Hunger was perhaps more acute in Madrid because the authorities had to feed a million civilians as well as an army. The writer Ángel María de Lera recalls that, by 1939, the food in the trenches of the University City "consisted exclusively of broths—at noon and at night—and a ladleful of water blackened by a few grains of toasted barley which was served for breakfast." The situation for the civilians was the same or worse: by the end of 1938 milk was no longer available, not even for children under the age of two. In January 1939, the daily food ration consisted of 100 grams of bread and 100 grams of lentils, garbanzos, and rice. In February, there was no wheat left.

The end of the war did not bring an end to the hunger or its associated physiological problems. Those who suffered the most were the Republicans imprisoned in Franco's jails and concentration camps, where constipation took on tragic dimensions. According to Eduardo de Guzmán, the prisoners, deprived of laxatives, had to make use of can openers to extract their constipation-hardened stools, which could cause hemorrhages. The weakened prisoners would frequently faint and fall into the latrines.

64. "PSYCHO-TECHNICAL" CELL, 1938–39, SALAMANCA

Adrian Shubert

This unusual prison cell was one of four so-called "psycho-technical" cells the Republic's Military Intelligence Service (SIM) had built in former religious buildings in Barcelona and Valencia during the final months of the Civil War. The concrete blocks on the floor were intended to make prisoners stumble when they attempted to walk and the bed, a slab installed at an angle of twenty percent, ensured that they fell onto the floor when they lay down. There was also a clock that ran fast and a metronome that was set at irregular rhythms. What is most striking, however, are the geometric patterns painted in brilliant colors that cover the walls.

After a Spanish art historian rediscovered the history of these cells in 2003, it was suggested that the wall paintings had been inspired by the work of Paul Klee and Wassily Kandinsky, and that their style had been appropriated as part of a program of psychological torture. There is no definitive evidence to support these claims, but we do know that the famous scene in Luis Buñuel's 1929 surrealist movie *Un Chien Andalou* (An Andalusian Dog), in which an eye is sliced by a straight razor, was shown in the *checas* (secret prisons) to terrify prisoners.

This cell was designed by Alphonse Laurencic (1902–39). He was a picaresque figure. Born in France to parents from the Austro-Hungarian Empire, he moved to Spain with his family when he was twelve. Later he enlisted in the French Foreign Legion, although he never actually wore the uniform. He went to live in Graz and then Berlin, where he earned his living as the leader of a jazz band and a designer. When the Nazis came to power in 1933, he returned to Spain and set himself up in Barcelona where he created a new jazz band, the 17 United Artists.

When the Civil War broke out, he worked as a translator, first for the CNT and then for the Republican intelligence services. He also found time to sell fake passports and embezzle public funds, activities that led to him being arrested and spending time in the Segorbe labor camp. He secured his release by claiming to be an architect and offering to work on what he called his "psycho-technical" cells. When the Francoists entered Barcelona in January 1939, he tried to sell them information but was arrested for being a Republican spy and having designed these cells.

Laurencic is a minor figure and his "psycho-technical" cells a small but striking anecdote. They do serve, however, to highlight two important issues. The first is the role of the Republic's secret prisons (the Francoists had theirs as well). Especially at the start of the conflict these were run by unions and political parties, beyond the control of the government, and they were the site of all kinds of abuses and crimes. Later on, the government took control of many of them, while the SIM created its own new ones where neither democratic values nor human rights were respected.

The second issue is the nature of Francoist propaganda. Laurencic's trial was described in R.L. Chacón's 1939 book *Why I Built the Barcelona "Chekas": The Court Martial of Laurencic*. Presented as a documentary account of the trial, the book quotes much of the testimony and the verdict, emphasizing "the multiple forms of physical and moral torture endured by the prisoners." It also claims that upon hearing the verdict, Laurencic yelled "Long live Generalísimo Franco!" More than a condemnation of this insignificant individual, the book is a condemnation of the Republic itself. First, it claims that the government not only knew about the existence of the *checas*, but actually encouraged their creation, and second, it suggests that Soviet agents were involved in them. Both claims were part of the Francoist narrative that the Republic was a cruel and inhuman regime subordinate to the Soviet Union and the creation of an international Jewish–Marxist–Masonic plot. In Francoist propaganda, only Republicans committed crimes.

Alphonse Laurencic was executed on July 9, 1939. According to Chacón, when he stood before the firing squad, Laurencic raised his right arm in the Francoist salute. This too was a Francoist trope. There are many similar books which show the vanquished recognizing and begging pardon for their crimes and, with their final breath, praising the Caudillo.

65. ZINC PLAQUE, MARCH 1939/ MARCH 1940, CASTUERA, BADAJOZ

Verónica Sierra Blas

Of the various items found at the concentration camp in Castuera, Badajoz, the most attention-grabbing are some zinc plaques—torn out of the walls reinforcing the wooden barracks—upon which the prisoners wrote their barracks number, their names, and the names of family members. Etched into the plaques with a pointed object and passed over afterwards with pencil, the irregular and disorganized writing contains but a handful of letters. There is, nevertheless, a certain calligraphic dignity to these subliminal attempts to humanize their otherwise cruel, dangerous, and hostile environment, where it was heroic merely to survive from one day to the next.

The name of one of the originators of this idea can be found on one of the best preserved plaques: "Antonio Rubio, Barracks n.º 53"/"Nati Rubio de Abertura (Cáceres)." Once he had written his sign, Antonio attached it to one of the slats on the facade of his barrack so that the deliveries that arrived for him, like the letters and packages sent by his wife, Nati, would not get lost. Receiving extra toiletries, food, and clothes from home, as well as reading caring and comforting words from loved ones, would have no doubt helped the prisoners to bear the difficult and distressing conditions of life in the camp.

The Castuera concentration camp was built just a few kilometers outside of the town, on a private piece of land called La Verilleja, in the northern foothills of the Benquerencia Mountains. It was operational from March 1939 to March 1940, and during those twelve months nearly 15,000 prisoners passed through it. There were many other Francoist concentration camps similar to this one: Albatera and in Los Almendros, Alicante; San Pedro de Cardeña, Burgos; San Marcos, León; La Corchuela and Los Merinales, Sevilla; Camposancos, Pontevedra; and Lavacolla, Santiago de Compostela. Thanks to the work of many researchers, the testimony offered by the prisoners and their families, and the laudable efforts of associations like the one for the Castuera Concentration Camp Memorial, the history of these camps is known in detail.

However, there are many camps about which there is scarcely any documentation, and that are partially or even completely unknown. According to Carlos Hernández de Miguel, there were around 300 camps in Francoist Spain, which contained somewhere between half a million to a million prisoners. The first camp, in Zeluán, close to Melilla, opened on July 19, 1936, mere hours after the military revolt in Morocco. The last one, in Miranda de Ebro, Burgos, closed in January 1947. There are records of even later camps, from the 1950s and 1960s, like the ones in Puerto del Rosario and Tefía, on the island of Fuerteventura. In contrast to the camps that operated during the war and the postwar era, these were not meant for imprisoning Republican Army soldiers but rather for isolating and controlling other "dissident elements," like homosexuals.

Some camps were temporary; others were more permanent. But all of them were, in the words of Javier Rodrigo, "illegal and extrajudicial detention centers run by the military administration and employees to intern and classify the prisoners of the war without a trial." Beginning in March 1937, the responsibility for organizing and managing the camps fell to the Inspectorate of Concentration Camps of Prisoners (ICCP), which was a part of the Mobilization, Instruction and Recovery Headquarters (MIR). They were also in charge of categorizing the prisoners, which was done in accordance with the so-called "classifying commissions" of the General Order of Classification from March 11 of that same year.

Even if it is impossible to specify the total number of killed, dead, and disappeared today, we know that the systematic mistreatment, overcrowding, hunger, and the proliferation of all types of diseases, together with the killing and exploitation of the prisoners in the labor battalions as well as in concentration camps themselves, were the principal causes of death.

The primary forms of forced labor undertaken by the prisoners of war during the conflict included hauling supplies and laboring on strengthening defensive installations. After the war they were put to work excavating canals, exploding mines, installing electric cables, performing agricultural and forestry tasks, and constructing or reconstructing monuments, roads, dams, reservoirs, bridges, airports, and railways. Lavacolla airport in Santiago de Compostela was one of these projects (see Chapter 71). In addition to benefiting the dictatorship, the labor of the prisoners also enriched numerous private companies.

66. ADVERTISEMENT FOR THE GURS CONCENTRATION CAMP, APRIL 1939, BARCELONA

Adrian Shubert

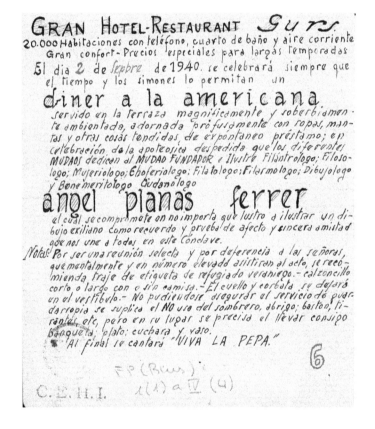

This handmade announcement, created by Fernando Rius, a member of the Unified Socialist Party of Catalonia (PSUC), in September 1940, ironically advertises the concentration camp in Gurs, France, just over 100 kilometers from the border with Spain, as a deluxe 20,000-room hotel, each with "telephone, bathroom, and air conditioning," that offers special rates for "long-term stays."

As the Republican resistance in Cataluña crumbled in January 1939, some 500,000 men, women, and children, civilians and soldiers alike, fled to France in what is known as the *Retirada*. The center-right government of Édouard Daladier, whose November 12, 1938 law mandated the creation of centers for "the reception of undesirables subject to strict measures of surveillance," responded by interning them in a number of concentration camps. The first were the primitive "sand camps" hastily thrown up on the beaches at Argelès-sur-Mer, which housed more than 180,000 refugees, Saint-Cyprien, and Le Barcarès.

Things changed following the appointment of General Menard to oversee the refugee situation. As well as improving conditions at the "sand camps," he had six new camps built. Some were located in existing facilities, such as the military training center at Rivesaltes that housed 15,000 and the First World War camp at Vernet built to house colonial troops. Others were newly constructed. These included Bram, where photographer Agustí Centelles was among the 17,000 prisoners, and Gurs, which at the outbreak of the Second World War had 14,977 inmates: 9,488 Spaniards, listed separately as "aviators," "Basques," and "Spaniards," and 4,530 members of the International Brigades from more than fifty countries. France also established internment camps in Algeria and its Moroccan protectorate for the Republicans who escaped there. French officials referred to them as "reception centres," "accommodation centres," "administrative camps," and "concentration camps."

Concerned about the costs of maintaining so many refugees, the French authorities encouraged as many as possible to leave the country and by the end of 1939, approximately 250,000 had done so. Many soon found themselves in Francoist concentration camps. Few other countries were prepared to accept the Republican refugees, although Mexico took 22,000 between 1938 and 1948, and the Soviet Union took a few thousand Communist militants.

The Spaniards who remained had to choose among four options. They could accept employment in a local business or on a local farm to make up for the Frenchmen who had been mobilized; enlist in the French Foreign Legion; join the Foreign Labor Companies (CTE), join militarized labor units run by the French Army; or join the special military units commanded by French officers. Some 5,000 Spaniards joined these units and 50,000 found themselves in the CTE. The number of Spaniards in Gurs fell quickly, especially after November 1939. By the time the Germans invaded France in May 1940, only ninety-two Spaniards remained.

The story of Gurs began with the Republican refugees but it did not end with them. The German invasion of France led to the imprisonment of foreigners the French government labeled "undesirables": 18,744 Spaniards, who arrived between May and September 1940, and 9,771 women, mostly German but also Poles, Romanians, Czechs, and Italians. Among them was Hannah Arendt. There were also 1,329 French males, including communists, pacifists, and pro-German defeatists.

Between October 1940 and August 1944, when Gurs was run by the Marshall Pétain's collaborationist Vichy regime, it held more than 18,000 inmates, including almost 14,000 non-French Jews. Between August 1942 and March 1943, 3,907 of those Jews were handed to the Germans and deported to Auschwitz-Birkenau. Vichy also sent its own "undesirables," including Roma-Sinti, prostitutes, and political prisoners. By the time the Bearn region was liberated, almost 60,000 people had passed through the camp. More than 1,000 of them died.

Gurs remained in operation for sixteen months after the liberation. During this period, it housed 310 German prisoners of war, 1,585 minor French collaborators, and, ironically, 1,475 anti-Franco Spaniards who had fought in the Resistance and taken part in the failed invasion of the Valle de Arán in October 1944. The Gurs camp closed on December 31, 1945.

Among the French camps, Gurs was special. At 80 hectares, it was the largest, and it functioned longer than any other. But it was not unique. Other camps that housed Republican refugees, like Septfonds and Rivesaltes, also later housed other types of prisoners, including Jews who were sent to the Nazi extermination camps. And like so much else of this difficult period of the country's recent past, it was forty years after the end of the Second World War before it began to occupy a place in France's historical memory.

The Francoist
Dictatorship

67. SKETCH OF JOSÉ ANTONIO PRIMO DE RIVERA'S COMMUNAL GRAVE, APRIL 1939, ALCALÁ DE HENARES

Jesús Espinosa Romero

On March 14, 1936, the new Republican Parliament was formed, with a majority of deputies belonging to the Popular Front electoral coalition. That same day, José Antonio Primo de Rivera, national leader of the FET-JONS, was detained in relation to a terrorist attack that had taken place two days earlier against the socialist deputy Luis Jiménez de Asúa that killed his bodyguard, Jesús Gisbert. By this time, there had been a qualitative change in the violent strategy of the Falange, Spain's primary fascist party. Primo de Rivera had decided to move on from what he called "the dialectic of fists and pistols" against his leftist rivals to strike at the very heart of the Republic's legislative power. Jiménez de Asúa, the father of the 1931 Constitution, who was about to be elected Vice President of the Congress in its inaugural session, was a highly symbolic target. Even after their leader was jailed, the Falange did not give up in the pursuit of this goal. Francisco Largo Caballero, the leader of the socialist parliamentary caucus, was attacked in his own home on March 15. Supreme Court member Manuel Pedregal, who wrote the verdict in the case of the Falangists who were convicted of the attempted murder of Jiménez de Asúa, was the next major target. He was killed on April 13 while returning home from a gathering at the Circle of Fine Arts. The Falange had decided to take yet another step forward in its assault against the Republic, this time by intimidating the Judiciary.

Primo de Rivera was implicated in various trials connected to his organization's violent activities, but the permissive visitor regulations allowed him to continue controlling his coreligionists from prison. This situation also permitted him to collude with other right-wing leaders who were in favor of a coup d'état. Despite being moved to the prison in Alicante on June 5, together with his brother Miguel and sister-in-law Margarita Larios, who were imprisoned for the same reasons, the Falange leader was still able to participate in these schemes. He instructed his most active militants to join the coup and informed General Mola, the organizer of the rebellion, of this. In turn, Mola kept Primo de Rivera apprised of the date of the revolt. The coup failed in Alicante, however, and on July 19 Republicans intercepted the Falangist fifth column from Callosa de Segura that was on its way to liberate José Antonio.

On October 3, he faced a new, much graver, accusation: military rebellion. He was informed about the indictment on November 14 and José Antonio, a lawyer by profession, provided his own defense. Instead of refuting the charges against him, he decided to explain the Falange's political program to save Spain, while at the same time denying any involvement in the coup. After two days of oral arguments, the jury, composed of fourteen members of the different political parties and unions that were loyal to the Republic, agreed with the prosecutor's charges, and on November 18 the Provincial Popular Tribunal of Alicante condemned him to death. Although the prisoner requested a pardon, he was executed two days later, together with four other prisoners. All of the cadavers were taken to the Alicante cemetery where they shared a communal grave. A drawing of the grave, replicated above, was done at the time of the first exhumation of José Antonio's body, in 1939. He would be buried three more times.

Although Franco, who now headed the FET-JONS, and the other leaders of the Falange knew about the execution, it was not made public until July 18, 1938. Thus "the Absent One," as José Antonio had come to be called by his party, now became known as "the Fallen," "the Prophet," and "the Martyr of the Crusade." Funerals were held across Nationalist Spain and the cemetery in Alicante was bombarded with flowers. The Falange began a practice of permanent mourning by changing the color of the tie worn with their uniform to black. After Nationalist troops entered Alicante, José Antonio's cadaver—relatively well-preserved thanks to the efforts of the city's fifth column, who had sprinkled silicates on the grave—was moved to a niche in the same cemetery.

At the beginning of November 1939, the Falange leadership decided to move José Antonio's remains again. On November 19, he was exhumed and carried on the shoulders of Falange militants for ten straight days to the monastery of King Phillip II's Escorial Palace—the stony metaphor of the Falange's imperial desire. This, however, was not José Antonio's last trip. On March 31, 1959, he was exhumed again and buried a few kilometers away in the Valley of the Fallen a day before its inauguration. His body has remained there ever since, although because of changes to the status of the monument following the passing of the Law of Democratic Memory in October 2022, his descendants requested that José Antonio's remains be exhumed and reinterred in a Catholic cemetery.

68. CASTILLO DE OLITE, JULY 1939, CARTAGENA

Antonio Cazorla-Sánchez

Do an online search for the words "Olite Castle" (or "Castillo de Olite") and you will get many hits. Nearly all of them will refer to the royal castle in Olite, Navarra. In contrast, you would have to try very hard to find a single entry about the greatest modern naval catastrophe on the Spanish coasts, one that claimed 1,476 lives, only a few less than the 1,503 who died aboard the *Titanic*.

It all began on March 4, 1939, less than a month before the end of the war. That day, the officers and crews in Cartagena, the only important naval base remaining in the hands of the Republic, rebelled against Juan Negrín's government. Negrín wanted to keep fighting at any cost, so that the war in Spain would run into the looming Second World War. Moreover, the government had just sent the communist officer Francisco Galán (brother of the Republican martyr Fermín Galán) to take charge of the base, but the sailors in Cartagena wanted an end to communist influence in the Republic. Taking advantage of this situation, a second insurrection was carried out by the fifth column in Cartagena, which proceeded to occupy nearly the entire city. By March 5, Cartagena appeared to be in the hands of the pro-Francoist forces. As a result, the Republican fleet set off to sea. It could have saved thousands of Republicans who just a few weeks later found themselves trapped in the city and at Franco's (scarce) mercy. But the ships did not return; they were interned in Bizerta, Tunisia.

On March 5, the leader of the fifth column, general Rafael Barrionuevo, sent a message to Franco assuring him that Cartagena was completely in his hands. But this was not true; in fact, at that moment the Republic was preparing to recapture the base. Despite the confusing situation, Franco took the hasty and fatal decision to send thirty ships and more than 20,000 men to occupy Cartagena. The soldiers embarked in Castellón, where the seasoned Division 83 from Galicia was stationed, and Málaga. March 5 was a rest day, and all of the soldiers were getting ready to watch a bullfight, but part of the division was ordered onto the freighter *Olite Castle*. Although the ship was in good shape (it had been launched in Holland in 1921) its radio was broken. It was among the last to leave on the so-called Cartagena Expedition. When it arrived in Cartagena on the morning of March 9, the pro-Francoist rebellion had already been squashed by Republican forces who had also taken control of the onshore batteries that guarded the port.

The convoy that was meant to take Cartagena waited at a prudential distance for orders to retreat, but nobody told the *Olite Castle* to stop its advance. Once it had almost entered the harbor, it came under fire from the La Parajola battery. The second shot, fired by captain Antonio Martínez Pallarés while held at gunpoint by captain Cristóbal Guirao, was a direct hit that detonated the munitions on board the ship. The explosion was horrible. Hundreds of men flew through the air while others drowned within the ship's hold.

Franco never took responsibility for the catastrophe and avoided the topic whenever he could. The official blame fell on Vice Admiral Francisco Moreno, whose prestige never recovered. Franco's General Headquarters did not even acknowledge the loss of the ship until March 23.

After the end of the war, on July 26, 1939, the regime erected a stone cross in memory of the dead on the coast near the location of the sunken ship. But in 1954, navy divers blew up the wreckage and the hundreds of cadavers that remained inside, and the steel plates were sold to a scrap metal company. In 1957, a new, more imposing cross was erected to replace the previous one: it was 10 meters tall with an altar at its base and preserved the bronze plaques from the original monument. It also included a sculpture of a woman as a symbol of consolation for the dead. Over time, the monument and the memory of the *Olite Castle*'s victims was forgotten. The final remains of the ship and its sailors were covered over by a new jetty in the harbor. In 2001, the location where the cross had been was turned into a quarry. The cross was dismantled and disappeared. The sculpture was restored in 2009 and relocated to Calvario hill, next to a hermitage. There is a reference to the sinking of a ship, but it does not expressly mention the *Olite Castle*.

After the war, Guirao, the Republican official who ordered the lethal shot, went into exile to France where he fought in the Resistance. He returned to

Cartagena in 2005 where he said that he knew perfectly well what could happen when he gave the order. He also told the local press that for years he had been unable to sleep thinking about captain Martínez Pallarés, the man he had forced at gunpoint to fire, who was then killed by the Francoists for fulfilling his duty—whether he had wanted to or not.

69. JULIA CONESA'S LETTER FROM DEATH ROW, AUGUST 1939, MADRID

Verónica Sierra Blas

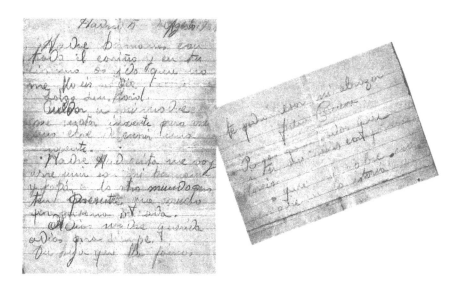

"May my name not be erased from history." This was Julia Conesa's request in the postscript of her final letter to her family, which she wrote from the chapel in Ventas prison while awaiting her execution. She was one of the thirteen young women collectively known as the "Thirteen Roses" who were shot on August 5, 1939, in front of the wall of Madrid's East Cemetery, known today as the Almudena Cemetery. Although Julia was not the only one who had to bid farewell to her loved ones by letter that fateful morning, hers is one of the few such missives that remain with us today. The request that she made of her mother and siblings soon became a motto of the anti-Francoist struggle and, after the arrival of democracy in Spain, an object of collective memory and one of the most potent symbols of condemnation of Francoism's crimes.

Julia and the twelve other women of the Thirteen Roses, all between the ages of 18 and 29, along with another forty-three young women known as the "43 Carnations," were judged and sentenced to death by the Permanent War Council Number 9. They all faced the same charge: participation in clandestine meetings of the Socialist Youth United (JSU). Their execution was "a hard-hitting response" by the Francoist regime, which wanted to take advantage of the July 29 assassination of Commander Isaac Gabaldón, his daughter and his chauffeur, to warn to those trying to reorganize the Communist Party in Madrid that their actions could have fatal consequences.

Like Julia, Carmen Barrero, Blanca Brisac, and Dionisia Manzanero—whose letters from death row have also been preserved by their families—insist on their innocence and deny the crimes of which they were accused. Although those condemned to death may commonly use their final words to defend themselves against false accusations, doing so was especially important for these women given that, unlike imprisoned men, the Francoist regime did not classify women as political prisoners but rather as delinquents, prostitutes, and thieves.

The punishments they faced were also different in kind. Some punishments, such as rape, and forms of public humiliation like having their heads shaved or being made to ingest castor oil, were specifically designated for "red women." They also had their own prison regime—the "cloistered prison." This was managed by religious orders and based on the pseudoscientific theories of psychiatrists such as Antonio Vallejo-Nájera and priests like Demetrio González Aguilar who believed that women were biologically and intellectually inferior to men, and who claimed that Marxism was a sickness that, given women's "weakness," made them more susceptible to crime.

It is very difficult today to calculate the exact number of women who were locked away in Francoist prisons. It is even more difficult to know the number of children who were born in the prisons and who remained there, as established in Order 30 from March 1940, until they were three years old. The *Spanish Statistical Yearbook* (*Anuario Estadístico de España*) from 1940 put the penal population of the country that year at 363,000. Studies undertaken since then estimate that between 20,000 and 30,000 of these were women, around 13.7 percent of the total.

The picture painted of these women by the official documentation reveals a gender-specific criminal typology. It also distinguishes, as the prisoners themselves did, between two different groups: those imprisoned during the war or in its immediate aftermath, who faced charges of economic crimes, for being accessory to the crime or "for inciting it"; and those imprisoned during the dictatorship for the crimes of rebellion against the security of the state, its property, or the socioeconomic and moral order.

Although information is often sparse and incomplete, when it exists at all, the lacunae and silence that exist around the reality of penal life under Francoism are alleviated by the testimony provided by the prisoners themselves, either while in captivity or afterwards. The letters written from death row are, without doubt, the most powerful example of how the memory of their authors and those who were incarcerated with them remains alive, thus helping to fulfill Julia's wish that their names not be erased from history.

70. PICTURE FRAME BELONGING TO A POUM PRISONER, DECEMBER 1939, BARCELONA

Arnau González i Vilata

On Christmas Day, 1939, there was little to celebrate and even less to say inside of Barcelona's Modelo prison. It was clear: Franco had won the war. The prison cells were an acronym soup overflowing with militants from conflicting political groups. The only thing that united them was defeat and certain repression.

Claudi Bou Roca, condemned to death for belonging to the Workers Party of Marxist Unification (POUM), was preparing a dramatic goodbye to his "unforgettable" fiancée Cinta Ramos Vidal as a "testament to the great love that I profess during the days of my death sentence." To hold her photograph, he made a picture frame in the colors of the Republican flag—a more than likely "last and final gift."

The prisoners were subjected to psychological torture. Each day some of them would be taken to the Boca Camp to be shot, while others endured a simulation of an execution. Any day could be one's last; it was better to say one's goodbyes while one could.

The war was eternal for many of them. Bou Roca was born in 1919 in Santa Maria d'Oló and grew up in Sant Vicenç de Castellet, close to the industrial town of Manresa and the mining areas of Súria, Sallent, and Fígols. A stonemason by profession, he developed leftist political concerns very early on. At his village's community center, he would harangue local residents about utopian projects that, with the outbreak of the war, seemed possible for the first time. The success of these projects was another thing altogether. Even before this, he had already learned from experience about the turbulence of his time. His area of Cataluña, the Alto Llobregat, experienced frequent anarchist rebellions. In 1932, a proclamation of libertarian communism in the mines was snuffed out by troops sent from Barcelona. Meanwhile, in October 1934, the town of Sant Vicenç witnessed the revolutionaries of the Workers' Alliance set fire to their church and attack the priest. And the mayor and councilors of Cataluña's Republican Left (ERC) would be jailed after declaring an independent Catalan state.

But all of this was before the war and the *true* revolution. In the few photographs that remain from those years, Bou Roca can be seen standing proudly underneath the statue of Columbus on the Ramblas in Barcelona, alongside some of his friends known collectively known as the "three inseparables."

Taken prisoner during the Battle of the Ebro, after the war he was condemned to death, but his sentence was commuted to five years forced labor. After surviving the prison camp at Belchite—known as "little Russia" given the ideology of its prisoners—his ideals began to take on a slightly different character. Eight long years passed from 1939 during which he spent time helping to build the new Belchite as well as constructing roads, like the one leading to the port in Monrepós, in Huesca. Adding another dose of punishment to this, the new regime required Republican soldiers to undertake a lengthy military service, which in Bou Roca's case lasted from 1944 until 1947. His freedom finally came with a pardon issued on July 19, 1948. But not before he endured a brief exile in Manreso, just a few kilometers away from his hometown of Sant Vicenç—proof of the Francoist bureaucracy's ignorance. A suggestion of exile in Brazil with a sister came to nothing.

Through all of this there were many photographs of his fiancée Cinta—his "negrita" and "Nineta"—the daughter of a Civil Guard turned railway conductor whose only faith was in the Catholic Church. Condemned to death in 1939, Bou Roca was able to avenge his captors by marrying this girl from the photographs. But the memory of defeat would never leave him, nor would the bad health he inherited from his time in prison. His house, where his son Jordi was born in 1949, was of all places located on a street previously called Migdia but now called Caudillo, in eternal homage to the dictator.

The young stonemason, again employed at a quarry belonging to one of his six brothers and which he would one day end up running, delved into social Catholicism and ended up as a member of the "socially committed anti-Francoist wing of Catholicism." What had happened to the POUM militant who had followed in the footsteps of the socialist Catalanist Josep Rovira? Did he find in the most progressive strain of Christian democracy something that resonated with his earlier socialist beliefs?

71. LAVACOLLA AIRPORT, 1940, SANTIAGO DE COMPOSTELA

Emilio Grandío Seoane

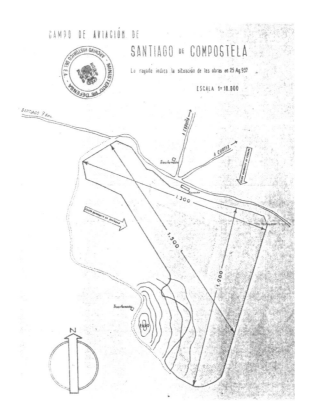

Thousands of people pass through Santiago de Compostela's Lavacolla airport every day, on their way to destinations in many different countries, including throughout Spain. They do not know that the runways they take off from or land on were constructed by prisoners, as part of the Franco dictatorship's policy of criminal redemption. In other words, Lavacolla was, for a time, a concentration camp.

National reconciliation was never a priority for the Francoist regime. Those who thought differently from the regime or who had helped defend the Republic had limited options, all of them bad: death, economic hardship, or imprisonment. Or all three. Given the immense number of people in Francoist prisons and camps, the regime made use of a new policy of redemption for one's sins. Something akin to a *reeducation* as a way of adapting to the New State through work. This was how the prisoners were to settle their supposed debt with Spain for their supposed bad actions. They were paid very little, as the real objective was to supply cheap labor both for public works, as in the case of the airport, and for the private sector, which benefited greatly from this privilege. Some of the most successful construction companies in Spain today have their origins in the postwar use of forced labor.

The new regime saw this policy as a winning formula, but perhaps the most important thing about it is how intensely it was used over the course of a few years, and then how quickly it disappeared, leaving no trace behind. There is a great hole, or worse, in the official memory.

Within the politics of national reconstruction of the transportation networks beginning in the 1940s, building an airport in Galicia was a top priority. The primary railway line in Galicia, which encompasses the entire Atlantic arc from Ferrol to Tui, was also constructed during the early 1940s. The need for transportation networks within Galicia was obvious, not just for the economic development of the area but also to assure military control over the peninsula by permitting rapid deployment of troops to strategic points. It is no coincidence that all of these improvements to the transportation network were undertaken during the Second World War, when the friendly relationship between Franco's dictatorship and the Fascist Axis gave rise to concerns about a possible Allied invasion through the north of Galicia.

Thousands of prisoners worked for years in the hills of Santiago de Compostela leveling out terrain. But practically no trace of their work remains. There are only a few plans, the physical location of the barracks— they themselves are not preserved—and some papers in the Santiago Municipal Archives documenting the payment of daily wages and other expenses to the employees. It is almost as if the work of constructing Galicia's main airport had never taken place—as if it had fallen from the sky.

Erasing evidence of their crimes was characteristic for much of the Francoist administration, proof of their willingness to suppress the memory of, or even annul, a conflictual past. It is not just that these acts were considered unimportant. Rather, those who served the regime—who believed it had been born of out of the struggle against chaos, crime, and to top it all off, called itself Christian—feared that they could be compromising in a post-Axis world. After 1945, the use of concentration camps as well as other totalitarian practices, now inconvenient, needed to be forgotten. For this reason, one of the most characteristic features of the Francoist regime was its silences. And this most relevant of Francoist methods, in a way, still persists. It is why the passenger who passes through Lavacolla today does not know that the land they walk on was worked by others who, in contrast to them, were not free. It is not their fault: there is no plaque or sign in the airport remembering this past.

72. DOUBLE-BOTTOMED PLATES AND PANS, 1939–45, ALBACETE

Verónica Sierra Blas

Following his victory, Franco began a forceful and indiscriminate policy of repressing and controlling the vanquished. While this had started during the conflict and lasted throughout the dictatorship, it reached its pinnacle between 1939 and 1945. During those "leaden years," prisons became the keystone of the Francoist system of repression. They were not just for subjugating and punishing the dissidents but also for bending, transforming, and converting them into people who embraced the principles of the New State. Visits from family members were thus severely limited and the exchange of letters between prisoners and their loved ones was prohibited or very closely guarded.

Norms of postal censorship established in 1937 remained in place (with some exceptions) until 1948, when new regulations were published. Prisoners could exchange letters only with immediate family members, just once a week, every fifteen days or once a month (depending on the time period and the prison). They could not make negative comments about the regime and had to limit themselves to describing the state of their health, their basic needs, the weather, their routines in prison (though not in too much detail) or asking after their family and any of their businesses or properties.

Additionally, there were specific days and times for letter exchanges that needed to be respected, as well as space constraints that varied with the different kinds of writing materials. In general, they would use postcards that their family could buy from the prison commissary, and which could hold at most ten-to-fifteen lines if squished together. Slightly longer letters were permitted when paper was not scarce. This often featured the prison letterhead, a portrait of Franco, and the familiar salute "Arise Spain!"

All correspondence had to be deposited into the mailbox of the prison's director, who would act as censor or else delegate the task to subordinates of their choosing. The censors not only read the letters carefully but were also required to submit a report whenever they encountered some anomaly: either when the content of the letter was inappropriate, or if they had discovered one of the many tricks that the correspondents used for exchanging news or messages clandestinely.

On August 4, 1943, the General Director of Prisons, Máximo Cuervo Radigales, sent out a secret notification to all the prison directors throughout Francoist Spain urging them to exercise the utmost "care and vigilance ... regarding the relations of the prison population with the external one." It also instructed them to use a "rubber stamp" to indicate that the letter had gone through the censorship process, and to alert those who wrote and received letters of the consequences of disobeying the established norms. Thus, on visitation days, there would often be posters on the prison door, or leaflets would be distributed, with messages like this one:

> Submitting something to the imprisoned person must be done in accordance with the law ... This is the first and only warning that will be given. Consequences for disobeying will be severe.

Nevertheless, the prisoners and their families were able to create alternative avenues of communication outside of the legal channels, and to exchange information behind the backs of the censors. Such clandestine communication had a two-pronged structure: one was internal, based on the solidarity among the prison population; the other external, made up first and foremost of families, as well as political organizations. Some of the most successful strategies were encoding messages, making invisible ink with which to write, or bribing the prison guards. Others included getting prisoners who were being transferred to act as messengers and slipping papers through the bars during family visits while the guards on duty were distracted. Finally, letters were also hidden and camouflaged in the most unexpected places, such as utensils and related objects of daily care—food and clothing—that the families had to provide. Thus, hampers and baskets, pockets and hems, bottles and cans, napkins and wrappers, and plates and pans with double bottoms, like the ones pictured above, could perform the miracle of allowing the prisoners to breathe a bit more freely, at least once in a while.

73. MONUMENT TO THE OATH OF LLANO AMARILLO (YELLOW PLAINS), JULY 1940, KETAMA, MOROCCO

Antonio Cazorla-Sánchez

The notorious Víctor Ruiz Albéniz (known as *El Tebib Arrumi*) was one of a number of Francoist mouthpieces who delighted in describing how the conspirators behind the Llano Amarillo military exercise of July 5 to 12, 1936 that took place near Ketama, Morocco, had ridiculed the local Republican authorities by asking them with increasing urgency for more "CAFÉ!" They were not referring to the drink (coffee) but were really saying "Camaradas, Arriba Falange Española!" ("Comrades, Arise Spanish Falange!"). The primary jokester was apparently Falange member lieutenant colonel Juan Yagüe, idol of the right since his repression of the Asturian revolution in October 1934, who later became sadly famous for the murder of some 4,000 people in Badajoz in August 1936. The victims of this unfunny joke were the acting High Commissioner in Morocco—"some guy named Buylla," as Tebib Arrumi condescendingly referred to him— and the head of the Colonial Army, general Agustín Gómez Morato. Arturo Álvarez-Buylla, a prestigious soldier and aviation pioneer, was shot by the rebels on March 17, 1937; he showed great integrity during this ordeal. His son and grandson are well-regarded scientists (the latter won the Prince of Asturias Research Prize in 2011). Gómez Morato was sentenced to prison. His life and career were ruined, despite having three sons and a son-in-law fighting with the rebels.

During the exercise at Llano Amarillo, in which 15,000 men took part, officers swore an oath to take part in the rebellion whenever General Emilio Mola, the brains of the operation, gave the order. Franco was at that time continuing to stall, and engaging the officers was necessary for ensuring that the rebellion would not fail. For this reason, on July 15, 1940, the authorities unveiled a grand monument celebrating this event. It consists of a winged obelisk featuring the then-official Spanish coat of arms in its center and is inscribed with the date July 12, 1936. A staircase ascends from its base, contributing to its great size. The monument boasts a certain artistic quality. In 1962, after a group of antifascists painted the words "Amnesty and Liberty" onto the monument, the Francoist authorities moved it to Ceuta, where it was placed at the base of Hacho Hill. Taking advantage of this move, the date on the inscription was changed to July 17, 1936. Why this was done is not clear, but it certainly simplifies the history and, at the same time, avoids the question of what people were actually doing at Llano Amarillo that July 12, five days before the uprising that initiated the Civil War.

During the conflict, Hacho Hill housed large numbers of prisoners while they awaited execution. To the 268 in Ceuta we should add 195 more in the Eastern zone of the Moroccan protectorate. Loyal soldiers and distinguished civilians were killed for defending the Republic. As in many other places, Falangist hit squads were prominent, sometimes acting with the help of rebel soldiers, and they applied the "escapee law" (*Ley de Fuga*), which gave them the right to shoot any prisoner who "was attempting to escape," with impunity.

The dictatorship also went to great lengths to erase their names and history from Ceuta's collective past, but they are remembered in Ceuta today. Despite hesitations and many contradictions, the city has launched a program of critical recovery of its past. It removed the famous "Franco's Feet" monument that marked the place from which, on August 5, 1936, Franco ordered the passage of "Victory Convoy" that transported colonial troops to the peninsula. In fact, the troops had already been traveling for over a week. It has also removed the mast of the gunboat *Dato* that protected the convoy.

Even more importantly, in 2006, it had the mass grave in Ceuta's Santa Catalina Cemetery fixed up and the names of the 169 people whose remains lie there added to it. That year also marked the beginning of a tradition unique in Spain which is repeated every year on the Day of the Dead in which local military and civilian authorities come together to pay homage to *all* of the victims of the Civil War: those executed by the Francoists, those killed by the Republican bombings, and those who died in combat.

Meanwhile, the monument to the Llano Amarillo Oath has been abandoned and is partially covered over with cement. It remains there, quiet, mutilated, and out of the geographic and mental space for which it was conceived. In this, it is not unique. As with so many other monuments and locations from the Civil War, it sits there without explanation, without contextualization, and without contributing to the historical knowledge and democratic culture of Spain's citizens.

74. JOSEP BARTOLÍ'S "CAMPS SKETCHBOOK," 1944, BARCELONA

Verónica Sierra Blas

Argelès-sur-Mer, Saint-Cyprien, Le Barcarès, Fort-Collioure, Bram, Agde, Rivesaltes, Septfonds, Gurs, Rieucros, Vernet d'Ariège, Noé, Le Récébédou, Mauzac, Saint-Sulpice, Fort-Barraux, Vallon-en-Sully, Le Chaìaut, Le Sablous, Les Milles, Nexon, Vénissieux … These are just some of the internment camps set up by Édouard Daladier's government to "receive and house" the half-million Spanish refugees who, between the end of January and beginning of February 1939, crossed the border into France. The penultimate of the five phases of the Spanish exile identified by Javier Rubio, this one, triggered by the fall of Cataluña, was the largest.

Among the thousands of people who traveled the many kilometers, crossing frozen mountains, and following roads crowded with cars and trucks, mostly by foot, to reach the border, was the artist Josep Bartolí i Guiu. Few others could draw the Republican defeat like he did. His drawings, populated by gaunt and elongated silhouettes, by famished, amputated and sick bodies, and by sad and desperate looks, is an unequaled historical chronicle of the *Retirada* (Retreat), as well as a scathing denunciation of the French authorities' vexatious, humiliating, and miserable treatment of the Spanish exiles.

Josep had to hide his first drawings in the sand on the beach at Le Barcarès when he was hospitalized with typhus. Luckily, he was able to recover them when he returned to the camp and they accompanied him on his first failed escape attempt, and then for the rest of his life as a political refugee. So did the drawings that he did later at the camp at Bram, to which he was transferred after being captured. Following his second escape attempt, he achieved his goal of reaching Paris, where he worked in the famous cabarets Folies-Bergère and Moulin-Rouge as a stage designer and poster artist. After the French capital was occupied by German troops, Josep went into hiding in Chartres, Bordeaux, Orléans, and other French cities until he was finally imprisoned by the Gestapo in Vichy. Just before being deported to Dachau, he escaped again and, after many vicissitudes, made his way to Marseilles from where he embarked on the *Lyautey*, which took him to Tunis. From there he went to Oran, from Oran to Casablanca, and from Casablanca to Mexico.

Between 1943 and 1945, Josep worked intensively and joined the circles of the most important Mexican artists: he collaborated with Frida Kahlo and Diego Rivera and became a member of the "Ruptura" group. His drawings from the camps were first published there. In 1946, he went to the United States. In New York he contributed to a number of newspapers and magazines, and joined the group "10th Street," of which Franz Kline, Mark Rothko, and Jackson Pollock were also members. He also worked as a set designer in Hollywood. Starting in the 1950s, he made repeated trips to Europe but did not return to his native Barcelona until 1977. In 1989, six years before his death, he sold a large part of his personal papers, including the drawing *Life in the Camp*, shown above, to the city of Barcelona.

Like Josep, other exiles were able to escape from the camps in France and Algeria and get a ticket to some third country, but the majority were repatriated to Spain, worked for French companies, enlisted in the Foreign Legion and in the Marching Regiments of Foreign Volunteers, or enrolled in one of the Spanish Workers Companies (CTE). Regardless of their final destination, their shared experience of imprisonment was the pillar on which the "imagined community" of Republican exiles was built.

The daily struggle that the exiles waged to sustain their ideas and values has its greatest reflection in what Francie Cate-Arries has called "barbed wire culture." Josep's drawings are a product of this culture. So, too, are the numerous cultural and educational initiatives that were born in the camps: people created, drew, wrote, read, taught the illiterate to read, gave classes on French and general culture, organized classes, conferences, talks, and workshops of all kinds, set up radio stations, created newspapers and news bulletins, held exhibitions, concerts and poetry readings, etc. In the face of the dehumanization, violence, indifference, criticism, rejection, and marginalization that they endured, the record of these activities that has reached us today constitutes the most beautiful homage to the bravery, utopia, and liberty that the exiles always carried as their flag.

75. RATION COUPONS, 1944, ALEGIA, VIZCAYA

Miren Llona

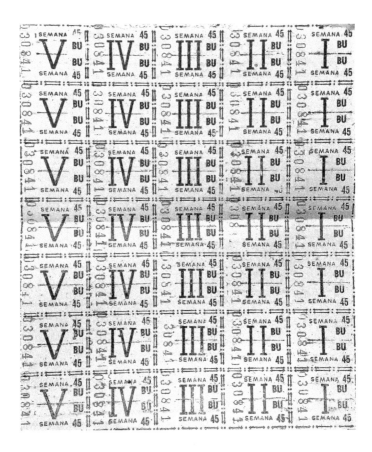

The misery did not end with the end of the Civil War; it was exacerbated by the interventionist economy consonant with the autocratic regime that Franco sought to create. On the one hand, this was a way to demonstrate that the new regime was self-sufficient and did not have to rely on other countries. On the other, self-sufficiency permitted him to favor the interests of the different oligarchic groups that had supported the rebellion and helped finance the war. The result was a situation of extreme scarcity, and the consequent need to ration most foodstuffs and other essential products.

Rationing was in force between 1939 and 1952, and it created a situation of generalized corruption as well as undermining the supplies that it was supposed to ensure. Although the dictatorship attributed this crisis to the destruction caused by the Civil War and the commercial upheavals of the Second World War, historical research has shown that the principle causes of scarcity were the monopolization of production and its deviation toward the black market. The consequences of the inefficiency and irrationality of this policy of autarchy were economic stagnation and the collapse of living standards for over a decade. Shortages, hunger, rationing, the black market, and corruption are, therefore, experiences inextricably linked to the postwar era and the beginnings of Francoism. In 1943, the book of ration coupons, which had originally been given to families, were given instead to individuals with the aim of preventing families from sheltering relatives who were hiding from other locations.

These ration books were the mechanism for regulating people's weekly food supply: bread, oil, sugar, rice, legumes, potatoes, bacon, cod, coffee, and ham. The books specified the quantities that should be given to each family. Women and people over the age of sixty received 80 percent of the daily ration of an adult male; children under the age of fifteen received half. In 1941, the Rockefeller Foundation calculated that the Spanish diet was only about one-quarter to one-third of what it should have been, especially due to its lack of calories and carbohydrates. In the collective memory of the long postwar era, the experience of hunger and of meager rations has remained firmly associated with the black market and paying two to three times the official prices for food.

For a select few, participating in the black market, what was commonly called "*estraperlo*," was an extremely lucrative activity from which they amassed great fortunes. Privileged sectors of society, like the landlords of the rural world and important players in commerce and industry of the cities, were able to monopolize the production of food and other essential items. They could also be sure that they could engage in their speculative activities without fear, and even, in a way, with the connivance of the provincial authorities, local governors, commanders of the Civil Guard, and even the police, who were lax about repressing sales at abusive prices.

For the humbler classes, however, the black market was a means of survival that the governing authorities worked hard to stop and punish. The poor people's black market, as some authors have called it, consisted of people hiding part of their harvest or not delivering their entire quota, transporting products from one place to another, and not removing themselves from the ration book when they should. The common denominator of these widespread practices was, on the one hand, the small quantities involved— one sack of flour, one basket of potatoes, a few bottles of oil, goods that did often did not surpass a few kilograms—and, on the other hand, the short distances they traveled, usually by foot or train, by bicycle or donkey. These small-scale black-marketers, many from the defeated Republican side, were persecuted by the authorities, had their goods requisitioned by the Civil Guard, received hefty fines and, on some occasions, were jailed for 100 days for crimes related to the illicit trading of essential items.

Women played a principal role in this black market of survival. In Almería, for example, 70 percent of the black-marketeers prosecuted during the postwar era were women. They would sew hiding places for food into their clothing and in this way were able to pass through the checkpoints that had been established in train stations and at the entrances to cities. Many were widows or had husbands in jail; others were simply married women who needed to bring in some additional income for their family's subsistence. Let's not forget that the Francoist regime worked hard to prevent women from having their own livelihoods.

76. MAUTHAUSEN FLAG, 1943–45, PERPIGNAN

Verónica Sierra Blas

On May 5, 1945, when the 11th Armored Division of the United States Army arrived at Mauthausen to liberate the camp, they found an immense banner written in Spanish flanking the entrance from side to side: "The anti-fascist Spaniards salute the liberating forces." Above it waved a Republican flag made by the Spanish deportees of the Mauthausen Liberation Commando (KLM), a clandestine organization made up of prisoners of various nationalities founded in 1943. Woven with infinite patience out of the linings of uniforms stolen from the laundry and carefully hidden away in a barracks, this flag became a symbol of resistance for the *Spaniers* (Spaniards). Even all these years later, one can still read the *Komando* acronym (twice) as well as the names and numbers of some of the prisoners who made the flag inserted haphazardly between the capital letters that make up its central message: "SPANISH REPUBLIC."

Among the signatures is the one belonging to Francisco Ortiz Torres. Born in 1919 in Santisteban del Puerto, in Jaén, he was one of the last to leave Mauthausen. Like many other Spanish soldiers of the Republican Army who escaped to France in the winter of 1939, Francisco was interned at the Septfonds concentration camp, which he left in May of that year upon enlisting in the French Army's Marching Regiments of Foreign Volunteers. He was taken prisoner in May 1940 and sent to the Stalag XII D camp, close to Tréveris, on the border with Luxembourg. In April 1941, he was deported to Austria, where he was sent to Mauthausen, close to Linz. After being liberated by the US troops, he remained in France, first in Champigny, on the outskirts of Paris, and then in Perpignan, where he made his living as a carpenter.

Like Francisco, many of the Spaniards who were exploited, tortured and killed in the extermination camps were Republican soldiers who had fought in the French army or fought with the Resistance, and were taken prisoner by the German troops, the Gestapo, or the police of the collaborationist Vichy regime. According to Benito Bermejo and Sandra Checa, there were 9,328 Spaniards in Nazi camps. The database created by the Democratic Memorial of the Generalitat, the autonomous government of Catalonia,[1] reports the slightly smaller figure of 9,161.

Although there were Spaniards in Auschwitz, Bergen-Belsen, Buchenwald, Dachau, Flosenbürg, Gross-Rosen, Mittelbau-Dora, Natzweiler, Neuengamme, Ravensbrück (a women only camp), Sachsenhausen, Stutthof, and Treblinka, about three-quarters—7,532 people—were in Mauthausen-Gusen. Of these prisoners, 5,185 died, 4,816 of them between 1940 and 1945. (According to the books of the Central Civil Registry, discovered by Gutmaro Gómez Bravo in 2019, this figure is 4,427.) They were the victims of hypothermia and starvation, punishments and beatings, the gas chambers, medical experiments, "exemplary" shootings and hangings, and forced labor.

Few objects are able to capture the fighting spirit of the Republican deportees who fell victim to the Nazis so powerfully as the flag waving at Mauthausen in 1945. Francisco, along with another 3,539 of his compatriots, survived that horror, and for this reason he never stopped remembering those who did not. He carefully preserved the flag for the rest of his life, bringing it with him, as long as his heath permitted, to each and every one of the commemorations of the liberation of the Mauthausen camp that different associations, like the Amical de Mauthausen, organize every year. Since his death in 2013, his son and grandson have continued to do so in his name, giving them the opportunity to tell their father and grandfather's story, accompanied by his guitar, his cello and, of course, by the "Mauthausen flag."

---

[1]See https://memoria.gencat.cat/ca/que-fem/banc-memoria-democratica/fons/deportats-catalans-i-espanyols-als-camps-nazis

77. "CIDADE DA SELVA" ("FOREST CITY") GUERILLA CAMP, 1946, CARBALLEDA DE VALDEORRAS, OURENSE

Emilio Grandío Seoane

The quick success of the military coup in Galicia, León, and Asturias, left many people who did not know where to go to escape the repression and death desperate. With the Salazar dictatorship in Portugal to one side and the Galician and Asturian coasts under surveillance, there were few options for leaving this northeastern corner of the peninsula. As early as August 1936, hundreds of individuals went into hiding in people's homes and, when they could no longer resist harassment by the military forces, they escaped to the nearby hills. To take just one example, hundreds of people went to the hills near the city of A Coruña hoping for a quick resolution to the conflict.

The formation of an incipient guerrilla organization had its origins in this border area. Armed resistance groups, accompanied by people escaping persecution or simply the suffocation of living under a dictatorship, roamed the Galician hills waiting for an end to the war. To these groups, the outbreak of the Second World War in the autumn of 1939 represented the international continuation of the fight against fascism, and Spain became a key objective for the Allies given the risk of the dictatorship allying itself directly with the Axis.

With Churchill's assent to power in May 1940, Great Britain activated its espionage and sabotage networks on the peninsula. This brought Spanish resistance forces into contact with British military and technical groups, who provided them with military as well as political training and structure. The first to organize in this way was the León-Galicia Guerrilla Federation, in 1941. They updated their tactics and began the process of expanding the guerrilla organization throughout the entire peninsula. When the British lost interest, the communists took control of the organization.

The geographic nucleus of the Federation's activities was the Casaio Mountains in Ourense province. Located between the mountains of Ourense, Lugo, León, and Asturias, this was a strategic location. And here, in the isolated and rugged Serra do Eixe, is where the Cidade da Selva guerilla camp was established. The Cidade da Selva had a long life: from the first months of the Civil War until its discovery and definitive disappearance in July 1946. With a defense and surveillance structure composed of numerous huts throughout various camps, this area was extremely secure for years. Regardless, it is now known that the guerrilla fighters did not always remain in the hills. They would spend a good part of the fall and winter far removed from their regular routes, hidden in people's homes with someone permanently keeping watch outside, and they would leave only infrequently.

For the last few years, an archaeological project to recover this area's past has been underway. The current excavations in the region—wild and hard to access, practically impossible to find by air due to the thick vegetation that surrounds it—reveal the harsh, difficult, and miserable reality of life in the Cidade da Selva, a refuge zone that expresses very clearly the brutality of existence as a guerilla fighter. Hundreds of people—harassed, surveilled, permanently suspicious—waited with a thread of hope and a rifle in hand for more than ten years for the defeat of Franco's military dictatorship. With the fall of the Axis, the idea that the guerrilla fighters would arrive in the cities as heroes finally seemed like a possibility. By this point, however, the dictatorship had sufficiently toned down its fascist features to achieve gradual recognition from the Western powers. In addition to the regime's efforts to achieve diplomatic recognition, the nascent Cold War also provided a context to combat the communist guerrilla group located in their own hills.

Even in the early 1950s, some armed resistance groups still remained in Galicia. Divided and distrustful of everything and everyone, they faced constant denunciations. The Cidade da Selva was dismantled, and time passed over its remains, its past buried in the earth and in time.

78. GERMAN UNDERWATER MINES, 1947, CÁDIZ

Sofía Rodríguez López

Bombs from the Civil War kept on killing even after the conflict had ended. The terrible explosion that occurred in an old torpedo factory in Cádiz in 1947 was a tragedy little known for decades outside of the city and neighboring provinces, even though the detonation had been heard from Ceuta and Seville to Huelva and Portugal. The Francoist dictatorship always made sure to hide bad news, especially if it had to do with military negligence. Not only this, but it intentionally propagated the idea that the detonation was due to "anti-fascist sabotage," and there was no lack of informants about a supposed Jewish conspiracy in Bern, the no less fictitious purchase of some delay mechanisms in Milan, a mysterious oil tanker that anchored in the waters of the bay the very night of the accident, and the ruthless actions of the Russian agent Larissa, who was linked to the Red Aid organization in the Campo de Gibraltar. Current research assures that the explosion was caused by the spontaneous decomposition of the guncotton that was present in fifty German WBD depth charges, whose use had been prohibited since the First World War.

In 2001, the journalist Antonio Burgos chronicled this event in *El Mundo,* making reference to "some Russian mines that had been taken from the Reds during the war that were being stored" in the city. These "Russian mines" had come from the arsenal requisitioned from the Popular Army on the Northern Front, which were then transferred to several munitions storage areas throughout the peninsula in 1938. They arrived in Cádiz from Cartagena between 1942 and 1943, coinciding with the deployment of Operation Torch—the Allied landing in North Africa. The warehouse affected by the explosion housed 1,737 underwater mines, depth charges, and torpedo heads, with a total volume of 200 metric tonnes of TNT and ammonium nitrate. Only 491 remained intact after the explosion.

The Francoists had accumulated these munitions out of fear of an Allied landing on their coasts during the Second World War. They created a defensive plan for the coast from Huelva to Almería where 16,000 mines were to be placed in territorial waters. Cádiz, where the Maritime Department's General Headquarters was located, ended up with only 15 percent of the planned amount. The project was abandoned after the invasion of Italy in the summer of 1943, but due to the lack of an appropriately large and secure storage facility, the bombs ended up stored in two warehouses belonging the Navy's Submarine Defenses Base. The director of the Carraca Naval Station had detected deterioration in the weapons when they arrived, but this was kept out of the official report. This was meant to be a temporary solution, until the bombs could be transferred to the mine shafts that had been acquired by the army in the San Cristóbal mountains, near Jerez de la Frontera. But time passed, while 100,000 unsuspecting residents of Cádiz lived quite literally next to a powder keg.

The night of August 18, 1947 was hot. A dance was scheduled at the Playa Hotel, as well as an Antonio Machín concert at the Los Rosales ranch. But at 9:45 p.m. the sky turned into an immense red mushroom. The epicenter of the explosion was in the San Severiano neighborhood, home to summer tourists, working-class houses, and the Hogar del Niño Jesús, where twenty-six minors, four nuns, and eleven assistants perished. The Radio Falange building became an improvised aid station, receiving trucks filled with the injured and naked children from the Casa Cuna orphanage. For his part, General Varela, the former rebel general and local strongman, rode his convertible through the streets yelling out: "Courage, people of Cádiz! Don't give up! Together we will come out of this miserable disaster!"

The accident left 148 dead and more than 5,000 injured and, despite the protection offered by the Puerta Tierra walls, the historic city center was so badly affected that it became a priority zone for the Regional Directorate of Devastated Areas.

The authorities abandoned any attempt at an exhaustive identification of the victims and processes initiated by military and civilian authorities produced no charges. The following year, in an attempt to raise the spirits of the population, governor Rodríguez de Valcárcel authorized the celebration of Carnival, something the Franco regime had prohibited.

79. BOXES OF REMAINS IN A CRYPT AT THE VALLEY OF THE FALLEN, APRIL 1959, CUELGAMUROS, MADRID

Jesús Espinosa Romero

Spain's relationship to its mass graves from the Civil War is complex and enduring. It began with the Republican government in the middle of the war. In May 1937, Prime Minister Negrín ordered that clandestine cemeteries must be located and their perpetrators prosecuted. This was an attempt to restore state authority in the face of the furious parastate violence that had taken place in the preceding months, especially in 1936. Although the political situation in Republican Spain led the search to end after only five months, by November 1937 the bodies of more than 2,000 opponents of the Republican government had been found—an estimated 3.6 percent of Republican violence—and 128 people were punished for the extrajudicial killings.

As the rebels came to hold more territory, they searched the enemy's rearguard for their coreligionists who had been killed or executed. After the end of the war they redoubled their efforts, not only to strengthen Franco's image of justice but also to unite the victors even more closely through the public recognition of their fallen, especially civilians, who were classified as martyrs of the New State. The victims were seen as having a privileged relationship with God, and the dictatorship promoted itself as the link between them by administering their remains and their memory. These dead—and only these—became an important instrument in the politics of victory. Suffice it to say that the New State did not search for the cadavers buried in graves across its own rearguard and unburdened itself of the bodies of its opponents in improvised burials in cemeteries, jails, and camps. These bodies were never returned to their families.

Cemeteries and villages became populated with mausoleums for the martyrs and crosses symbolizing the blood of the soldiers and civilians spilled for the construction of the new political community in Spain. This was the mental paradigm in 1940 when Franco ordered the construction of the basilica of the Valley of the Fallen, a sacred space built by the "keeper of memory." Meanwhile, the complex was constructed by Republican prisoners who in this way atoned for their supposed guilt.

With the inauguration of the Valley of the Fallen imminent, the mortuary policy of the dictatorship was reactivated. In October 1958, the Interior Ministry was charged with getting all municipal governments to contribute their quota of remains, in theory with the permission of their families. On April 1, 1959, Franco presided over the grand inauguration of what has come to be called "the stoney expression of National-Catholicism." The immense, granite, reliquary took in the first 9,000 remains which were transferred in boxes locked with a key, as shown in the photograph above.

According to the Valley's Book of Burials, it houses more than 33,000 cadavers. (In reality the total is not clear, as the identification of the bodies was hasty and inaccurate.) The final remains arrived in 1983. Remains found in Republican graves were also moved there, but these do not share space with either the fallen Nationalists or the martyrs. The regime was also not interested in identifying its enemies, much less asking their families for permission to move the remains. The fallen and the sacrificed were placed to Christ's right-hand side—the side of the Gospel—while the others were placed in the nave of the Epistle, where the Christian message, faith, and conduct are taught. They may have been pardoned from a religious perspective, but not from a legal one. Another ten years would have to pass before Franco decided, in 1969, to pardon the enemies he had defeated three decades earlier.

After Franco's death, some family members of the Republicans lying in mass graves were able to start recovering their remains. However, it was not until the year 2000 that a powerful social movement emerged whose objectives include finding, identifying and dignifying the human remains that had been looked down on by the Francoist regime and ignored by democratic Spain in the name of peaceful coexistence. Twenty years later, the various associations devoted to maintaining the memory of the victims of Francoism have recovered some 10,000 cadavers, or 7 to 8 percent of the estimated total produced by the "White Terror" during the war and the following years. Many of the cadavers remain in the Valley of the Fallen despite the wishes of the families. Meanwhile, from November 1975 until its exhumation in October 2019, Franco's body lay in a central tomb in front of the altar of the basilica, surrounded by his alleged supporters, and their victims.

80. *ON THE EMPTY BALCONY (EN EL BALCÓN VACÍO)* BY JOMÍ GARCÍA ASCOT, 1962

Vicente J. Benet

On the Empty Balcony is the most important movie about the Spanish exile of 1939. Some of those who left Spain became quite successful in the film industries of the Latin American countries that took them in, and their status as exiles left its mark in movies such as *La barraca* (Roberto Gavaldón, Mexico, 1945) and *La dama duende* (Luis Saslavsky, Argentina 1945). But only in *On the Empty Balcony* is the traumatic experience of expatriation at the film's heart.

Filmed in Mexico, the movie is a reflection on memory, uprootedness, awareness of a truncated life and nostalgia for a lost country. Filmed in 16mm on a tiny budget, it was made during the team's free time over the course of forty Sundays between 1961 and 1962 and was produced thanks to the enthusiastic collaboration of some of the filmmakers' friends. José

Miguel (Jomí) García Ascot directed the film and María Luisa Elío, was the lead actress and also wrote the text that accompanies the images. The two were a couple and connected to the intellectual circles not only of exiled Spaniards but also of some of the great Latin American literary authors, like Alejo Carpentier, Álvaro Mutis, and Gabriel García Márquez, who dedicated no less than *One Hundred Years of Solitude* to them. Moreover, García Ascot had participated in some of the first projects of Cuban cinema following the revolution, and was in contact with many of the filmmakers who had gone to the island at the end of the 1950s and beginning of the 1960s. One of these was Joris Ivens, the Dutch documentary maker who directed *The Spanish Earth*, who supplied García Ascot with documentary images of the Civil War that he ended up using in the film. It had a limited circulation, although it won a prize at the 1962 Locarno Festival.

When the war broke out, García Ascot and Elío were children who had to hastily leave their homes. The trauma caused by this uprooting and the period of their childhood that they definitively lost are the central themes of the film, which has a marked autobiographical tone. It is divided into two distinct parts. The first is anchored on the experiences and gaze of a young girl, Gabriela Elizondo (played by Nuri Pereña), who confronts a series of situations too complex for her young mind to understand but that are quite clear to the viewer. In Pamplona, following the victory of military coup, she observes the attempted escape of a fugitive who is finally captured by the Civil Guard after being informed on by a neighbor; hears rumors about the disappearance of the father, which a friend tells her family; watches a "Red" prisoner being humiliated by children and learns the next day that he has been shot; and goes mute during a disturbing interrogation by a policeman who interrupts her while playing in a park. She also endures having to hastily leave her home, escaping through the mountains and returning to the Republican zone, the Republican defeat and escaping again to France, and finally, arriving in Mexico. The scenes follow one after the other like paintings with a predominant static quality and a density corresponding to her need to focus her memories and consolidate them into concrete pieces. Objects in the film take on a symbolic value which is revealed very precisely in her memory: a glass stopper that she takes as the only souvenir of her childhood, clocks, and her dolls which she lovingly dresses from her bed after just having left her home forever. The movement of the camera also subtly exploits the complexity of the spaces and the density of the unfailing passage of time.

The second part of the film takes place twenty years later when Gabriela (now played by María Luisa Elío herself) reveals her anguished feelings of uprootedness in Mexico and finally returns to visit her old home. She finds the walls bare, the bedrooms empty—spaces crossed by rays of light and dense shadows. Occasionally it seems as if a memory or a return to the experiences of childhood may, precariously, emerge. But this, the film shows, is impossible. The entire segment makes use of a voice-over to express the character's inner thoughts, revealing the pain of being unable to recover one's childhood, the trauma of not remembering, the impossibility of reliving what has been irredeemably lost. And this is where the evocative strength and unforgettable melancholy of the experience of exile captured by the film emerges with greatest force.

81. *TO DIE IN MADRID (MOURIR À MADRID)* BY FRÉDÉRIC ROSSIF, 1963

Vicente J. Benet

At the beginning of the 1960s, the Francoist regime succeeded in normalizing its relations with other countries and began opening the doors of the country to mass tourism. Spanish society found itself on a path of profound economic and social transformation. For its part, the devastated landscape of Europe following the Second World War remained hidden behind the comfortable views of economic growth, the consumer economy and the welfare state built by these countries that had been ferociously fighting with one another only one generation prior. The tragedies of the past were beginning to fade: the celebration of young cultural pop icons and mass entertainment media were a clarion call for hedonistic enjoyment of the present, in which memory was practically mute.

The considerable impact made by Rossif's 1963 documentary was perhaps related in part to Alain Resnais' *Night and Fog (Nuit et Brouillard)*—a film about the Nazi concentration camps—from seven years earlier. Putting the latent pain of these increasingly ignored images into the public forum produced a shock. In the case of the more limited memory of the Civil War, *To Die in Madrid* brought to the fore an uncomfortable issue that, in the context of reconstruction and the Cold War, the government of Spain, as well as international organizations, preferred to ignore: the Francoist regime's violent origins and its undeniable connections with European fascism of the 1930s. As Nancy Berthier points out, the film put the memory of the Spanish exiles into the public space: their myths reflected in heroic battles, their victims, their most charismatic personalities and, especially, the daring of the International Brigades, who came *to die in Madrid* (as referenced in the film's title). And this occurred, moreover, at a moment when, alongside the stability produced by the country's economic growth, the regime demonstrated its most repressive side, with the execution of Julián Grimau for what the dictatorship claimed were crimes committed during the Civil War, and the persecution and disparagement of the democratic opposition forces that had met in Munich in June 1962.

In principle, Rossif had received permission from the Francoist authorities to shoot in Spain and to access material from the archives because he had told them his intention was to make a film about the "eternal Spain." There are remnants of this original idea in the film, with the presence of some clichéd romantic images of the country: shots of timeless peasants with cracked faces accompanied by their backlit carts and beasts of burden, in the shadows of the naked landscape of the Castilian plateau. However, these images serve only as occasional framing for the film's primary visual component: a compilation of archival footage obtained both from Spain as well as from international newscasts.

Rossif's use of this material follows the cannon of propaganda films in its use of editing, that is, the selection and combination of images. Thus, the viewer confronts an amalgam of images from difference sources (including some from fictional movies and staged scenes), almost always decontextualized and only distantly related to the events being discussed. Their meaning is fixed with the help of a narrator or descriptive voice, as well as the use of an expressive musical score, this one by Maurice Jarre. These techniques serve to construct the events and direct the meaning of the story. In Rossif's film, sympathy for the Republican cause is evident, and it very specifically highlights the significance of Nazi Germany and Fascist Italy to the Francoists ultimate victory. It alludes, moreover, to the conflict's principal battles and symbolic places: Madrid's University City, the Alcázar of Toledo, the Northern Front, Gernika, Brunete, Belchite, Teruel, and the Battle of the Ebro, as well as some of its more emblematic figures who had international reach: poet Federico García Lorca, philosopher Miguel de Unamuno, Communist leader Dolores Ibárruri, "La Pasionaria," and French writers André Malraux and Georges Bernanos.

The movie was a considerable success. It was nominated for an Academy Award and won France's Jean Vigo prize as well as one from BAFTA in the United Kingdom. The Francoist regime's attempt to have the film censored in France was in vain; it resorted instead to the strategy of responding to Rossif's film with its own battery of movies, like *Morir en España* (Mariano Ozores, 1965), *¿Por qué morir en Madrid?* (Eduardo Manzanos, 1966) and *Franco, ese hombre* (José Luis Sáenz de Heredia, 1964) (see Chapter 82). These films tried to reassert the Francoist memory of the war by making use of two essential discursive elements in the new context: the victory in the fight against communism and the economic development that had come to Spanish society since the end of the war. These would form part of the fundamental argument of XXV Years of Peace, the regime's greatest propagandistic campaign, launched the year after Rossif's film.

82. *THAT MAN FRANCO (FRANCO, ESE HOMBRE)* BY JOSÉ LUIS SÁENZ DE HEREDIA, 1964

Vicente J. Benet

The XXV Years of Peace campaign planned by Minister of Information and Tourism Manuel Fraga sought to offer a modernized image of the Francoist regime as much to the external world as to the new generations of Spaniards who had not experienced the Civil War. This new image was based on an updating of concepts, where the term "victory," which had legitimized the Francoist state since 1939, became tied to the more conciliatory and ambiguous word "peace." Much had happened over the previous twenty-five years. The implicit acceptance of the regime in the international sphere, the signing of bilateral agreements with the United States, the beginnings of economic development and the invasion of mass tourism were all significantly changing habits and customs of Spaniards. The dictatorship, meanwhile, could barely hide its anachronistic character; surviving as a Fascist-inspired authoritarian state amongst countries that had managed to establish stable democracies after the turbulence of the Second World War.

The campaign thus tried to renew the state's image, impregnating all spaces of daily life, from postage stamps to television. In addition to the *No-Do* newsreels, the campaign's main cinematic output was the film *That*

Man Franco by José Luis Sáenz de Heredia, who had previously directed the film *Raza* (1940) that was based on a screenplay by Franco himself. Beginning with its title, the film identifies Franco's leadership at the pillar supporting this beneficent state of peace. As the *No-Do* series had also done over those years, the film's opening credits present a series of photographs of Franco reflecting his more human side. He is shown as a loving grandfather with his grandchildren, as a fisherman, painter, and amateur filmmaker, playing cards—a kindhearted image associating him with the idea of peace sought by the campaign. These images form a bookend with the film's finale, which features a short interview of Franco by the obedient director where he offers some trivial observations on the qualities of the Spanish people. In any case, the dictator's image again stands out: dressed in civilian clothing, at home and relatively approachable, after having watched the film of which he is the star.

Between these bookends, the film makes use of the annual military parade commemorating the end of the war as its narrative spine, and as a metaphor for the Francoist regime itself. The parade from the year the film was made is said to be different in meaning from previous ones. According to the text written by Sáenz de Heredia and José María Sánchez Silva, the 1964 parade "Speaks of peace and of victory, but a different type of victory, more difficult than one brought about by arms. A total victory, in which there is no pain on the part of the defeated, in which there is room for everybody's joy. This is the victory of peace."

Woven throughout images of the parade is the story of Franco's trajectory, covering all of the commonplaces of the myth that surrounded him. Using archival images supported by a totally hagiographic text, the film shows his rapid climb through the ranks due to heroism and divine providence, his capacity for sacrifice and leadership during his time in Africa, and his talents as an organizer in the consolidation of the Legion and the founding of the General Military Academy. The abundant material provides a detailed tour of his career. But just after describing the chaos generated by the Second Republic and the justification for the July 18 military coup, the film takes an unexpected turn that reveals its true propagandistic intentions. The director himself appears, surrounded by film canisters that he claims contain documentary images of the war but that he will not show. His justification for this unexpected ellipsis is contradictory, since it combines the ideas of shared pain and the extirpation of an evil. On the one hand he states that: "In Spain there was a war inserted between two irrefutable realities: the chaos of 1936 and the happy reality of 1964. To reach this shore of a better Spain 1 million Spaniards, on both sides, gave their lives." He later adds that the war was an "inevitable surgery." Then, instead of showing a cascade of archival footage, there is an interview in which journalist and diplomat Manuel Aznar summarizes the war. The meeting takes place at another setting fundamental to the propaganda aims of the campaign: the Spanish Pavilion at the 1964 New York World's Fair, which is shown in detail.

After Franco's death, Sáenz de Heredia tried to make a final film about the dictator entitled "The Final Fallen One" ("El último caído"). He never finished it.

83. MARÍA MOLINER'S DICTIONARY, 1966, MADRID

Miren Llona

The Civil War created a human wave of exiles who sought refuge in places as different as France, Mexico, Great Britain, Cuba, and Argentina. However, a significant portion of the Republican population was condemned to spend decades experimenting with an "internal exile," a kind of estrangement experienced from within Spain itself. The dictionary that María Moliner created during the Francoist dictatorship is the fruit of precisely this type of exile, which, in the words of the journalist Inmaculada de la Fuente, helped the author to "resist elegantly, in silence, while creating." Moliner recounted how, after harsh years of sanctions, being purged from jobs, and ostracism, "one fine day I took my pen and a notebook and began to outline a plan for a dictionary."

But before Moliner found refuge in words books had been her great passion and being a librarian her vocation. In 1922, she passed the civil service exams for archivists and librarians and began a career in which her contributions to create easily accessible books for the public culminated, during the Second Republic, in the Pedagogical Missions Trust (1931). Through this project, which sought to bring culture to Spain's villages,

Moliner organized a network of rural libraries in Valencia, which she personally inspected and for which, in 1937, she published *Instructions for the Service of Small Libraries*, a small manual to help those who were not professional librarians. During the Civil War she was also in charge of running the University of Valencia Library and the Office of Acquisitions and International Publications Exchange. As a result of her experience, in 1939 Moliner published the first *Plan for the General Organization of State Libraries*, a project whose final objective was, as she put it, to make it possible for "any reader anywhere to obtain any book that interests them." In 1939, Moliner watched as Nationalist troops entered Valencia.

The plan prepared by Moliner was abandoned during the Francoist period. Given her involvement in the Republican regime she was punished and prohibited from holding positions of authority or trust. In 1946, she was transferred to the library of Madrid's Engineering School, where she remained until her retirement in 1970. From her internal exile, Moliner devoted herself to organizing words instead of books, a task that she undertook alone, at home, as a means of escape that had no limits. The initial objective was to define words anew, "bringing to bear all of the resources offered by the language," by grouping together entire families of terms that share the same root: love, to love, love someone, love affair, loving ... This project turned into *The Dictionary of Spanish Usage,* the lexicographical value of which was highlighted by Gabriel García Márquez in 1981 when he called it "the most complete, useful, diligent and entertaining dictionary of the Castilian language." The *María Moliner*, as it has commonly been called since the publication of its first volume in 1966, is a masterpiece, of which its author said:

> Finally, here is a confession: the author feels the need to declare that she has worked honorably; that to her knowledge she has not been careless about anything; that, even to the nit-picky details which, to no detriment whatsoever, could have been cut short for sanity's sake, she devoted time and effort to resolving the difficulties they presented disproportionate to their value, out of obedience to the irresistible imperative of scrupulousness; and that, finally, this work, which, due to its ambition and given its novelty and complexity, is denied perfection, approximates it as much as the author's efforts have permitted.

Nevertheless, the dictionary remained the homemade work of a woman, librarian, and mother of four, not connected to the state-sanctioned authority, the Royal Academy of the Spanish Language, many of whose scholars were unaware of its existence. The philologist Rafael Lapesa tried to break this misogynistic tradition by getting support for Moliner to be admitted to the Academy. In her column in the newspaper *Ya*, Josefina Carabias claimed that "If Mrs. María Moliner had been a man, she would have been in the

Academy for a long time already." But, like Gertrudis Gómez de Avellaneda in 1853 and Emilia Pardo Bazán in 1912, Moliner was denied admittance in 1972. In a letter to Lapesa regarding his support for Moliner, Camilo José Cela, one-time Francoist censor and future winner of the Nobel Prize for Literature, informed him that he would not under any condition vote for her "given that I don't share her spineless [feminine?] criteria of lexicography."

84. DEBOD TEMPLE GARDENS, 1972, MADRID

Jesús Espinosa Romero

The Debod Temple is one of Madrid's main tourist attractions. In 2019, before the COVID-19 pandemic, nearly 240,000 people visited it. Many of these visitors ascend a short staircase to get a glimpse of ancient Egypt and to admire the views of the Casa de Campo Park, but they what they do not know is that they are walking on the grounds of one of the Spanish capital's primary sites of historical memory. There is no explanatory sign, but the base of the staircase features a sculptural ensemble made of bronze composed of a prostrate and mutilated human figure located in the center of a wall make to look as if it has been built out of sandbags. There is a similar lack of explanation about the terrain on which it is located: that of the Montaña Barracks, nerve center for the coup d'état in the capital.

The rebels' plans to take Madrid were quite flimsy. They had been ordered to conceal their moves, coordinate with the troops quartered in Carabanchel and wait for reinforcements. At noon on Sunday, July 19, the Reservist general and right-wing deputy Joaquín Fanjul—who was to direct the operations—as well as officers from other barracks, Falangists and monarchists arrived at the barracks. After Fanjul gave a short speech, the rebels prepared to deploy throughout the city when they ran into a crowd of armed civilians who were attempting to seize the light arms stored in the barracks, but they were stopped by machine gun fire. The crowd withdrew to the Plaza de España.

By the early morning of July 20, the coup in Madrid had failed. The Montaña Barracks remained under siege. After a shell fell in the patio, some white flags appeared in the windows. Believing the rebels in the barracks were surrendering, the crowd began to approach but were met by more machine gun fire. Accounts from the time as well as the photographs taken by Alfonso Sánchez Portela are testimony to that day's gruesome orgy of blood, between those killed by the rebels and those who died due to the actions of the vengeful crowd.

Due to its location on the frontlines of the Battle of Madrid, the Montaña Barracks fell into a state of near complete ruin by the end of the war. One month after Franco's Army entered the capital, the Junta for the Restoration of Madrid was formed. It approved a Plan for Urban Renewal drafted by Pedro Bidagor, one of the most important representatives of Falangist urban planning. Initiated in 1941, the Bidagor Plan proposed the construction of a megalomaniacal building to house the central headquarters of the FET-JONS on the site where the demolished barracks stood, thus cementing over the ground watered with the blood of those who had "fallen for God and for Spain" as the slogan of the new regime put it. With the addition of this new building, the three principals of the New State would be seen represented from the banks of the Manzanares River: religion, represented by the Almudena Cathedral; the state, represented by the royal palace; and hierarchy, represented by the new Falange headquarters.

The Bidagor Plan was finally approved in 1946 but never executed in its entirety, and some of its most significant projects, like the Falange headquarters, were abandoned despite having had Franco's initial approval. The future palace of the Falange remained as the demolished barracks that it was—an intact memorial site on which to venerate the "fallen" of July 20.

This space that had been reserved for glorifying the dead was later threatened by development, as plans to build new housing called for its complete destruction. The National Movement's own press protested this profanation of its sacred ground, and the Francoist state respond by stopping the project and creating the urban landscape that we see today. The space meant for the Falange headquarters was repurposed by the Mayor of Madrid, Carlos Arias Navarro, as a place for leisure. On July 18, 1972, Juan Carlos de Borbón, the prince of Spain and Franco's designated successor, inaugurated the new urban complex and its sober, modern, and symbolic monument.

85. DIARY OF A MOLE, 1976, SANTIAGO DE COMPOSTELA

Emilio Grandío Seoane

Life changed from one day to the next. The strange and the singular became quotidian. They had never imagined that they would spend their lives locked up inside their homes, their futures paralyzed, all of their prospects cut short. Living day after day in a present that extended no further than a new and routine morning. Watching those close to them die, their friendships and relationships disappear in an ever narrowing circle. And further, the passage of time only increasing the level of surprise caused by someone previously "disappeared" returning to the village.

Although certain recent films have taken up the subject of the moles, one of the greatest sources is Jesús Torbado and Manu Leguineche's book *The Moles (Los Topos)*, published in 1977, during the early phases of the transition to democracy. The book connects the changing world of the mid 1970s to the experiences of those who suffered forced captivity and are stuck forever in the past. The protagonist of this chapter, Gonzalo, does not feature in that book as he died before he could be interviewed, but he very well could have. Surreal situations; reality that seems more like fiction. This is the story of a mole who hid for years just a few hundred meters from Franco's summer home, the Pazo de Meirás.

Gonzalo and Manuel Antonio Becerra Souto were two brothers from the municipality of As Nogais, in Lugo. Gonzalo, the elder of the two, was an anarchist who worked driving mining trucks between Fabero and Ponferrada, where he came into contact with the local unions. After the military revolt, news spread that the rebels were going to impose mandatory conscription. The brothers decided to hide, first near their house, then in other people's homes. Finally, they returned to their own house. As was the case for many others as well, their house and family members were under constant surveillance. The authorities even detained their father while they searched for the brothers. But he didn't speak, and they were saved.

The two brothers spent twenty-two years together in hiding. Desperate, Manuel Antonio succeeded in obtaining a false identity and in 1958 left for Madrid. But not Gonzalo. He remained in his family home, hidden in an excavated enclosure of 2 square meters, which he would leave at night to take walks. All the while, he kept a diary that ran from July 1936 until Franco's death in November 1975. He did not trust the pardon of 1969, whereby the regime absolved its opponents the way it had given amnesty to its own people in 1939. Only when Franco dies does Gonzalo decide to leave his hideout. But his life as a free man is very short: he dies just a few months later, on February 12, 1976.

Gonzalo spent forty of his seventy-six years in hiding. Writing his diary—proof of his imprisonment—was as much a type of therapy as a demonstration of a fighting spirit, and an attempt to preserve the memory of his life. The pages of the diary were kept between the hard sheets of missals provided by the parish church, which protected them from the harsh climate. Behind all of this written work is the natural impulse to survive his "living death."

This sad story does not end here. More than thirty years after Gonzalo's death, the research group Names and Voices (Nomes e Voces), dedicated to the study of Francoist repression in Galicia, was notified about a series of papers from those years that had been found in potato sacks, and whose importance had been unknown. This is fairly common: whether due to ignorance or lack of guidance about the need to preserve this heritage, such documents are often thrown out by family members. Happily, this specific material was recovered. But we must ask ourselves how many thoughts, how many feelings, and how much testimony to other lives have been lost.

Democracy

86. *THE OLD MEMORY* (*LA VIEJA MEMORIA*) BY JAIME CAMINO, 1977

Vicente J. Benet

...work for three or four days

Jaime Camino's film *The Old Memory* (1977) is one of the most significant cinematographic documents for understanding how the memory of the Civil War was dealt with during the turbulent years of the transition to democracy. Its very title already suggests ambiguity regarding the value that can be given to individual testimony when it comes to understanding the events of the past. The film consists primarily of interviews with political and military leaders from both sides of the conflict, which appear intertwined and without continuity, framed only by titles defining the themes to be discussed. Some of the interviewees were still in exile when the film was made and had not returned to Spain since the end of the war. In addition to these witnesses, the film makes use of a range of archival material, photographs, and clips from films and the press.

Most of the interviewees had been high profile figures during the war or the Francoist period, and some of them had returned to take up political roles during the Transition. Such was the case for Dolores Ibárruri ("La Pasionaria"), who was elected as a member of parliament in the first elections of 1977, and Josep Tarradellas, president of the newly restored government of Cataluña, the Generalitat. Others, like Enrique Líster, Raimundo Fernández Cuesta, and José María Gil-Robles, had disappeared almost entirely from the political scene.

The witnesses narrate and interpret the most significant events after the creation of the Second Republic. The film focuses particularly on the events of the middle of July 1936: the military conspiracy; the reaction to the outbreak of the conflict; the fight to defeat the rebels, especially in Barcelona; and the uncertainty of the first days of the war. The final images are dedicated to the defeat and exile. The most notable aspect of the film is the way in which Camino directs and molds the voices of the witnesses. He does away with the usual presence of the interviewer or voice-over and instead works with their testimony directly so that they talk among themselves, either complementing or contradicting each other, despite the fact that the subjects are in reality separated from each other in both time and place. Given the variety of points of view, the reconstruction of the events that comes out of this dialogue is complex, at times indeterminate, heterogeneous, and divergent. Through this process of stitching the different voices together, the film articulates a sequence of events that leaves room for viewers to judge, to compare, and to arrive at their own conclusions about that they are being told.

To a certain extent, this strategy reveals caution in the face of eye-witness testimony, which could otherwise prove too powerful and captivating. In other words, this editing strategy is intended to distance the viewer from the witnesses' words so that they may judge for themselves. Camino also makes use of musical commentary, through a wonderful score by Xavier Montsalvatge, which by turns distorts, highlights, or introduces irony over what is being said in the moment. One example is the terrifying testimony provided by José Luis de Vilallonga, who, at his father's express request to the colonel of his Requeté regiment, was made part of a firing squad when he was barely sixteen years old. There is no doubt that his testimony tries to express the horror and brutality of the situation. Nevertheless, this refined and seductive man, with a notable capacity for relating events lightly, provides a narrative that comes to seem almost too carefree. At this point Camino's editing intervenes to punctuate the testimony with real images of the executions and the pain of the victims, which Montsalvatge's score emphasizes further.

In sum, the reflective distance introduced by the film helps to separate the viewer from the hypnotic warmth of literal memory provided by each witness and gives them instead a bird's-eye-view from which to judge the fault lines and different perspectives offered on the same events, as well as the weaknesses and inexactitudes of memory. By highlighting these contradictions, the clash of different memories, these impossible dialogues, and exploring the cracks between them without offering any reconciliation, Camino tries to go beyond mere empathy and rejection, to make the memory of this past an exemplary one.

87. STATUE OF FRANCO, 1978, MELILLA

Antonio Cazorla-Sánchez

"From Melilla, to the commander of the Legion, Francisco Franco Bahamonde, 1921–1977." This statue—erected in 1978, made of bronze and stone—and its accompanying inscription not only tell a lie, they also contribute to the enormous hole in knowledge regarding the terror, that is never discussed yet which is often thought to be known. This gap extends beyond Melilla and summarizes the relationship between Spanish society and its violent past beginning in 1936. For this reason, this chapter could easily fit into any part of this book.

The lie is, perhaps, the least important part. The statue was erected following a resolution of the municipal government on December 4, 1975, two weeks after Franco's death, as an homage to "our glorious Caudillo Generalísimo Franco." In reality, Franco did not save Melilla from the July 1921 attack by Abd el-Krim's troops following their frightful defeat of the Spanish Army at Annual. Franco was part of the force that came to the city's aid, but he was not in charge of anything: he was simply an officer, the second in command of the Legion. Military figures much more celebrated than he, such as General Sanjurjo and his then-superior, lieutenant colonel Millán Astray, were present. Franco was made into the savior of Melilla, of Spain and of the world by his press office which, already in 1936, in the middle of the Civil War, was inventing his messianic past which it would later expand and revise according to the budding dictator's needs. Just like this lie, the statue in Melilla—the last one of the dictator displayed in public before its removal in 2021—perpetuated a sugarcoated and manipulated version of Franco's memory as it defied the 2007 law prohibiting the display of rebel symbols.

But worse than this is what the statue and all of the city's public history do *not* tell; what they hide. The regime used to refer to Melilla as "The Advanced" (*La Adelantada*) because this is where, in the early afternoon of July 17, 1936, the military rebellion began. It is also where the first defenders of the legal regime—soldiers loyal to the Republic and badly armed and defenseless civilians—were murdered, where the first hit squads operated, and where the New Spain opened its first jails and first concentration camp. Anyone who has not made the effort to read a history book, including the majority of the local population, will know nothing about this horrible reality, and there is a simple reason: while there is room in Melilla for a statue that tells lies, there is none for explaining the horror that Franco and his minions unleashed in those very streets.

To win in Melilla, the rebels had to use unbridled terror. They were a numerical minority. In this city of fewer than 65,000 people, the Popular Front had won more than 72 percent of the votes in the February 1936 elections. The Republicans controlled the local institutions. They had to be killed. The city's commanding general, Manuel Romerales, was also loyal to the Republic, and thought the same of his "sons"—as he called the officers whom he had taught in the academy. They killed him, just as they killed many other commanders, officers, non-commissioned officers, and troops who remained loyal. And then there were the civilians. At least 316 were killed. There is no statue remembering them, nor the many people killed at the Rostrogordo fort or the Victoria Grande fort which served as a women's prison (a restoration in 2016 erased the final traces of this sad history). The bodies of dozens of people "taken for a walk" by Falangists and rebel soldiers—who were given carte blanche for their misdeeds by Colonel Luis Solans—appeared along the Alfonso XIII highway. Yet there is no plaque to indicate this. Neither is there one in the Batería Jota Civil Guard Barracks, where prisoners were horribly tortured; nor on the walls of the cemetery, from which many more watched their final sunrise. There is no signage outside of the city to direct a visitor to the Zeluán concentration camp, where thousands of prisoners languished and died of abuse, hunger, and suicide.

There are barely any Jews left in Melilla. Who among them or their neighbors can recall the supposedly *voluntary* donations of money and jewels to the Glorious National Army, the antisemitic screeds on the radio, the theft of their property, their murder and exclusion from public office? The Francoists always said that they left the Jews alone. In Melilla, at least, this was just another lie.

As is true of millions of other Spaniards, the people of Melilla want to learn about their history and honor their victims—if they are allowed to. In February 2004, when Carlota Leret visited the city to present the book *A Woman in the Spanish War* written by her mother, Carlota O'Neill, the citizens of Melilla crammed into the exposition hall to hear and honor the daughter of Captain Virgilio Leret—the pride of Spanish aviation who was executed by his colleagues for defending the Atalayón hydroplane base—and his wife, who spent four years locked in the Victoria Grande jail.

Melilla was the birthplace of the war, and with it the horror, the lying, and the forgetting that continues to plague Spanish society today. The most unsuspecting places and objects are full of history that should be known.

88. THREE MONUMENTS AT PUNTA HERMINIA, 1994, A CORUÑA

Emilio Grandío Seoane

There cannot be many places in Spain with three monuments within little more than half a kilometer of each other honoring the victims of Francoism. But this does occur in one place, Punta Herminia, in the city of A Coruña. This location is a short distance from the provincial prison, which housed one of the greatest concentration of prisoners in Galicia. Its relationship to the three monuments is clear: the ample outdoor space was the site of shootings, both as sentences following military tribunals, as well as extrajudicial ones. Beginning in the summer of 1936, "walks" and "reverse justice" were tragically unified every morning in the sound of gunfire that reached all the way to the city's urban center.

The first place this sound of death would reach was the Monte Alto neighborhood, the heart of the local labor movement, where many dozens of people were in hiding. The victims would walk there in the middle of the night, accompanied by the roar of the ocean battering the rocks near the Tower of Hercules lighthouse. At dawn, illuminated by the headlights of trucks, came the constant routine of executions. The taste of salt and blood. Multiple and continuous explosions coming from what was during the 1930s considered the outskirts of the city, away from the more luminous part the port that was the center of city life.

The first of the monuments is called *Menhirs* (Standing Stones) *for Peace*, created by the Galician sculptor Manolo Paz in 1994. The Celtic reference in the area surrounding the Tower of Hercules—declared a World Heritage Site by UNESCO in 2009—is clear, almost inescapable. The menhirs can be seen to represent the idea of souls departing the earth. Placing them next to the Tower of Hercules—the world's oldest functioning Roman lighthouse—adds a dramatic allusion to the events that occurred there after the military coup of July 1936.

This idea was later reinforced by the addition of another monument that more explicitly honors the victims of Francoist repression: a cromlech (a circle made of stones) called the *Monument to the Murdered of the Civil War* created by Isaac Díaz Pardo. While the Celtic reference is again clear, this monument is much more directly about the victims. Its inauguration on April 15, 2001, brought together a large group of people around the idea of recovering the Republican message that had been destroyed there. Díaz Pardo himself, who lived for years in Argentina, was by then a symbol of what Galicia could have been but for the disappearance of so many of its most talented people. At the inauguration he described the monument as "the memory of those who were killed and all of the blood that ran for no reason other than ideological differences." The monument includes a reproduction of a photograph of an execution by firing squad taken by a prison guard that summer of 1936. This simple addition, together with two poems, endows the space with an unmistakable and direct meaning.

The third monument is a memorial that includes the names of people from the city and surrounding area who were persecuted between 1936 and 1939. The sculpture, *Embryos of Peace and Freedom* by Xosé Val Díaz, used the research carried out by a working group with results obtained by the inter-university project Names and Voices (*Nomes e Voces*). Unlike in the previous cases, the instigator of this idea was not the city itself, which granted the space, but a civil society through a project by the Coruña Commission for the Recovery of Historical Memory, which was financed by the Office of the Prime Minister in 2010.

Together these three monuments clearly illustrate the evolution that has taken place since the 1990s of how the victims of Francoism are memorialized. The subject is presented elegantly yet almost unconsciously. This has changed into something much more direct, portraying the collective suffering through individuals who are no longer presented as mere ideas or cold statistics, but rather as people with names, who lived lives, had families, and loved.

89. *LAND AND FREEDOM* BY KEN LOACH, 1995

Vicente J. Benet

There are a number of elements related to the production of Ken Loach's *Land and Freedom* (1995) that help us understand the film's significant reception and influence, both outside as well as inside Spain. The first is the very way it approaches the Civil War, supplanting the mythical narrative that was especially popular in the English-speaking world and separating itself from the simple romanticized and elegiac idealism of the young people who went to the arid fields of the Iberian Peninsula to fight against fascism. This reading, crafted through war journalism, political propaganda, and inescapable cultural references—discourse linked to prestigious names like Ernest Hemingway, John Dos Passos, Robert Capa, and many others—had been hegemonic outside of Spain.

In contrast, the narrative approach employed by *Land and Freedom* offers a more complex vision, one inspired more by the experiences described by George Orwell in *Homage to Catalonia* (1938). In Loach's film, the romantic vision of the war is colored by the complexities, and even the misery, of political life at the time. In particular, it focuses on an important issue that had been previously mostly neglected in films directed at a general audience: the conflicts between the different ideological factions on the Republican side, and more specifically, the clash between the Anarchists and the POUM's revolutionary and collectivist objectives, on the one hand, and the Stalinist dogmatism of the communists, on the other. According to a report on the festival by Ángel Fernández Santos on May 23, 1995 for *El País*, the film's accusation that communists had felled these revolutionary dreams still angered a number of the intellectuals and film critics who attended its premiere in Cannes. Despite this, the film won the International Critics' Award, which helped its distribution afterwards.

A second element is linked precisely to the film's polemics regarding the memory of communism. Little more than five years after the fall of the Berlin Wall, the denunciation of communism's political legacy had become commonplace in academic and intellectual circles.

A third piece of the film's relevance is related to its narrative structure. This brings us to a term that has recently began to appear in academic writings: "post-memory," that is, the continuation of the conflict and an emotional connection to it on the part of the descendants of those who lived through the actual events. Thus, the primary story of the film, which is centered on the war, is framed on both sides by the present, where the granddaughter of the protagonist, a former combatant, learns about his history through documents that she finds in an old suitcase. This is how she comes to understand and accept his legacy. In the final scene, which takes place at his funeral, the girl recites a poem by William Morris and pours the handful of Spanish earth that her grandfather had kept all of those years over his coffin. Finally, she raises her fist as a final gesture of goodbye, signaling the ongoing relevance of this struggle from the past for new generations.

Formally, the film expresses its main theses by means of rather predictable methods. The viewer's perspective is always tied to that of the young idealist, who soon encounters political conflicts that often disconcert him. These are expressed primarily by his fellow soldiers, who together make up a mixed cultural and ideological microcosm. He also experiences the extreme scarcity of means they have for fighting the enemy, generous sacrifices, the friendship that arises among the comrades-in-arms, and, of course, a love affair with a tragic ending. The death of the militia woman with whom he was having a relationship at the hands of an old comrade who joined the Communist-dominated Popular Army is a melodramatic metaphor that seeks to align the essential political message with the emotional highpoint for the viewer.

In contrast to this more conventional aspect, the film also includes scenes of notable veracity. One that stands out in particular shows a debate over the collectivization of land after the militiamen occupy a small village in Aragon. The truthful approach to the debate, the mixture of languages that, nonetheless, does not impede the arguments from advancing, and the fact that Loach did not use professional actors, all serve to produce a memorably intense scene.

90. MONUMENT TO ALEXANDRE BÓVEDA, 1996, A CAEIRA, PONTEVEDRA

Emilio Grandío Seoane

Alexandre Bóveda was a well-known member of the Galeguista Party during the years of the Second Republic. After placing first in the civil service exams for the Treasury in 1924, he left his native Ourense for Pontevedra, where he got married, had five children, and became a leading member of local society. He was a core member of the party leadership and believed that the construction of democracy and adapting to new realities required new frames of reference. He had never advocated violence, although he was one of the group that barricaded itself in the Civil Government building of Pontevedra at the time of the military revolt of July 20.

Bóveda's execution, like that of so many others, was yet one more piece of the tsunami of violence that shook Spanish society—a wave that washed away everything in its path. The norms of coexistence in local communities established over decades now had to be reconfigured, and, with the fracturing of the state provoked by the military coup, unforeseeable and uncertain situations arose. There was nothing to hold onto, or, more accurately, hold onto those who were the strongest, who could offer the greatest protection. If this could be achieved at all.

Along with many others, Bóveda was charged in a summary war tribunal on August 13 as a representative of the Republican regime in the city. He was administered the famous "reverse justice" whereby those who defended the legal government until the end were accused of rebelling against the state. Bóveda was shot on August 17 in Caeira (Poio), on the other side of the estuary from Pontevedra, facing his own city. Exactly one month had passed since the rebellion had begun in Africa. His death was considered a warning, a cautionary tale for the community. If the rebels killed well-regarded people like Alexandre Bóveda, if they executed for rebellion those who prior to the coup had been considered the most respectable and honest, then it was clear that they could kill anyone against whom the authorities decided to press charges. The justice or injustice of the acts was beside the point. The defenses that were offered in the trial, if there was one at all, served for little or nothing. Bóveda's execution was a clear signal to demobilize, to incite fear, and to provoke panic in the face of arms that operated with impunity.

In Pontevedra and throughout Galicia, Bóveda's death came to symbolize the brutality of man and his atrocious capacity for self-destruction. Bóveda's family remained well-respected among a majority of people in Pontevedra, perhaps even more so because of the injustice committed against him. As with other families who survived the drama, they retained a permanent air of dignity. Among the local population's intimate conversations, one word stood out: "respect."

With time, Bóveda has turned into a symbol of the fight against barbarism. He was one of those potent reminders of the repression whose reputation lasted through the dictatorship practically without blemish. After Franco's death and with the transition to democracy, numerous organizations throughout Galicia began to vindicate his legacy. In 1990, a foundation, to which several of his family members belong, was created in his name. Six years later, on August 17—the anniversary of his execution—a monument was erected near the place where he had been killed. Since 2006, on this same date, the Galicia Martyr prize has been awarded in recognition of those who work to recover the memory of the victims of the repression.

Bóveda's death was one among hundreds of thousands. One day after he was executed, far from Galicia, Federico García Lorca was executed in his native Granada. The two men, so different, so innocent, became permanent reminders of the great tragedy that bloodied Spain in 1936. And after.

91. PRIARANZA MASS GRAVE, 2000, LEÓN

Emilio Grandío Seoane

Silence, silence, and more silence. The heavy feeling of not speaking about what should not be spoken about. Dirt over the bodies, locations never mentioned out loud and communicated only in whispers. Confusing at times, they form part of our most intimate past. A fragile memory. The doubts appear when new mass graves are found and old injuries begin to heal. This is what happened on October 21, 2000, in Priaranza del Bierzo, in the province of León, when after contacting local historians, Emilio Silva unearthed the remains of his grandfather. Silva and others belong to the Association for the Recovery of Historical Memory (ARMH). The news of what happened that fall was amplified with the excavation of even more graves in the area in the summer of 2001. Social networks and people interested in this past—about which little or nothing is said—were newly confronted with the physical reality of the human remains. Little more than two shovels-full under the earth. And all of this happened through volunteer efforts and a new way of constructing social networks.

This was not the first time that such exhumations had taken place. In the first years of the Spanish transition, numerous families awaited Franco's death and the arrival of democracy to arrange for their family members' and relatives' eternal peace. The majority of these efforts were personally facilitated and financed thanks to the initiative of family members as well as anonymous persons. With barely any resources. The state's reparations to the victims of Francoism during these first years were limited to homages and the paying of pensions to members of the Republican Army. Neither those who spent years in exile nor, of course, those lying in the ditches, received their homages or compensation. After the attempted coup of February 23, 1981, these first state initiatives ended. News of those brief efforts, from memories of open graves, continued until the beginning of the twenty-first century. But these were diluted over time, as society gave priority to constructing and consolidating democracy.

With the turn of the millennium, a quarter-century after the death of the dictator, the grandchildren of the victims were now the ones asking questions and demanding the "normalization" of their parents' long-lasting doubts. As if in a snowball of acceptance and commitment, these first attempts brought the past to the fore. And not only the years of war; they also directed the spotlight of analysis onto how the transition to democracy had taken place: a new regime constructed despite the fact that the existence of the "disappeared" had not been resolved and was being ignored by the state, and with no consistent set of public policies to cement the country's democratic identity. The concept of "memory" was coined in that moment by Spanish historians working on this subject. We know that this was not a uniquely Spanish phenomenon, and that "memory" as a way of remembering the victims' past was greatly effective in media throughout the world. The emergence of new technologies and the expansion of the internet without a doubt also contributed to this.

The change regarding the perception of the conflictive and inconclusive past that remains with us today has been radical. The perception of the Civil War has veered from equidistance and "everyone was responsible" to the search for "humanitarian" referents. Surveys reveal huge percentages of social support for this new approach. Unfortunately, reparations will not arrive in time for many. The law of life acts inexorably upon those who know the locations of the remains and who told us firsthand about that tragic time. Soon the only references that will remain will be the records of military trials. These are very valuable, but they should be approached with much caution, attention, and thoughtfulness, since the intentions of their protagonists—accusers, accused, and witnesses—were sufficiently complex in those dramatic moments of impunity to require a great exercise of contrast and analysis.

Despite this, too many cadavers still remain in the ditches. More than eight decades after the fact.

92. THE FINGERPRINT OF THE IRON BELT, 2005, VIZCAYA

Miren Llona

The Aterpe (Refuge) 1936 association was founded in 2005 with the goal of creating a place of memory with which to recognize the people who defended liberty and the authority of the Basque government and the Second Republic during the Civil War. The project was initiated by like-minded people from different political parties and unions, combatants and guerrilla fighters, exiles, family members of the victims of Francoism, and the children of the war. The association asked the artist Juanjo Novella to come up with an idea for a sculpture to "squarely face the past and obtain for the future all of the lessons that we can extract from it." The monumental piece that Novella created—an enormous fingerprint made of carbon steel measuring 8 meters high and weighing 8 tons—is slightly curved, thereby transmitting through its use of space the ideas of shelter and protection that the sculpture, popularly known as the "The Fingerprint," aims to project.

Since 2006, on June 17—the day on which, in 1937, the Francoist Army succeeded in entering Bilbao—the Fingerprint welcomes all of the people who unite around it with their small bouquets of flowers to pay homage to the youth who gave their lives for their principles and for liberty during the Civil War. As 97-year-old José Moreno Torres, from the Basque Workers Solidarity (STV) San Andrés battalion, said at the 2015 commemoration, "We were persecuted for being Republicans, Nationalists, socialists, anarchists, or communists, in short, for defending the value of liberty. The past is past in time, but we should make it remain present in our memory, and that is the reason we are united here, in this Aterpe 1936, in this refuge of memory." According to historian Jesús Alonso Carballés, this is a good example of how the memory of a tragic past can be turned into a principle of action and the defense of human rights in the present. Such exemplary use of the past is even potentially liberating, and the lessons of past injustices can thus be made use of to fight against those produced today.

All of this comes from Novella's interest in creating not just a sculpture, but "a space," as he says, "that makes sense and in which the city that it's located in can see itself. Where the pieces fit in such a way with the surroundings that the people who view it come to think that it has always been there." The Fingerprint has succeeded in growing roots and becoming an indissoluble part of Bilbao's current urban landscape. It is no coincidence, then, that the Fingerprint is located in an emblematic place, the Artxanda mountains, in whose foothills Bilbao is located.

Artxanda was part of the defensive line more than 80 kilometers long called the Iron Belt that was constructed to protect the city as well as the heavy industry and arms factories located on both sides of the Nervión estuary. The defensive belt was made up of trenches, forts, machine gun emplacements and refuges that proved unable to resist the bombardment of artillery by the Francoist troops and Italian and German airplanes. Further, the Iron Belt's weak points became known to the rebel troops after one of the engineers involved in its construction, Alejandro Goicoechea Omar, crossed the frontlines in February 1937, taking the plans of the installations with him, thereby facilitating the fall of Bilbao. Mount Artxanda was the scene of the Republican troops' final battles in defense of Bilbao, and for this reason it is a place of memory of the Civil War in the capital of Vizcaya.

In 2019, the Basque government declared the Iron Belt and the Civil War-era defenses of Bilbao as a Cultural Good, in the Monumental Complex category.

93. CANADIANS' WALK PLAQUE, 2006, MÁLAGA

Antonio Cazorla-Sánchez

"In memory of the help given by the people of Canada, through Normal Bethune, to the people of Málaga who fled in February 1937."

The inauguration of the Canadians' Walk in Málaga took place in February 2006. The mayor of the city and the Canadian ambassador were both present. As can be seen in the image above, the plaque expresses gratitude "to the people of Canada" for the help given "to the people of Málaga who fled in February 1937." Both in what it says and what is does not, the inscription reflects how the historical memory of the Civil War has developed both in Spain and abroad. Already from the beginning, there was controversy. The original text, which was later modified, referred to those fleeing as "fugitives," as if they had committed a crime.

The date of the inauguration was no accident; it came along with the birth of historical memory in Spain and throughout the West that began in the new millennium. The mayor of Málaga's attendance is notable given that, shortly after, his Popular Party objected to the passing of the Historical Memory Law of 2007, and when it took power in 2011, left it without funds, thereby hindering its application. Also notable is the presence of the Canadian ambassador, given that in reality his country—that is, "the people"—not only washed its hands of the Spanish Civil War but also prohibited Canadians from traveling to Spain, and upon their return punished or marginalized the volunteers who went to fight for the Republic. The great majority of the more than 1,500 Canadians who volunteered to fight in Spain, mostly in the International Brigade's Mackenzie-Papineau battalion were, moreover, recent immigrants to Canada.

And then there is the ambiguity in speaking of "the people from Málaga who fled." A visitor who does not know very much about the history of Málaga would surely ask themselves who those people were and from what they were fleeing in February 1937. What the plaque does not say is that they were as many as 150,000 terrorized people who were trying to escape in the face of the Francoist advance that took the city. The forces of the rebel army then continued along the coast until they were stopped *in extremis* by Republican troops in the province of Granada. The people from Málaga call this humanitarian disaster "the rout" (*"la desbandá"*). It was terrible; in addition to fighting hunger, the cold, and exhaustion, the civilian refugees were bombarded and machine-gunned without mercy by the Francoist Army over more than 200 kilometers. The air force and navy stand out in particular in the commission of this war crime, which took the lives of at least 5,000 people.

Even though it was the greatest civilian tragedy of the war until the enormous floods of refugees that left Cataluña for France during the terrible winters of 1938–39, it received very little official recognition until recently. As with other similar cases, only recently has the suffering of civilians become the principal concern of those who study or commemorate the Civil War. Every February since 2007, historical memory organizations have held a commemorative march along the road from Málaga to Almería.

The majority of the refugees went to Almería, though many continued their journey, some even relocating to Barcelona. During the Francoist dictatorship and even afterwards, people in Almería would speak of "those from Málaga" cautiously and in private with a mix of pity and horror. Orphans inhabited the city, lost children who never reunited with their families, if they were even still alive. The refugees were also spoken about as desperate people who would steal, destroy, or even kill to get food to eat or out of vengeance. In one of his radio harangues while the crime was taking place, General Queipo de Llano made the supposedly witty quip that he had sent the airplanes "to accompany [the Republicans] in their flight and make them run faster." Later, during the Franco dictatorship, it was as if they had never existed. Even today, the brief mention of the Civil War in Madrid's Naval Museum speaks even-handedly of the repression carried out in the city by both sides, but neglects to mention the role played by the ships *Almirante Cervera*, *Baleares*, and *Canarias* in the merciless shelling of the refugees.

That we have any images of this war crime is thanks to the photographs taken by Hazen Sise, a member of doctor Norman Bethune's medical team, who helped transport the weakest and sickest to Almería in his ambulance. These photographs have been half-forgotten for decades in the library of McGill University in Montreal.

94. THE CASARES QUIROGA HOUSE MUSEUM, 2007, A CORUÑA

Emilio Grandío Seoane

Santiago Casares Quiroga was an important Galician and Spanish political player. Educated in Galicia during the first decades of the twentieth century, the "prince" was destined to govern and lead. Following the death of his older brother, Arturo, Casares Quiroga "inherited" the responsibility of playing a leading role in A Coruña society, as his father, Santiago Casares Paz—a distinguished member of local Republican circles who had briefly been mayor of the city—had done before him.

Casares Quiroga was part of the generation that received a civic and secular education in A Coruña's central high school, Eusebio da Guarda. He was schoolmates with people such as Picasso, Salvador de Madariaga, and Novoa Santo, among others. Like Casares Quiroga, a good number of people from this generation left Spain to get a better education. They saw the world and upon their return tried to apply what they had seen.

After becoming a point of reference for republicanism and the smallholders movement in Galicia before the 1920s, he spent the years of the Primo de Rivera dictatorship (1923–30) under house arrest in his family home, which is today the Casares Quiroga House Museum. It was in those years, as well as his final ones spent in exile in Paris, that he had his deepest relationship with his second daughter, the actress María Casares.

From the final years of the Primo de Rivera regime, Casares Quiroga became the reference point of Galician republicanism. The creation of the Autonomous Galician Republican Organization (ORGA), a mixture of moderate leftist republicanism with elements of nationalism, gave him even greater prominence. He inserted himself into the national circles of opposition to the monarchy and formed part of the first provisional government on April 14, 1931, after spending time confined in Madrid's Modelo prison. He became one of the strongmen of the Republic: Minister of the Interior in the first legislature and Prime Minister in the third.

He was also one of Manuel Azaña's greatest confidants. And this is precisely the cause of the greatest discrepancies in analyses of his actions on July 18, 1936. For some, Casares was the one whose indecision in the face of the news of the military coup provided the rebellion time to gain traction while at the same time projecting an image of weakness. For others, he will be the sacrificial lamb from that cabinet in order to try to negotiate a peace with the rebels through the abortive government of Diego Martínez Barrio. This strategy failed after protests by workers over the dismissal of the Casares government. The cabinet returned to power practically in its entirety, but without its leader, who had presented his resignation days before July 18 and had been replaced by José Giral, another of Azaña's confidants.

And from there, a new silence falls over him. Or perhaps, not as much as has been thought. During the first months of the Civil War, Casares Quiroga became the parliamentary spokesman for the Republican Left party, and he remained in Madrid until the first months of 1939. He was essential for maintaining agreements with the labor movement, especially with the PSOE.

Casares Quiroga's discrete position after July 1936 is due more to the fact that his first daughter and granddaughter were under house arrest in rebel-controlled A Coruña. They were not allowed to leave the city until 1954—four years after Casares Quiroga had died in exile in Paris. Casares Quiroga was also one of the few Republican leaders who did not write his memoirs, despite receiving offers. There was clearly a connection between these two things.

Today, the Casares Quiroga House Museum collects items linked to him and to the Republican movement in Galicia and A Coruña. It is one of the few house-museums dedicated to a leader of Spanish republicanism. Preserving it was not easy. It was one of the "looted homes," its notable library having been expurgated. Casares Quiroga's shadow loomed large in the Francoist city, not only for the weight he carried during the years of the Republic but also because of the drama surrounding the prolonged confinement of his descendants. After having been occupied by different businesses, by the end of the twentieth century the house was in a bad state of repair. The municipal government had it refurbished, and it opened to the public in 2007.

This house had belonged to Santiago Casares Quiroga and his family, including his daughter María, who left amazing memoirs in which she tells of this uprooting, and the forgetting, in a very intimate and direct way. To read it is to take a delicious walk through the memory of her "homeland" (*patria*) and her childhood, with her father showing her, intelligently and with love, how to open herself to the world. Without fear.

95. THE VOID OF THE FORMER SATURRARÁN PRISON, 2007, GIPUZKOA

Miren Llona

Between Bizkaia and Gipuzkoa, facing the Cantabrian sea, there is an empty cement esplanade opening onto the beach at Saturrarán. Between 1938 and 1944, the old Saturrarán baths and neighboring buildings were converted into the Women's Central Prison. In the six years that it was operational some 4,000 prisoners passed through, more than half of them accompanied by their children. When it closed, the official death toll surpassed 177, including women and children. All of the buildings that had formed part of the prison were torn down in 1987. With the demolition, the life and suffering of these women were buried under the gray asphalt. However, since 2007 their historical experience has been remembered with a commemorative plaque organized by the Ahaztuak (Forgotten) 1936–1977 Association, as well as by a monolith by the sculptor Néstor Basterretxea that was sponsored by the Basque government.

In her book *Down with the Dictatorships*, the Galician prisoner Josefa García Segret describes her memory of the place: "A cheerful and enchanting little valley, lashed by the wind, sweetens in the soft breeze the troubles and bitterness that rests in our hearts ... Triangular in shape, with no exit but to the sea or the entrance to the prison, [it] is a very beautiful place that captivates one's view wherever one looks." It is comforting to think that the breezes coming off the Cantabrian sea could offer some comfort to the women locked up in the Saturrarán prison, who suffered deprivation, illness, and hunger, as well as inhumane treatment.

The majority of the prisoners were housewives, but there were also teachers, seamstresses, nurses, servants, shopkeepers, and students. They came from all over Spain: Asturias, Castilla, Cantabria, Andalucía, Cataluña, Madrid, as well as the Basque Country. Some, like Rosario Sánchez Mora, "the Dynamiter" (*la Dinamitera*), were considered highly dangerous; others were foreigners from the International Brigades; and though a minority, there were also women belonging to political parties and unions. Saturrarán was a prison for serving out sentences. All of the women had been judged and condemned for crimes relating to the war, and were known as "anterior" prisoners, in contrast to the "posterior" ones who were punished for their political activism during the Francoist dictatorship.

The image of the "red woman" as depraved and who must be punished to be redeemed echoes through the prison files. Many of the women were imprisoned because of their relationships as mothers, sisters, wives, and daughters of Republican men, accused of "helping the rebellion" and "collaboration." Others were condemned for "agitating and propaganda," for having distributed songs praising Republican leaders or making fun of the Francoists. Some were servants, concierges, and neighbors who had been betrayed by enemies of the Republic. The militia women were condemned for transgressing public morality: for living with men outside of marriage, for wearing overalls and pants, for carrying arms, or generally for having acted like men. It seems that, when it came to women, they were punished more for social insubordination than for political militancy. The women who came to Saturrarán had been condemned to death, but later had their sentences reduced, some to thirty years in prison, but most to twenty, twelve, or six years.

For some of the women who were sent to Saturrarán it was a relief to come to a prison for serving out one's sentence where nobody was taken out to be shot and where no acts of violence were perpetrated by uncontrolled groups. However, life in the prison was very hard. The Mercedarian nuns ran the prison, and in the prisoners' testimony there are constant references to their inhumane treatment, their ironclad disciplinary control, and the arbitrariness of their punishments. The prisoners died of typhus, tuberculosis, pneumonia, and in many cases, of hunger and malnutrition.

Many prisoners arrived with their children; others gave birth in the prison. According to the municipal records of Mutriku, as many as 161 children were born in Saturrarán. After March 1940, in the absence of direct family, children under the age of three were put in the care of the Juntas for Child Protection. This legal provision meant that parental authority could belong to the state or to a Catholic family loyal to the regime. For the prisoners, this was the worst punishment possible. Some of the babies baptized in Mutriku were taken care of by local people who took charge of them. Some of the mothers entrusted their children to family members of close friends. But others lost their children forever.

96. TYPEWRITER, 1937, GIJÓN

Verónica Sierra Blas

According to Andrey V. Elpátievsky, by the start of Operation Barbarrosa, in June 1941, there were some 4,500 Spanish refugees in the Soviet Union. Between 700 and 800 of them enlisted in the Soviet Red Army, the guerrilla or the Popular Militias during the Second World War. Many more contributed their efforts to the fight against Hitler in the rearguard, working nonstop in the factories and in the fields, fortifying villages and towns, doing nighttime watches and contributing to social assistance programs.

Although the majority of the refugees, including some of the Republic's political and military leaders, arrived in the Soviet Union in 1939 after the end of the Civil War, many others, like the 2,895 children evacuated between March 1937 and October 1938, came earlier. What was initially conceived of as a stay of just several months, for most turned into an exile that lasted for the rest of their lives: few returned to Spain and those who did had to wait at least twenty years, as the first return expeditions did not begin until the 1950s.

Stalin ordered the Narkompros (the People's Commisariat for Education) to organize and manage Children's Houses for the Spanish refugees. In these grand mansions, located in idyllic locations and filled with all types of services, the children lived and studied with Spanish teachers and caretakers. Their development continued with Spanish-focused activities: talks about

Spain and Spanish customs, choirs and orchestras for traditional music, dance groups for regional styles of dance, classical and popular theater productions, book clubs for reading *Don Quixote,* etc. This was part of the general lifestyle in all of these children's homes, as the final objective of the Spanish and Soviet authorities was for the children to not forget their roots.

Among the 1,110 children evacuated in the third of the four organized expeditions, which left Gijón on September 24 and arrived at Leningrad (now St. Petersburg) on October 4, 1937, were Libertad ("Liber") Fernández and her two brothers. Born in Langreo in 1927, Liber was eleven years old when departed the El Musel port to escape the bombs. She was one of the oldest of her group and perhaps for that reason she had with her a rather heavy and unusual object compared to what was in the rest of the children's luggage: a typewriter. It had been given to her by her father and it would be witness to everything that happened after the children fled Asturias until they returned to Spain, which Liber did in 1991, after having traveled all over the world together. For this reason, when Liber decided to write her memoirs, she wanted this typewriter to be the one to relate in her name everything that she had lived through. The typewriter is currently being preserved by her family, but it has passed through many hands prior to this, and its keys bear the fingerprints of all of them.

After arriving in the Soviet Union, Liber and her brothers were sent to the Pravda House in Tishkovo, on the outskirts of Moscow. Nearly 500 Spanish children lived there for four years until the outbreak of the war, when they were evacuated to Moscow, then to Privolskoye (Kukkus) in the Volga German Autonomous Soviet Socialist Republic:

> We found ourselves in a practically deserted place whose last inhabitants are being evicted by a NKVD company ... Cows, pigs and chickens roamed the streets ... There was no electricity or running water [and] winter was coming.

In the summer of 1942, the Fernández siblings were separated. Liber was sent to Sarátov near Stalingrad (today Volgograd), where she began working as a nurse in a hospital. Her vocation of being a doctor—a profession she practiced for the rest of her life—was born from this experience.

The cold, the lack of food and medicine, and the bombings were the principal causes of the numerous casualties suffered in the Soviet rearguard, including 750 Spaniards who died—500 of them children and young people—in just the first year of the war. Another 200 to 215, depending on the sources, lost their lives on the Russian Front, including 66 of the 135 Children of War who took up arms. Since 2003, an homage to them all exists in the form of a monument by Antonio Mije in Moscow's Pobedy Park. The plaque reads: "To the Spaniards who died in the Great Patriotic War, 1941–1945."

97. *DR. URIEL* BY SENTO LLOBELL, 2013–16

Vicente J. Benet

Carta y sobre, con el cuño de censura, en la que un familiar de Luis Florén le comunica que le ha llevado unos libros y le facilita una dirección a la que puede escribir cartas

El alférez Pablo Uriel en Belchite

The last quarter of the twentieth century saw a great proliferation of memoirs written by some of the protagonists of the Civil War, as well as general interest and academic publications aimed at a popular audience. At the turn of the century, cinema took center stage when it came to relating the Civil War in popular culture. And most recently, the leadership role in communicating historical memory has been taken up by comics and graphic novels, following the path pioneered by Carlos Giménez during the Transition. Those made by descendants of the people who experienced the conflict stand out in particular. They tend to combine their documentary goals with narrative strategies that seek to establish an emotional connection with the reader through the experiences transmitted through their protagonists.

Sento Llobell's comic is one of the best examples of this genre. It first appeared in three installments between 2013 and 2016, before finally being released in a single volume in 2016 by the publisher Astiberri. Its plot is based on the memoirs of the protagonist, Pablo Uriel, as reflected in the book *There is No Shooting on Sundays*. Uriel was a recently qualified young doctor substituting the lead doctor in a village in Logroño when the military coup takes place. Once back in Zaragoza, he is drafted into the Nationalist ranks despite his Republican sympathies. These make him suspect, and he is jailed in a military prison, where he experiences the anguish of constant shootings and the terror imposed by the Francoist authorities. He is finally freed thanks to arduous efforts by his family. Given his fear of being retaliated against, he volunteers to go to the front, where he believes he will be safer. His is sent to a company fighting in Belchite, where he rises to second lieutenant. He describes the Republican offensive in Aragón and the resulting battle in all of its cruelty. When the Republicans conquer the town, Uriel is taken prisoner but is miraculously saved despite all of the captured Nationalist officers being shot. He is again captured near Valencia, where he spends the rest of the war maintaining his stoicism in the face of the extreme situations that have made up his life's journey.

The volume is almost 400 pages long and includes an additional twenty-five pages of documentation such as letters written by Uriel to his family, photographs from the time, IDs, certificates, current photographs of the places where the events took place, and other material referencing this history. The balance between truth and fiction is present throughout the project. The essence of the story is based on Uriel's memoirs, but we can also see inventions and conventions of the genre that are used to make the story more accessible to a general reader. Further, sone of the objects and documents that appear in the story serve a purely narrative function, thereby strengthening the truthful effect that sustains it. In this way, the little ivory box made by a prisoner and the watch recovered from his brother who has been shot are highlighted in the story and appear in the documentary appendix as elements establishing an emotional connection with the past.

In a certain way, the story itself begins with an exercise of memory, which, moves from the family realm into the public sphere. Indeed, as Pablo Uriel says in the introduction to the first edition of his memoirs, the motive for writing them arose in response to the propaganda campaign XXV Years of Peace in 1964. Worried about the distorted vision of the events that his children would receive, he typed up manuscripts based on notes that he had taken during the war so that they would understand "how much misery and terror were hidden behind that beautiful peace." In 1964 it was not possible to make these impressions of the war public, and the story remained restricted to the family sphere. In fact, the first edition of the book—a single typed copy prefaced and bound by family and friends in 1975—was a gift to the author. His daughter, Elena Uriel, provided the illustrations and it remains a treasured family item. It was published a few years later with a preface by Ian Gibson and this edition served as the basis for the graphic novel by Sento Llobell, for which Elena Uriel again contributed to the illustrations.

98. *THE LINCOLN BRIGADE* BY CARLES ESQUEMBRE, PABLO DURÁ, AND ESTER SALGUERO, 2018

Vicente J. Benet

The great bloom of graphic novels and comics about the Civil War of recent decades share an interest not only in emphasizing the memory of the victims, the exiles, and those victimized for their loyalty to the government of the Second Republic, but in doing so pedagogically and with as much documentation as possible. We can place the subject of this chapter—a crowdfunded homage to the Americans who formed part of the Abraham Lincoln Brigade—in this lineage. Through the journeys of the avatars of some of the most representative personalities, the authors vindicate the legacy and the sacrifice of these combatants in a language that is accessible to younger generations. Although centered on specific events lived by the American battalion and above all its actions on the Brunete and Jarama Valley fronts, it also makes space for more fantastical or allegorical elements relating to popular culture that are directed to a younger audience. It also projects some of the political issues of the 1930s towards questions of a more contemporary sensibility, like the struggles for gender equality and against racial discrimination.

The story centers fundamentally on Oliver Law, the well-known African American volunteer who ended up becoming the battalion's commander and who died in combat at Brunete. The story begins with his participation in the labor protests in Chicago in the context of the 1929 crisis and his connection to the Communist Party. The military coup against the Republic required the mobilization of antifascist volunteers and the story describes his voyage to Europe, his arrival in Spain, the precarious military instruction done with outdated rifles and a complete lack of ammunition, and finally, his participation in battles in which some of his comrades die. It does not fail to cover the thorny issue of how the commanders squeezed the International Brigades, a shock force frequently used for actions requiring enormous sacrifice and, from a military perspective, suffering the worst conditions.

As is common in narratives about war, the protagonist is profiled through his relationship with his comrades-in-arms, who together form a microcosm of motivations and diverse psychological profiles. In this case, all of Law's fellow unit members are combatants from the Lincoln Brigade whose biographies can be perfectly traced in the archives. Some of them achieved a certain recognition, like the commander Robert Merriman, or the novelist and Hollywood screenwriter Alvah Bessie who was persecuted during McCarthyism. Others are hardly known except to specialists, although some like Harry Fisher and Harry Hakam left written testimonies of their experiences in Spain; as well as figures like Walter Grant, a young man who joined the Communist Party after witnessing a lynching of two African Americans in Marion, Indiana in 1930.

The graphic novel also includes references to some of the celebrities who circulated through the Spanish battlefields, like the inevitable Ernest Hemingway, the African American nurse Salaria Kea, the driver Evelyn Hutchins, and the photographer Gerda Taro. Indeed, there is a fictional conversation between Taro and Law that serves to project antifascist political themes toward more contemporary issues, like feminism and antiracism. Moreover, after Law's death the story connects the meaning of the fight in Spain to other contemporary movements: for civil rights in the 1960s, the protests against the Vietnam War, etc. The story ends with a group of elderly veterans who, after Franco's death, return to the battlefields that marked their lives. The stones under which the bodies of their fallen comrades rest rise up to form the image of a closed first.

The book's cover features a poster by Juan José Parrilla, an important graphic artist who designed a series of commemorative posters for the International Brigades.

99. ANTONI CAMPAÑÀ'S PHOTOGRAPHS, 2018, BARCELONA

Plàcid García-Planas

At the end of 2018, two boxes with almost 5,000 unpublished photographs of the Civil War were found hidden in the back of a garage. The two boxes contained the story of a photographer who was searching for beauty but discovered reality, who ended up renouncing beauty and voluntarily forgetting reality inside of these two boxes.

Before the outbreak of the war, Antoni Campañà Bandranas (1906–89) wanted to conquer the world: he was the artistic Spanish photographer who, at the beginning of the 1930s, had the most works exhibited abroad and had won the most prizes. From Indianapolis to Tokyo, through Budapest and Cape Town. In 1934, one of his photographs was featured on the front page of the magazine *American Photography*. In the light, drenched in chemistry, he was searching for beauty. And, like a flash, all of a sudden came the Civil War, a conflict that was fought for the first time with printed photographs like rifles in newspapers across the planet.

A Catholic, a Republican, and a Catalan Nationalist, as well as an official representative of Leica cameras, Campañà took nearly 5,000 photographs during the war, especially in the city of Barcelona, with a foray into the Aragón Front. And he photographed it all. Everything that Robert Capa and Agustí Centelles did not: the destruction caused by Fascist airplanes and women complaining that they did not have enough food for their children; Republican refugees who arrived broken from Málaga and anarchists destroying churches; great portraits of Stalin, and youth skating half naked to forget their pain; triumphant parades, and people rummaging through garbage to find food.

In contrast to the foreign photographers who landed in Spain knowing the assaulted and torn apart country that they were going to photograph would be done only superficially or not at all, Campañà had his finger on the pulse of his country: it was the country photographing itself, in a sublime way. His war photographs appeared in *La Vanguardia, L'Humanité, Die Volks-Illustrierte, Catholic Standard, American Photography*, and *L'Espagne Antifasciste*. They were also displayed in the mythic Republican Pavilion at the Paris International Exhibition in 1937, and the German antifascist artist John Heartfield used them in his legendary photomontages (using a refugee from Málaga in Barcelona as a victim of the Gernika bombing).

At the start of the war, using Leica and Rolleiflex cameras and approaches characteristic of the Russian avant-garde, Campañà took the most beautiful portraits of the CNT-FAI militiamen and women. Appearing in newspapers and magazines across the world and on libertarian postcards printed in various languages, they were the most widely published photographs of the anarchists. And here is the paradox: a practicing Catholic, a man of the church, took the best photographs of those who burned churches and murdered priests.

In the final year of the war, Campañà served as a chauffeur for the Republican Air Force. After the defeat he chose to stay and suffered no consequences. Between 1940 and 1942, seeing that Francoism used his images as propaganda against the losers—as the anarchists and communists had done before—he locked his 5,000 negatives of the war into two red boxes and hid them in the back of the garage at his home in Sant Cugat del Vallès, near Barcelona. He wanted to forget. He wanted to live. He turned away from pain and renounced his artistic gaze, and from then on focused his camera on the Barça football team, SEAT cars, skiing, and tourism. Along with Joan Andreu Puig Farran, another of the great photographers of the war, Campañà was the first to produce touristic color postcards on a mass scale for all of Spain. It was as if the war had not existed. Neither did he want to return his gaze to the years 1936–39 when a retrospective of his work was organized in 1989, a few months before his death. While others were reclaiming themselves, Campañà never wanted to be known for his sensational images of the war.

Once the boxes were found, the photographs escaped their captivity to close the circle: surprisingly—or not—the reasons for which Campañà locked away his images still apply in their own way today. Just like eight decades ago, the rescued photographs have been interpreted by people molding them to their current political interests: from readers of the conservative press denigrating the Republic thanks to images of the mummies of nuns that the anarchists had put on public display, to the purely aesthetic and uncritical reading and appropriation by anarchists regarding the sensational portraits of the CNT-FAI.

One day, while photographing anarchists in the Barcelona Bruch barracks—renamed Bakunin—a scapulary that he had been wearing fell on the floor.

"Campañà," a militiaman warned him, "this amulet …"

100. MEIRÁS COUNTRY HOUSE (PAZO), 2020, SADA, A CORUÑA

Emilio Grandío Seoane

Meirás. Just the name of this place in the municipality of Sada, A Coruña, where Francisco Franco—in his capacity as head of state—had his summer home, incites a whole series of feelings: of a summer court, peace, tranquility, a bucolic Galicia with stable values, where nothing ever changes … The same idea that the dictatorship wanted to portray of itself. It was said that this was a singular political regime for a singular society, one that would always feel threatened by change. The country house was a necessary resting place for the warrior, for the "Leader of the Peace."

The country house landed in Franco's hands after a complex process where the intention the leading forces of A Coruña's capital city was always to ingratiate itself with the dictator. In the first months of 1938, the Junta for the Country House was created with the help of representatives from the A Coruña municipal government, the Civil Government, the A Coruña provincial council, the Chamber of Commerce and other key institutions in the city. A separate institutional entity was never established, but the public weight of its representatives is evident just in reading their names. Their intention was clear: to get the Meirás Country House for the Caudillo. To do this they established a "popular fundraising initiative"—which followed the traditional model of the requisitions from the Civil War years—among the province's civil servants, as well as private donations to subsidize the cost. The estate had belonged to the famous novelist Emilia Pardo Bazán (1851–1921); it had hosted many of her literary gatherings and was home to her amazing library. Since the full amount for the house was not raised, the rest of the money was advanced by the Pastor Bank, through its director Pedro Barrié de la Maza—an old personal friend of Franco's. The house was transferred to Franco and his wife in a widely covered ceremony on December 5, 1938, in his capacity as "Head of State, Generalísimo of the Armies, and Leader (*Caudillo*) of Spain." Since the "voluntary" donations had been insufficient, the remaining funds were obtained by apportioning parts of the budgets of every municipality in the province of A Coruña, deducting a certain percentage to reimburse the bank for the amount it had advanced.

The war ended. The Junta for the Country House disbanded. But on May 24, 1941, a second contract for purchasing the house was formalized—the first had been made between the Junta and Pardo Bazán's heirs—which this time turned the offering to the head of state into Franco's private property. During the years that Franco and his family resided in the house, all of its expenses were paid by the public treasury. Despite this, the country house never became official state property.

After Franco's death, Meirás became a highly symbolic place: one of those elements that the process of the transition to democracy in Spain had left at a loose end. After many years, the state finally reclaimed the property and the surrounding estate from Franco's family. This was possible thanks to one of the greatest social movements regarding the recovery of the past that has ever occurred in Spain. There were many attempts to recover the country house for the public after Franco's death, but this required first reaching an economic agreement with Franco's family. Finally, their behavior in 2017, against the Xunta de Galicia's proposal from a few years earlier to turn the house into a Place of Cultural Interest, provoked a massive response by civic movements, institutions, historians, lawyers, universities … Proposals were unanimously approved by the A Coruña Civil Council, numerous municipal governments—especially in Sada and A Coruña which were directly implicated in the initial purchase—and in the Galician parliament. Historical legal reports were also prepared for its public reclamation. And this was not the only case of Franco family property being reclaimed: see the reclamation processes regarding the Maestre Mateo statues—located in the Meirás Country House—by the city of Santiago and the Casa Cornide by the city of A Coruña.

In September 2020, the courts ruled in favor of declaring the Meirás Country House a Place of Cultural Interest. The verdict represented an enormous triumph for Galician society and a vindication of the work of historians. Today, it can be considered a victory for the citizens that allows Spanish society to move forward with one less albatross around its neck and fewer stones tying it to the past.

IMAGE CREDITS

1. © Museo del Aire, Madrid
2. © Museo del Ejército, Toledo. Signatura: 23017
3. Personal Archive of Jesús Espinosa Romero
4. © Sergi Bernal
5. © Personal Archive of Eduardo Albéniz
6. Personal Archive of Plàcid García-Planas. Photograph: Juan Luis Toledo
7. © Museo del Traje. Centro de Investigación del Patrimonio Etnológico, Madrid. Signatura: MTCE032887
8. Personal Archive of Vicente J. Benet
9. Personal Collection of Arnau González i Vilalta. Photograph: Juan Luis Toledo
10. © Museo de los Mártires Claretianos de Barbastro, Huesca
11. Wikipedia/Hugo22
12. Personal Archive of Miren Llona
13. © Agencia EFE
14. © Ministerio de Cultura y Deporte, Centro Documental de la Memoria, Salamanca. Signatura: Incorporados, 754, 3
15. © Sociedad Aranzadi. Photograph: Lourdes Herrasti
16. © Museo de la Escritura Popular, Terque, Almería
17. Private Collection of the Luis Ortega Family, Santa Fe de Mondújar, Almería
18. Wikipedia/Dura-Ace
19. © Archivo de la Fundación Canaria Juan Negrín
20. © Personal Archive of Alfredo González
21. © Museo del Ejército, Toledo. Signatura: 202663
22. © Personal Archive of Alfredo González
23. © Album
24. © Bethune Memorial House National Historic Site, Gravenhurst, Canada
25. © Personal Archive of Alfredo González
26. © Biblioteca de Catalunya, Barcelona, subfons del Servei de Biblioteques del Front. Signatura: BNC_DSC9510
27. © Ministerio de Cultura y Deporte, Centro Documental de la Memoria, Salamanca. Signatura: Biblioteca_Hemero, Bibl. F, 3999
28. © Ministerio de Cultura y Deporte, Centro Documental de la Memoria, Salamanca. Signatura: Discos, Caja 1, 11, 1

29. © The History Collection / Alamy Stock Photo
30. © Ministerio de Cultura y Deporte, Centro Documental de la Memoria, Salamanca. Signatura: Objetos, 90
31. © Ministerio de Cultura y Deporte, Centro Documental de la Memoria, Salamanca. Signatura: Objetos_43, 1-69-91
32. Personal Collection of Adrian Shubert
33. © Ministerio de Cultura y Deporte, Centro Documental de la Memoria, Salamanca. Signatura: Causa General, 1813, 3, 18, 4
34. © Cabildo de Gran Canaria
35. © Biblioteca Nacional de España, Madrid, Dibujos infantiles de la guerra civil. Signatura: BNE/Dib/19/1/524
36. © Josu Santamarina Otaola
37. Personal Archive of Johanna Arzoz
38. © The University of Southampton. Signatura: MS 404 A4171/4/6
39. Photograph by Faustino Vázquez Carril from his family archive, in Grandío, E. (2011, ed.), *Las columnas gallegas hacia Oviedo. Diario bélico de la guerra civil española (1936–1937)*, Nigratrea, Pontevedra
40. © Javier Marquerie Bueno
41. © Special Collections and Archives, Glucksman Library, University of Limerick
42. © Archivo General de Palacio, Sección Casa Civil Jef. Estado, Leg. 29
43. Personal Archive of Vicente J. Benet
44. © Biblioteca de Catalunya, Barcelona
45. © Personal Archive of Alfredo González
46. © Panteón Civil Municipal de Morelia, Michoacán, México
47. © Ministerio de Cultura y Deporte, Centro Documental de la Memoria, Salamanca. Fotografía del Fichero General
48. © Ministerio de Cultura y Deporte, Centro Documental de la Memoria, Salamanca. Signatura: Fotografías-Kati_Horna, foto. 102
49. © Museo de la Escritura Popular, Terque, Almería
50. Personal Collection of Arnau González i Vilalta. Photograph: Juan Luis Toledo
51. © Ministerio de Cultura y Deporte, Centro Documental de la Memoria, Salamanca. Signatura: Causa general, 1547, 1, 385
52. © Candela Martínez Barrio
53. © Ministerio de Cultura y Deporte, Centro Documental de la Memoria, Salamanca. Signatura: Biblioteca_Hemero, Bibl. Fa, 01239
54. Personal Archive of Plàcid García-Planas. Photograph: Rosina Ramírez Rosillo
55. Personal Archive of Sofía Rodríguez
56. Mascarenyes-Rubiés Family Archive. Photograph by Juan Luis Toledo
57. Personal Archive of Vicente J. Benet
58. © Memorial Democràtic de la Generalitat de Catalunya, Barcelona

59. Personal Archive of Plàcid García-Planas
60. © MUHBA – Collecció Filatèlica Ramon Marull. Signatura: MGPB 006968
61. © Personal Archive of Alfredo González
62. © Ministerio de Cultura y Deporte, Centro Documental de la Memoria, Salamanca. Signatura: Objetos, 170
63. © Personal Archive of Alfredo González
64. © Ministerio de Cultura y Deporte, Centro Documental de la Memoria, Salamanca. Signatura: Causa General, 1633, 1, 158
65. © Asociación Memorial Campo de Concentración de Castuera (AMECADEC), Castuera, Badajoz
66. © CRAI, Biblioteca Pavelló de la República, Universitat de Barcelona
67. © Ministerio de Cultura y Deporte, Archivo General de la Administración, Alcalá de Henares, Madrid, AGA, 33, F, 806, 9. Aut. Ké mer
68. © Salvador Merino Archive. Photograph by Joé Casaú Abellán
69. © Family Archive of Julia Conesa, Madrid. Photograph: Museo Virtual de la Memoria Republicana de Madrid
70. Bou-González i Vilalta Family archive. Photograph: Juan Luis Toledo
71. © Archivo Histórico del Ejército del Aire, Villaviciosa de Odón, Madrid
72. © Junta de Comunidades de Castilla-La Mancha, Archivo Histórico Provincial de Albacete, Colección fotográfica, Fondo documental de la Asociación de Expresos y Represaliados Políticos Antifranquistas (AEXPA). Signatura: AHPAB 34.094/9
73. © Ministerio de Cultura y Deporte, Archivo General de la Administración, Alcalá de Henares, Madrid, AGA, 33, F, 1213, 31. Fot. Cifra
74. © Arxiu històric de la ciutat de Barcelona, Fondo Josep Bartolí i Guiu. Signatura: AHCB3-235/5D19-24928
75. © Alegiako Udal-Artxiboa
76. Francisco Ortiz Torres Family Archive, Perpignan
77. © Proxecto Sputnik Labrego
78. © Photograph: José Antonio Aparicio Florido
79. © Fototeca de la Agencia EFE. Signatura: 5841135
80. Personal Archive of Vicente J. Benet
81. Personal Archive of Vicente J. Benet
82. Personal Archive of Vicente J. Benet
83. Personal Archive of Miren Llona
84. Flickr / adele71. All rights reserved
85. Fondo Gonzalo Becerra, Arquivo Nomes e Voces. Universidade de Santiago de Compostela
86. Personal Archive of Vicente J. Benet
87. © Album / EFE
88. Wikipedia/Diego Delso
89. Personal Archive of Vicente J. Benet
90. Colectivo Ollo de Vidro, Fundación Alexandre Bóveda, A Coruña

INDEX

Page references for images are in *italics*.